MAKING A GLOBAL CITY

MAKING A GLOBAL CITY

HOW ONE TORONTO SCHOOL EMBRACED DIVERSITY

ROBERT C. VIPOND

UNIVERSITY OF TORONTO PRESS
Toronto Buffalo London

© University of Toronto Press 2017
Toronto Buffalo London
www.utppublishing.com
Printed in Canada

ISBN 978-1-4426-3195-3

Printed on acid-free, 100% post-consumer recycled paper with
vegetable-based inks.

Munk Series on Global Affairs

Library and Archives Canada Cataloguing in Publication

Vipond, Robert Charles, author
Making a global city : how one Toronto school embraced diversity / Robert
Vipond.

(Munk series on global affairs)
Includes bibliographical references and index.
ISBN 978-1-4426-3195-3 (cloth)

1. Clinton Street Public School (Toronto, Ont.) – History – 20th century.
2. Public schools – Ontario – Toronto – History – 20th century.   3. Immigrant
students – Ontario – Toronto – History – 20th century.   4. Multiculturalism –
Ontario – Toronto – History – 20th century.   5. Toronto (Ont.) – Ethnic
relations – History – 20th century.   I. Title.   II. Series: Munk series on
global affairs

LA419.T6V56 2017   371.0109713'541   C2016-906942-7

University of Toronto Press acknowledges the financial assistance to its
publishing program of the Canada Council for the Arts and the Ontario
Arts Council, an agency of the Government of Ontario.

Canada Council   Conseil des Arts
for the Arts   du Canada

ONTARIO ARTS COUNCIL
CONSEIL DES ARTS DE L'ONTARIO
an Ontario government agency
un organisme du gouvernement de l'Ontario

Funded by the   Financé par le
Government   gouvernement
of Canada   du Canada

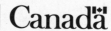

For Susanna –
and the many other graduates of Clinton Street Public School

Contents

Foreword

Why would we publish an ethnographic and political history of one inner city Toronto school in a book series on global affairs? One hint is found in the subtitle to Rob Vipond's lively history of Clinton School: "Making a Global City." The history of this one school helps tell the wider story of how a bastion of Anglo culture, once known as "Toronto the Good" (read "monolithic" and "bland" and "buttoned up"), became one of the most vital and diverse urban centres on earth.

But the story is even more "global" than the civic history would suggest. In 2016, the year that saw the rise of Trumpism, the shock of Brexit, a Hungarian referendum that ratified a refusal of an authoritarian government to take any refugees on a continent overflowing with need, this fresh story of Clinton School provides a much-needed counterpoint. It is the story of bottom-up mutual accommodation, of shifting demographics that prompt constant evolution in how a community is built and maintained, of a construction of citizenship that is both inclusive and bounded.

Professor Vipond traces remarkable Canadian immigration shifts over the course of the twentieth century that produce three distinct periods in the life of Clinton School, what he calls "Jewish Clinton," "European Clinton," and "Global Clinton." Somehow, in each period, students who were "new Canadians" were made to feel that they were "somebodies." When the Ontario government created regulations that sought to reaffirm a dominant Protestant culture in the 1950s, the local school community resisted and found ways to ensure that Jewish students and their families felt welcome. In the early 1960s, when children of Italian immigrants came to dominate the school numerically, communications from the school and from its parent committee were routinely sent out not only in English but in Italian (and later in other languages as well). In the 1980s, when Global Clinton emerged, the school's parent committee struggled to balance a commitment to ensure that new immigrants learned English quickly while supporting their desire to maintain their original language and culture.

The twentieth-century history of Clinton School reveals a complex, daily negotiation of what came to be called "multiculturalism." Vipond's story is not a simple "progressive" narrative, for it frankly acknowledges failures and conflict. Not all the former students interviewed had fond memories; many told stories of exclusion and bullying. Teachers sometimes remembered stronger academic commitment than the students could recount. Yet, despite the imperfections, Clinton School managed in successive generations to create forms of respect that allowed new Canadians to feel part of a "receiving" culture without sacrificing personal and community histories. As Vipond concludes: "Finding the right balance at Clinton between acculturation and adaptation was all part of the daily routine." Every day was a practice in the construction of civic identity.

A single school in a single city can tell us much about some of the biggest issues of our own era. How can new waves of immigrants find a place in their new countries? Is a "nation" made up only of those who share a common history and culture? Can shared identity be built through education? What does it mean to be a citizen? In this first monograph in our Munk Series on Global Affairs with the University of Toronto Press, Vipond demonstrates vividly that the history of public education can provide helpful ways to ponder these fundamental questions. Little Clinton School in the heart of Toronto has global significance.

Prof. Stephen J. Toope
Director, Munk School of Global Affairs

Acknowledgments

This is a book I had no intention of writing. It is not the culmination of a career-long scholarly interest in the history of public education. It does not draw on a deep reservoir of research money generated by national granting agencies. And it does not fit squarely into a well-established genre of writing in my home discipline, political science. It owes its existence, rather, to a more or less chance conversation that I had, in the spring of 2012, with Wendy Hughes, principal of Clinton Street Public School in Toronto. Wendy intercepted me one morning as I was leaving the school after dropping my daughter off at her Grade 5 classroom. "Are you interested in history?" she asked. There was, of course, only one possible answer to that question, and before I knew it I had volunteered to be part of the committee charged with organizing the program for the school's 125th anniversary in 2013. I want to thank her for getting me hooked and for keeping me hooked.

I soon discovered that the school held a complete set of registration cards that provided demographic information about every child who had attended the school between 1920 and 1990, a well-organized archive that had been assembled at the time of the school's centenary in 1988, and loads of graduates of all ages eager to share their school and childhood memories – rich resources all. I have spent most of my scholarly career reading and writing about political speeches, constitutional cases, and the like, so this project and these materials deposited me in a sort of scholarly *terra incognita*. I would probably still be there were it not for the generosity of friends and colleagues who know their way around. It gives me great pleasure, at long last, to be at the stage where I can thank those who have helped turn an idea into a research project, and a research project into a book.

In 2012–13, a half-dozen undergraduate students in political science at the University of Toronto signed up for a year-long seminar on the history of Clinton Street School. We spent the first term reading about some of the themes that animate this book – the history of education, theories of citizenship, and the politics of multiculturalism among them. In the second term, the students produced major research papers based on archival research and interviews with former students and school trustees. The work they did was superb. More importantly, their work confirmed that there really was a book waiting to be written about Clinton School. To those students – Jordan Kamenetsky, Scott Kilian-Clark, Taryn McKenzie-Mohr, Alissa Saieva, Nicole Stoffman, and Abby Vaidyanathan – I am deeply grateful.

While these undergraduate students were working their way through the secondary literature and digging into the archives, a group of recently minted MA students had begun the task of organizing, coding, and analysing the information contained on the student registration cards preserved by the school. Led by Korryn Bodner and James Michelson, their tireless efforts produced a remarkable data set, the content of which forms the backbone of this study. I am deeply indebted to Korryn and James and their colleagues Lauren Hudak, Conrad Koczorowski, and Adrian Philp, both for the quality of their work and their loyalty to Team Vipond.

Good data raise as many questions as they answer, and the deeper we drilled down into the information gleaned from the registration cards the more questions I had. So began the archival phase of the project. I am deeply indebted to a Clinton parent, Audrey Douglas, who, in 1988, assembled, organized, and so preserved a wealth of material relating to Clinton's first century. Without her efforts, I would have had much, much less material to work with. I am also grateful to Sonia Antunes, Clinton's current principal, the legendary Zilda Silva, who made sure I had ready access to the archives room, and Marlene Danicki, whose remarkable institutional memory helped me put names to faces in many photographs. Greg McKinnon and (especially) Marie Passerino at the Toronto District School Board

Archives were extremely helpful under trying conditions. Melissa Caza made working at the Ontario Jewish Archives a pleasure.

The registration cards also fed my desire to hear from former students and teachers about what it had been like to learn and teach at Clinton. In the end, I conducted about seventy-five interviews in person and connected with many others via e-mail, telephone, or in Jane Jacobs-style casual encounters on the street. People invited me into their homes or travelled to meet me downtown. Whatever the venue, they all gave generously of their time and shared their stories of Clinton and the neighbourhood. I can't thank them enough. Nor can I forget my colleagues Don Schwartz (who helped me work out kinks in the interview guide) and Elspeth Brown (who shared her knowledge of how to conduct oral histories).

As the manuscript began to take shape, chapter by chapter, many friends and colleagues were kind enough to read and comment on what I had written. My thanks to: Ryan Balot, David Cameron, Nancy Cardwell, Randy Gangbar, Jane Gaskell, Julie Guzzo, David Harrison, Wendy Hughes, Anna Korteweg, Jeff Kopstein, Ted Magder, Rita O'Brien, David Rayside, Jim Stathopoulos, Phil Triadafilopoulos, and Bernie Yack. I want to extend special thanks to Jason Ellis, whose prodigious knowledge of the history of public education in Toronto and careful reading of the manuscript saved me from many errors. Others, like Roberto Perin, were kind enough to let me read their works in progress. Anonymous readers answered the call from University of Toronto Press; I thank them for their helpful comments and support. And the comparative political development workshop at Oxford University provided a congenial venue to test drive the book's argument.

Once the data were organized, Fahd Husain, Conrad Koczorowski, and Anthony Sealey transformed them into graphs and tables, while Zack Taylor and Jeff Allen expertly produced the various maps. Vincenzo Pietropaolo's knowledge both of photography and of the neighbourhood helped mightily as I selected photos. I learned an enormous amount from all of them.

The University of Toronto has been my home away from home for some thirty-five years. I still don't understand its many nooks and crannies, but I do know that the place has an uncanny knack for finding, choosing, and cultivating strong academic leadership.

Lou Pauly, chair of the Department of Political Science, has been a booster throughout. Good political economist that he is, I relied on his creative suggestions to help fund my research. Janice Stein, director emeritus of the Munk School of Global Affairs, was enthusiastic from the outset, helped with research funding at a crucial moment, and suggested the title. The Centre for Jewish Studies, led at the time by Jeff Kopstein, chipped in as well. And David Cameron, friend and dean, has always been there when I really needed him.

I'm not quite sure how to describe Ken Alexander. Patron saint, interlocutor, friend, and editor – he is all of these wrapped into one. Ken loves the craft of writing. His careful reading of the manuscript, first in pieces then as a whole, was spectacularly helpful. I have come to spend a lot of time recently at the University of Toronto Press and have been completely impressed with the combination of enthusiasm and professionalism that I have found there. No one better exemplifies that combination than Jennifer DiDomenico, my editor, who believed in the project from the start and saw it, very patiently, to the end. And I want to thank Stephen Toope and other members of the editorial advisory board for the Munk/UTP series in global affairs, of which this is one of the first volumes.

My siblings – Mary, Fran, and Doug – provided suggestions about footnoting, tips about sources, and moral support. Over the course of this project, I spent many a Friday evening with Cliff and Donna Orwin – Clinton parents, fine scholars, and wonderful friends. They were always eager to hear what I had discovered and gave me the time and space to articulate even quarter-baked ideas. I can't thank them enough for their friendship.

One of the few regrets I have about writing this book is that my wife, partner, and friend, Gina Feldberg, died before it was conceived. She would have loved this project, though I suspect she would have done it differently – and a whole lot better. I missed her every sentence of the way.

My final debt is to my dear daughter, Susanna. There were many moments when the project took over our home ("Not Clinton again! I'm leaving!") and many others when her father was so preoccupied that he wasn't quite all there. So to her this book is dedicated – in her own way. Susanna (being Susanna) didn't want this to be all about her. And she's right.

1

Introduction

In June 1955, Toronto's director of education, C.C. Goldring, was asked to deliver the keynote address to a convention of Ontario school trustees. Nearing the end of his career, Goldring used the occasion to reflect on the current state of public education in the province and the future shape of public schooling in "this confused, scientific, speedy, exciting world."[1] He thought that in general "the children in Grades I to VI in the typical Ontario school receive as good an education as is available in any publicly supported school system in the world,"[2] but, just the same, this was no time for school boards to rest on their laurels. Ontario's schools might be doing an adequate job in their "ordinary classes," but if public education hoped to redeem its democratic promise to include "all the children of all the people,"[3] it would have to pay more attention to those who had special needs. This included "new citizens":

> We have received into this country during recent years, tens of thousands of people from Europe with little understanding of the English language or Canadian ways and ideals. Most of them wish to become good Canadians. We have a duty to provide evening classes for adults to teach them the English language as quickly as possible and to give them some knowledge of Canadian ways of life, traditions, and beliefs.

"In the anxious times in which we live," he observed, "it is of importance to strengthen our country in every way we can and one opportunity lies in providing evening classes for the purpose of integration for the many willing Europeans who have come to our shores during recent years, with the intention of becoming useful, loyal, Canadian Citizens."[4]

Goldring mused about the state of the educational system from the comfort of a conference podium. About a mile west of his College Street office, the teaching staff at Clinton Street Public School had no such luxury; they were living Goldring's story daily. Established in 1888, Clinton is a public school in downtown Toronto that, at the time Goldring spoke, served about 1,000 students from kindergarten through grade 8. The neighbourhood from which it drew was a "gateway" community for immigrants for much of the twentieth century. This includes the 1950s, when it attracted more than its fair share of those "tens of thousands of people from Europe" to whom Goldring referred. Clinton became their children's school. Indeed, almost 80 per cent of Clinton students in the 1950s were either first- or second-generation immigrants to Canada.

The challenge that Goldring threw down was a challenge the school embraced. At least in the estimation of Noel Pollard, Clinton's principal through the 1950s, the results were largely positive. "Scholarship worries me somewhat," he admitted in his farewell address to the school, but these reservations were offset by other considerations. Clinton was a "warm, friendly school" that boasted a "happy relationship" between school and community, "few quarrels," and strong extra-curricular activities. "We are especially proud of [the school's] record because our pupils come from many lands and a great many of them are just learning *our language and our ways*." It was no small accomplishment, he concluded, that "most of our children are trying to be good citizens."[5]

This book is about Clinton Street School and the ideas, debates, and practices that informed its attempts, from the end of the First World War to 1990, to "create" citizens in Toronto from a highly diverse, immigrant-rich population.[6] It is both a biography of a school and a window into some of the most basic questions of citizenship in a liberal democracy: about who belongs, under what terms, and to what end.

It may seem a bit eccentric to probe core questions of civic identity through the history of a single school in one city at a particular historical moment. It really isn't. Public schools have always been considered crucibles of citizenship; they still are.[7] And when their students include large numbers of immigrant children, this function takes on special significance (as the testimonials from Director Goldring and Principal Pollard attest). As a result, schools provide a wonderfully revealing venue for watching how different ideas and practices of citizenship play out. Clinton School, which served as a gateway for thousands of immigrant children in the course of the twentieth century, provides a particularly good vantage point from which to reconstruct those debates and practices in a fine-grained way.

The advantage of viewing citizenship *historically* is that one is forced to confront the fact that what citizenship means, the ideal of citizenship, has changed significantly over time. Principal Pollard's statement that Clinton School tried hard to help immigrant students learn "our language and our ways" reflected the long-standing and widely held view that immigrants should assimilate to Canadian life. In essence, assimilation was a one-way street. The onus was on immigrants to adapt to "our ways," and teachers were crucial to the process of transforming "them" into "us." As we will see, the consensus around assimilation began to fray in Toronto in the 1960s as educators began to question whether it was necessary or healthy or even possible to expect immigrants to check their identities at the Canadian door. Integration, rather than assimilation, seemed like the better option, and from there it was but one further step to extend accommodation for cultural diversity into a full-blown project of multicultural citizenship.

If this were all there were to it, we'd be left with a story of diversity and citizenship that chronicles how, in public schools, assimilation gave way to integration, which in turn morphed into multiculturalism – a stylized Canadian story in miniature. Put this way, the basic story line is like a well-known pop song or a favourite hymn. We may not remember the words to all the verses, but we certainly can, and do, hum the tune. Alas, the story of how Clinton embraced diversity over the years isn't quite so easy to hum. It's more like a jazz improvisation or, if you prefer, a fugue. There is a melody, but what gives the music its character is the way the tune interacts with other voices (counterpoint) and the way different voices impart a different pace and rhythm (syncopation) to the musical line. The citizenship "tune" – from assimilation to integration to multiculturalism – is still recognizable at Clinton, but dissenting voices and different rhythms are interwoven in ways that may come as a surprise to listeners who are expecting a simple and tuneful melody.

Put slightly differently, the story of Canadian citizenship and civic identity is not a neat and tidy narrative in which one idea gives way to another, only to be replaced by a third, each more progressive than the one that preceded it. It is, instead, a story about the ways in which different ideas are "layered" historically one on top of another. The top and most recent layer, multiculturalism, is the most visible, but it rests on, and has not entirely displaced, a foundation created by what came before – assimilation and integration. What the developmental story of Clinton Street School shows so vividly is the way in which these layers interact, sometimes producing friction, sometimes harmony. The very untidiness of the story may actually be a good thing. At a time when, across the globe, multicultural citizenship is under fierce attack from those who see diversity as a threat to shared citizenship, maybe, just maybe, the experience of Clinton Street School provides an alternative and more promising way to think about how to embrace diversity in a global city – a way that does not require throwing out the (citizen) baby with the (multicultural) bath water. Such is the basic argument of this book.

According to the 1881 Canadian census, Toronto had just over 86,000 residents. By 1891, just a decade later, its population had more than doubled to just over 181,000.[8] This population boom reflected the solidification of Toronto's status as an industrial city, an agricultural hub, and a commercial centre rolled into one, and as the population grew, the original physical and mental boundaries of the city simply did not fit any longer. Lake Ontario meant that expansion to the south was impossible, but expansion in the other three directions was not just possible, it was inevitable. Pushing west faced two obstacles, however. The first was that most of the land was controlled by a few wealthy landowners who had to be persuaded to sell their estates into partitioned lots suitable for modest but comfortable single family homes. Quickly enough, the penny of self-interest dropped. One by one these landowners sold their land, leaving their names behind on the newly created streets – Denison, Ossington, Crawford, and Shaw among them. The second obstacle to westward expansion was that until 1880 the mainstay of the city's public transportation system, horse-pulled streetcars, only went as far west as Bathurst Street. If the need for housing pushed Toronto's growing population farther west on weekdays, the pull of bucolic High Park lured residents still farther west on the weekends. For both reasons, the argument to extend the route beyond Bathurst Street was compelling. The College streetcar broke trail west of Bathurst in the 1880s, and once it was electrified (as it was by the 1890s) there was no looking back. Builders and home buyers soon followed,[9] and to serve their needs, both material and spiritual, shops and churches soon appeared in large numbers as well along the College Street strip.

Clinton Street School was built to serve the children of families who settled in this newly accessible west end of Toronto. The land purchased for it was well situated – five short blocks west of Bathurst Street, half a block north of College. This meant it was close enough to College Street to draw teachers from beyond the neighbourhood. (One former student said that in the early days the streetcar driver would wait at Clinton Street at four o'clock until all of the teachers had made their way down from the school to catch the tram home.)[10] The school's location meant, as well, that it was strategically placed in the middle of a large square bounded by Bathurst on the east, Grace. (or sometimes Shaw) on the west, College on the south, and Bloor on the north (see map 1.1). This was the school's catchment, and while the sides of the square have expanded and contracted somewhat over the years (especially on the west), Clinton Street School remains what it was originally designed to be – a neighbourhood school for children growing up in the central west end of Toronto.

The community originally served by Clinton is sometimes described as working class, sometimes as "solid middle class." In fact it was quite mixed from the beginning. Take, as an example, Markham Street, the first street west of Bathurst and the current eastern boundary of the Clinton catchment. The first houses on the street north of College were built soon after the streetcar pushed past Bathurst in 1880 and became home to mail clerks, travelling

Map 1.1 Clinton School Neighbourhood – 1920–1990

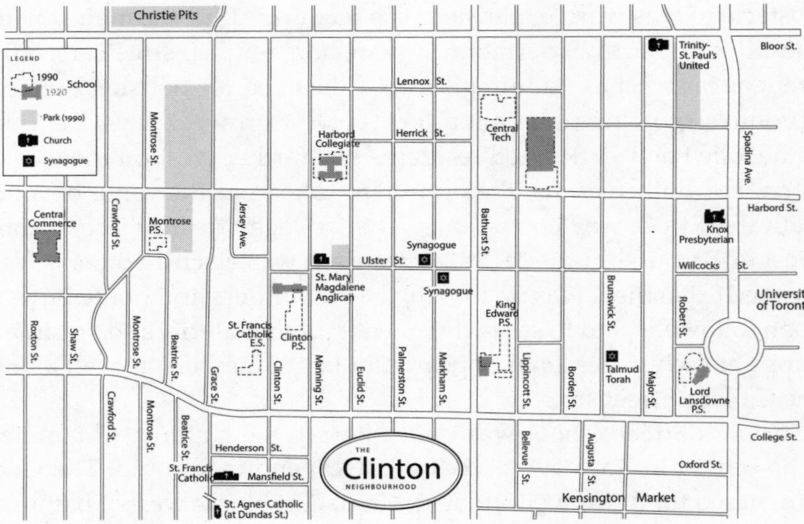

Source: Clinton data set

salesmen, and bookkeepers. The houses built a decade later farther north on the same block appealed to a different class altogether – typically, executives of medium-sized manufacturing companies headquartered in Toronto. The next street to the west, Palmerston Boulevard, was Toronto's early version of a gated community: grand, important, and stately. Next to it is Euclid Avenue, whose two- and three-storey brick, semi-detached houses were more like those on lower Markham and were occupied at the turn of the twentieth century by clerks, "travellers," and tradesmen. And on it goes, each street expressing its own character. At times in Clinton's life, as we will see, the same families lived in the same houses for decades. At other times, the neighbourhood was more like a transit stop on the way to somewhere else. But throughout, it remained socio-economically heterogeneous.[11]

The original Clinton School, which opened in 1888, was a two-storey, eight-room brick building that faced onto Clinton Street (hence the name).[12] It was, alas, too small for the number of students it had to accept more or less from the day it opened its doors. Some classes were outsourced to rented space in a local church; others were overloaded, fifty students to a room; and some students in the neighbourhood were simply turned away.[13] Soon enough, plans were developed to add a third floor. But even this addition could not meet the demand. Thus, in 1913, the original Clinton School gave way to a much larger, three-storey Edwardian brick school that comprised seventeen rooms and took over most of the block between Clinton and the next street to the east, Manning Avenue. Even this was not enough, so in 1923 an annex was built connecting the original school with the 1913 school. When that building began to deteriorate irreparably, it was replaced by the current structure: a two-and-a-half storey, ranch-style, cinder-block building facing Manning Avenue. When it opened, in 1966, the "new" Clinton was considered a state-of-the-art urban school.[14]

In many ways, Clinton was a typical urban Canadian school, embedded in a complex educational ecosystem that was both hierarchical and interdependent. Given this circumstance, it would have been difficult for any one school to have charted its own course unconstrained by its place in the system. Like other schools, Clinton followed a curriculum prescribed by the provincial department (later ministry) of education. Like other schools, its teachers and principals were hired by the city's board of education, which also framed many of the rules and routines that defined the school's daily rhythms. Like other schools, it had a parent council that waxed and waned over the years. Like other schools, it was profoundly affected by the two world wars. (One surviving artefact is a stunning lithograph, prepared by Group of Seven artist A.J. Casson, honouring graduates who served in the armed forces.) As in other schools, life at the school was deeply gendered; principals were almost always men, teachers were mainly women, and until 1965 boys and girls used separate entrances. Like many other schools, Clinton had and has always maintained a connection to special education, beginning with classes for the deaf in 1925. Like other schools in Toronto, Clinton helped to pioneer kindergarten; pre-school education has been a fixture there since 1898. And like other schools, Clinton has produced its share of graduates who have gone on to distinguish themselves in various ways in their adult lives – in the media, politics, medicine, business, law, and music, among other fields.

Yet for all these similarities, Clinton *was* distinctive in several ways and on several key occasions charted its own course despite the constraints imposed by "the system." What made Clinton (and other downtown Toronto schools) different was its ethnocultural diversity, fuelled by the waves of immigration that ultimately transformed Toronto, and indeed Canada, over the twentieth century. As we will see in due course, one can define and measure diversity in a number of ways. At Clinton's founding, however, there was only one distinction that mattered, namely whether you were Canadian- or British-born on the one hand or "foreign" on the other. By that standard, both Clinton Street School and the larger Toronto in which it was nestled were remarkably homogeneous. According to the 1891 census, 95 per cent of Toronto's residents were either Canadian- or British-born; by 1921, the same categories still accounted for 91 per cent of the population.[15] Clinton was no different. At the end of the First World War, 90 per cent of the student body came (in more or less equal numbers) from families that were either long-standing Canadian residents or whose parents had emigrated from the British Isles.[16] This last statistic deserves emphasis. From the beginning, Clinton was a "gateway" school for immigrant students because its neighbourhood was a reception area for recent (or relatively recent) arrivals to the country. But until the end of the First World War, almost all of those newcomers came from the British Isles. The transition to a school system that celebrated Empire Day and that hoisted the flag to commemorate British victories in the War of 1812 would not have jarred their sensibilities.[17]

And then things changed – at least at Clinton (see figure 1.1). While the rest of Toronto became less British only very gradually over the next three decades, Clinton changed, and changed dramatically, into what I will call Jewish Clinton. The transformation was both swift and deep. In 1920, approximately 10 per cent of Clinton students were Jewish. By 1930, fully 50 per cent were Jewish, and until about 1950 Jewish students accounted for at least half the student population – and often well more than that. (A graphic

Figure 1.1 Clinton Street School – Ethnicity by Father's Birthplace – 1910–1980

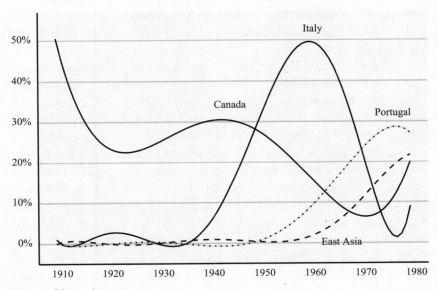

Source: Clinton data set

representation of this trend can be found in chapter 2.) Some of these students were first-generation immigrants; they had been born abroad. Many more of them were second generation, the sons and daughters of eastern European Jews who had come to Canada in the decade or so before the First World War. As we will see in chapter 2, the Clinton area was popular both because housing was relatively cheap and because it was close to Spadina Avenue, the centre of the textile trade. The parents worked hard, earned little, nurtured their Jewish identity in manifold ways, and placed great value on education. But they had to negotiate a school system that set out to teach students how "to live in a democratic society based on the Christian ideal." The tension created by this way of defining the school's mission came to a head in the 1940s when Ontario's premier, George Drew, promulgated regulations that required every public school in Ontario to teach religion and that provided lesson plans that conveyed the message that the Jews were responsible for killing Jesus. Chapter 3 will tell the story of how the "Drew Regulations" mobilized the Canadian Jewish community to articulate the connection between religious freedom and citizenship. At Clinton, the religious regulations inspired quiet resistance to a policy that was simply out of place.

And then, in the early 1950s, the ethnocultural composition of Clinton changed again. Having lived through the Depression and the deprivations produced by the Second World War, many of the Jewish families in the Clinton area were only too happy to take advantage of the post-war economic boom to head "up the hill" to the suburbs. And who built the suburbs? In many cases, the Italian immigrants who now settled in the very houses around Clinton that the previous generation had left behind in their flight to Bathurst Heights. As we will see in chapter 4, Jewish Clinton thus gave way to European Clinton as recent Italian (1950s) and Portuguese (1960s) immigrants moved into the area, began building families, and sent their children to Clinton Street School. The transition was again dramatic. In 1953, 35 per cent of incoming Clinton students were Jewish and 35 per cent were Catholic (of which most were Italian). By 1960, just a few years later, only 5 per cent of incoming students were Jewish while 75 per cent were Catholic. That is how quickly the neighbourhood – and hence the school – changed.

As the vignette with which I opened the book suggests, the challenges created by schools like European Clinton seized the attention of educators throughout the system. In this case, as we will see in chapter 5, Clinton was both a leader and a follower. It was a leader in developing English as a second language (ESL) programs in the 1950s, more or less from scratch and with minimal help from the school board. It was largely a follower in the 1960s, as policy makers, especially at the Toronto Board of Education, took the lead in rethinking the role of the larger school system in helping "New Canadians"[18] succeed. Their attempts to tease out the difference between "assimilation" and "integration" were particularly important in this regard. All of this preceded, then ran parallel to, the official turn to multiculturalism announced by the federal government in 1971.

Yet as one physical Clinton Street School replaced another, so European Clinton gave way, in the mid-1970s, to what I call Global

Clinton. This transition was more gradual than the ones that had preceded it, but the effects on the school were equally decisive. Building on its Italian and Portuguese base, Global Clinton came to include a significant number of recent immigrants from Latin America and East Asia. But now it included, as well, a growing number of "Canadian" students – the children of young, professional couples who were returning to the very downtown neighbourhoods their parents had left behind. The result was a polyglot, hyper-diverse, multicultural school that had no parallel before and that has not been rivalled since. Chapter 6 tells the story of Clinton's multicultural moment. It also sets the context for chapter 7, in which I describe how the Clinton community explored, and ultimately defined, what it considered the appropriate extent of, and limits to, multicultural education. Here again the Clinton community resisted the policy of its "betters" – in this case a proposal favoured by the school board to integrate so-called heritage language instruction into the school day. Unlike the school's quiet resistance to the Drew Regulations, this resistance was noisy, passionate, and sometimes angry.

The distinguished Catholic theologian Bernard Lonergan liked to compare his scholarship to the blades of a pair of scissors. The lower blade is the data gathered from the particular text being interpreted, the upper blade the larger theory or context to which the data speak. The challenge, as with scissors, is to bring the two blades together productively.[19] Lonergan's metaphor describes my method and this book. The lower blade is the granular story of Clinton Street School, divided into the three eras I have briefly sketched above: Jewish Clinton, European Clinton, and Global Clinton. The upper blade is an alloy created from the linked ideas of integration, diversity, and citizenship.

"Immigration is transforming the societies of North America and western Europe in ways that we could not have predicted a few decades ago."[20] Immigration has been transformative in part because there is simply more of it. According to the United Nations Human Development Programme, which tracks international migration, the number of people worldwide living in a country different from the one in which they were born reached 244 million in 2015. This marks an increase of 40 per cent from the year 2000 alone.

Almost 14 per cent of western Europeans, 14 per cent of Americans, 22 per cent of Canadians, and 27 per cent of Australians and New Zealanders qualify as migrants by this definition.[21] Of course, migration takes several forms and varies in size from country to country. Countries like Canada and the United States have tended (especially recently) to favour potential immigrants who possess certain skills, the financial capacity to create jobs, or both. Most of the Scandinavian countries, on the other hand, have given priority to refugees or asylum-seekers forced from their homelands by war, poverty, or persecution. One way or the other, however, the supply of people wanting and needing to resettle in another country is only going to rise. Between the need for developed countries to attract immigrants in order to maintain economic growth and generate tax revenue and the surge of refugees seeking asylum, global migration is bound to increase.

But it's not just about the numbers. "One consequence of these population movements has been the rise of ethnic, religious, and racial diversity in societies that previously thought of themselves as homogeneous, along with its permanent expansion in societies where immigration was already part of the national story."[22] To say the least, this diversity has become a lightning rod for mobilizing anti-immigration sentiment in many countries, including those that are usually described as "classic immigrant societies." Scratch the surface of the anti-immigration backlash – associated with names like UKIP in Britain, the National Front in France, and Donald Trump in the United States – and you usually find anxiety about the growing diversity of the population. The events of 9/11 (and its corollaries) and the circle-the-wagons response to economic crisis only reinforce this fear.

Yet while the anti-immigration story dominates the headlines, there is a parallel story about immigration and citizenship which, though quieter, is no less important. As Marc Morjé Howard and others have shown, over the past thirty years there has been an incremental but significant change in citizenship laws in many European countries that have not traditionally attracted large numbers of immigrants and that have not traditionally made it easy for immigrants to become full citizens. The basic conclusion to be drawn from this line of research is that it is now easier than it was a generation ago for immigrants – and their children – to become citizens in many European countries.[23] To be sure, not every country has made citizenship easier to acquire and many of the reforms are deeply contested, but in general there has been a liberalizing trend across Europe over the past three decades.[24] The fact is that, like it or not, more and more immigrants and refugees are able to become full-fledged citizens in their adopted countries.

These three trends – increased immigration, greater diversity, and easier citizenship – mean that more and more countries face the crucial "macro" question that Clinton School, in its own "micro" environment, has had to confront over the course of its history: how are new and future citizens best integrated into their new national political communities? This is, clearly, not a simple question to answer. For one thing, integration is by its very nature a dynamic process. It entails a movement or change along a path from one point (the newly arrived immigrant) to another (the integrated citizen). In order to assess whether integration has occurred, we need to be able to measure it in a way that will allow us to identify "before," "during," and "end" points. Beyond this, the process may be slower or faster, and more or less successful, depending on the unit of measurement we use. It is all well and good to plot change, but we have to be sure that the change we are measuring goes to the heart of what it means to "belong" to a given political community. Which measuring rods are the right ones to assess this change?

Finding a way to measure integration has produced a rich and extensive scholarly literature over the years. Broadly speaking, two sorts of answers have emerged. The first is essentially socioeconomic. If you want to understand how or even whether immigrants integrate into their new society, look to see how long it takes (usually counted in generations) for immigrants to improve their social and economic position to the point that they are essentially comparable to native-born citizens. If some immigrants remain locked into low-paying jobs even after a generation or two, for instance, then this immobility may be evidence that assimilation is "segmented" or partial. Since income and education are related, another way to measure integration is to track educational status.

Do members of immigrant groups attend college and university at the same rate as other members of the population? If not, why not? Not all measures are directly connected to economic status, however. Some scholars, for instance, study rates of inter-marriage or residential segregation or language acquisition as ways of assessing the extent of integration. However the rate and quality of integration are measured, the usual goal is to understand how comparable "new" citizens are to "established" ones.[25]

The second general approach to understanding integration focuses to a greater extent on more directly political characteristics.[26] Since voting is often seen as a barometer of active citizenship, one might analyse whether newly minted citizens vote as much (or, these days, as little) as other citizens, or whether they join political parties (and which ones), or whether they run for office with the same frequency (and whether they win). The events of 9/11 generated considerable scholarly interest in, and popular concern about, how long it takes for citizens who grew up in authoritarian regimes to acquire liberal democratic values – or whether this sort of value transference is possible at all. As Christopher Cochrane has observed, "critics of Islam in Canada and across the Western world often frame anti-Islamic positions as a defense of tolerance against intolerance, and equality against inequality."[27]

One particularly interesting measure of political integration focuses on the acquisition of citizenship itself. Not all immigrants who qualify for citizenship decide to become naturalized in their "new" country of residence, and not all immigrants who become citizens in their adopted country do so because they feel a strong attachment to it. Sometimes these decisions simply reflect pragmatic calculations. Still, for most people becoming a citizen is not a casual decision. Does the decision to move from potential citizen to naturalized citizen itself provide a useful way of measuring integration? And if so, then why do some countries consistently "convert" more immigrants into citizens than others? Irene Bloemraad has studied this phenomenon in her comparative study of citizenship in Canada and the United States, *Becoming Citizens*.[28] Working with census data, she has calculated what she calls the level of naturalization in the two countries – the percentage of foreign-born adults who have become naturalized in each country, decade by decade. The data suggest that, for most of the twentieth century, the levels were reasonably similar north and south of the 49th parallel. At the start of the 1970s, slightly more than 60 per cent of foreign-born adults in both countries were naturalized. Thereafter, however, a striking "naturalization gap"[29] appeared. In the United States, the level of naturalization dropped dramatically over the next three decades; by 2000, only about 40 per cent of all foreign-born adults in the United States were American citizens. In Canada, the level of naturalization also changed, only in the opposite direction; by 2001, over 70 per cent of foreign-born adults had become Canadian citizens.

What accounts for this stark Canadian-American difference? Why are immigrants to Canada so much more likely to become Canadian? There are several possibilities. Bloemraad's intriguing (and largely persuasive) answer is that Canada tends to do more than the United States in "providing material and symbolic resources that assist in political incorporation."[30] Material assistance comes in the form, for example, of funding for ethnocultural associations that help immigrant populations learn to mobilize successfully in the Canadian context. (We will encounter a textbook example of how this works in chapter 6, where I relate the story of the creation of Centro Clinton daycare in 1974.) Symbolic assistance comes in the form of Canada's official policy of multiculturalism, which provides "recognition" for "immigrants' diverse identities, ethnicities, and cultures within a framework of *future citizen* rather than *foreigner* or *alien*."[31] It turns out, she argues, that federal assistance to immigrant groups plus the centrality of multiculturalism as an official ideological principle actually do make a difference.

Now, Bloemraad is mainly interested in explaining the naturalization gap that emerged between Canada and the United States between 1970 and 2000; but a rather different puzzle emerges if you look at the Canadian picture alone over a longer historical sweep. As Bloemraad shows, the proportion of naturalized citizens rose in Canada between 1971 and 2001. Yet even at its apogee in 2001, the level of naturalization – around 70 per cent – is actually lower than in either 1941 or in 1951.[32] How come? The high rate of naturalization just before and after the Second World War can't be attributable to the warm glow produced by multiculturalism; that came later.[33] What was it about the war and the years immediately following it that persuaded more foreign-born residents to take out Canadian citizenship? Maybe the sense of common cause associated with the war effort prompted more immigrants to declare their connection to Canada and produced a sort of citizenship dividend. And perhaps the post-war rise in the naturalization rate had something to do with the passage of the Canadian Citizenship Act in 1947. Is it possible that some immigrants were more enthusiastic about taking out citizenship because they found it more attractive to think of themselves as *bona fide* Canadians rather than as "British subjects residing in Canada," which is how Canadians had been known pre-1947?

Perhaps. But don't these historical puzzles also expose a deeper question about the effect of the passage of the Citizenship Act in 1947 on the very meaning of citizenship itself. After all, the new Citizenship Act had the effect, literally, of changing the boundaries and definition of citizenship in Canada – and changing it for everyone. Before, we were British subjects; after, we were simply Canadian citizens. The change is important. Most scholars and commentators interested in immigration focus on the processes of integration. In the patois of social science, they are mainly interested in the independent variable. They want to explain under what conditions immigrants become integrated (or not) into their new milieu, and they want to explain why differences occur from place to place – as, for instance, in the contrast between conversion rates in the United States and Canada. For those who are policy oriented, all this makes a difference; to be able to identify which integration policies work and which don't has real importance on the ground – especially as the pulse of migration quickens.

These are undeniably important questions. But, logically, there is another question that precedes this one about integration. Before we can understand how immigrants fare on the path to becoming full and equal citizens, why some do well and others stumble, we have to know where the path leads and what the destination is. Citizenship, after all, is more than a legal status, the right to hold a passport, or have your name on an electors' list. It entails an effort to create a shared civic identity with specific norms, practices, beliefs, and expectations, even if these norms are contested and changeable. The point is that before we can know how immigrants "become" Canadian, we need to know what it means to "be" Canadian. We need to know what constitutes citizenship before we can judge or measure whether and why immigrants have "made it" to that destination.

The problem is that the meaning of citizenship, the dependent variable (to use the language of social science), is dynamic; it is constantly in flux. The Canadian Citizenship Act of 1947 is a particularly vivid and blunt example of this dynamism. Before 1947 Canadian citizenship meant one thing, defined in large measure by Canada's connection to the British Empire. After 1947 it had the potential to grow into something quite different, which is exactly what happened. But if the definition of what constituted citizenship changed, then what integration meant must have changed as well. It wouldn't make much sense to judge whether immigrants successfully integrated into post-1947 Canada by checking off the integration scorecard drawn up for the pre-1947, British-is-best, "for-King-and-Country," colour-it-Orange citizenship regime. In other words, citizenship is not just a more or less stable "background condition" for developing strategies of integration and figuring out what works best. Rather, citizenship is itself "the object and outcome of contests over power and principle, whose ebb and flow can, in time, illuminate some of the most important questions" facing liberal democracies.[34]

This is why the history of a school like Clinton is so interesting and revealing. It serves as a window into the multiple efforts, in this case of a school located within a wider educational regime, to define and construct citizenship over a period when both the population of citizens and the very meaning of citizenship changed quite significantly. As it turns out, each of the three Clinton communities that I have identified engaged a signature issue that crystallized ideas about, and kindled controversies surrounding, the definition of citizenship. Jewish Clinton was provoked by the provincial government's imposition of system-wide religious instruction to define and mark the place of religious minorities as equal citizens. European Clinton began to work out the difference, both in theory and practice, between integration and assimilation, a critical distinction that (when applied more generally throughout the country) led directly to the rise of multicultural citizenship. And Global Clinton, in the face of mounting pressure to include heritage language instruction as a regular part of the curriculum, set about to define (and constrict) the boundaries of multicultural citizenship. What were the dynamics and logic of these debates? How did one lead to the next? And how, if at all, do these debates illuminate our own situation? This is where the two blades of the scissors (Clinton School and ideas of citizenship) meet – and cut. I will argue that, taken together, the Clinton model of citizenship deserves to be refreshed and restored because it provides an attractive and coherent alternative to the terms of the current debate in Canada – and perhaps elsewhere – about what citizenship entails in a diverse, indeed global, city.

A Note on Method

I said at the outset that this book is a biography of a school. Institutional biographies of this sort tend to come in one of two forms. On the one hand, many individual schools have produced lively accounts of their history, typically in the context of a significant anniversary. Most of these school histories were written for (and often by) former students, and serve as vehicles for reflection, reminiscence, and celebration. At the time of its centennial in 1988, Clinton Street School produced such a history (vignettes from which are sprinkled throughout these pages), and I have profited enormously from the published histories produced by neighbouring schools.[35] On the other hand, there are institutional biographies, though far fewer in number, that tell the story of a school either in order to explore a particular socio-political phenomenon in depth or to advance a larger argument, for instance about youth culture or social change.[36] It is here that *Making a Global City* is situated because I want to suggest that the history of Clinton contributes to a larger story about the history of education, about diversity, and about ideas of citizenship. The difficulty – and one of the reasons this genre is so underpopulated – is that arguments, unlike reminiscences and celebrations, require systematic evidence and data on which to build. The old quip that "the plural of anecdote is not data" expresses the challenge nicely.

The fact is that I wouldn't have embraced this project or written this book had I not been confident that I could make accurate empirical statements about, for instance, the demographic composition of the student body and how it changed over the years. My discovery that Clinton School compiled and still holds a complete set of student registration cards that covers the period bookended by this study, 1920 to 1990, was, therefore, a godsend. For most of the twentieth century Clinton, like other Toronto schools, created registration cards for every student who enrolled at the school. In Clinton's case, this amounted to approximately 22,000 cards for students who attended the school between 1918 and 1990. While there is some variation over the years, these cards typically list the student's name, birth date, birthplace, home address, grades attended, and rooms assigned; the parents' names and birthplaces, occupation(s), and religion(s); when the student left the school and where s/he was bound. The information they contain has made it possible, through analysis of a large random sample, to generate a fine-grained, demographic snapshot of the school, as well as descriptive statistics that show how the school changed over seventy years.[37] There are, presumably, other complete sets of registration cards for other schools both in Toronto and elsewhere, but I don't know of any other collections that have been refined into a data set of this sort.

While the empirical data provide the foundation and framework for this study, the stories told by former students supply the narrative arc. The individual student (and teacher) stories I gathered came from several different sources. In a few cases, like Alan Borovoy's memoir *At the Barricades*,[38] graduates have written about their time at Clinton. A significant number of students responded to invitations, especially the one sent out by the committee organizing the school's centenary in 1988, to record their memories in written form. But the stories on which I have most relied for this book come from approximately seventy-five semi-structured interviews that I conducted over a period of two years, more or less evenly divided among the three Clinton eras. The oldest graduates with whom I spoke entered kindergarten in 1928, the youngest graduated in the late 1980s. As I quickly discovered, their memories, often startlingly vivid and detailed, provided a depth, colour, and texture to the Clinton story that the statistical evidence alone could not supply.[39]

But can one really learn much about citizenship and diversity from the history of a single public school in a particular Canadian city? Clearly, it would be dangerous to generalize from the story of Clinton Street School to all schools in Toronto – much less to schools in Vancouver or New York or London or Amsterdam. Clinton embraced diversity earlier and more vigorously than many schools in Toronto. In this descriptive sense, Clinton was indeed "exceptional," and I don't want to claim that Clinton's experience can be taken as representative of the universe of public schools. Still, shining the klieg lights on a single school like Clinton has significant advantages, most notably the potential to yield a story that is much more nuanced and polyphonic than a general treatise on citizenship and diversity might be.

Most of the studies on citizenship and diversity in Canada – including those that deal with education – approach these issues from a policy perspective: how policy is made, how it is delivered, and the normative goals it embraces.[40] Given this orientation, most policy studies naturally enough proceed from the top (the state) down (to the citizen). The advantage of an institutional biography like this one is that it reverses the narrative flow to tell the story in a way that pays more attention to the voices of teachers, parents, and students. This approach is important, it turns out, because more often than not it is this state-citizen interaction that shapes and drives the dynamics of citizenship. Sometimes Clinton led policy; at other times it followed. Sometimes it embraced broader policy; at other times it resisted. But in every case, this interaction (and sometimes collision) between policy makers and policy takers, state and citizen, served as a catalyst for rethinking the terms of citizenship.

Public schools don't exist in a vacuum. They are institutions of the state (one reason we call them public), nested among other state institutions (most notably school boards and, in Canada, provincial departments or ministries of education) and the citizens they serve.

For someone like me, a political scientist, schools are particularly fascinating because they are the one state institution with which many citizens have daily and recurring interaction. Most citizens are called for jury duty only occasionally, deal directly with the police infrequently, and encounter their elected representatives rarely. But for parents whose children attend a kindergarten-to-grade-6 public school, interaction with the state is all part of the daily routine – from drop-off in the morning, through calls from the office, e-mails from teachers, and volunteering for field trips, to pick-up in the afternoon and homework in the evening. As a consequence, schools are wonderful laboratories for observing how citizens and the state relate to each other, and for understanding how future citizens are constructed. Mostly, the liberal state approaches individuals, its subjects, as fully formed adults with more or less set attitudes and preferences and ways of behaving. Schools are the one institution where future citizens are really moulded into citizens, where the state helps to make them what they are.

As it turns out, a signature issue crystallized the ideas and controversies surrounding citizenship in each of the three Clinton eras surveyed in this book. For Jewish Clinton the issue was the place of religion, punctuated by the Drew Regulations (1944) that made religious instruction a required part of the curriculum for all students in Ontario. European Clinton was defined by the need, sudden but pressing, to develop programs for large numbers of students who spoke little or no English. This led first to pioneering programs in ESL, then to the emergence of a pivotal distinction between assimilation and integration. And in Global Clinton, the controversy over heritage language programs brought the citizenship question to a head once again. So what follows is the story of Clinton Street School told in three (largely) symmetrical parts. Each part has two chapters. The first sets out the social and demographic context and describes what school was like from era to era. The second concentrates on the signature issue that, I believe, defined the citizenship debate in each era. Together, they provide an account of how one Toronto school, in different ways at different times, embraced diversity.

2

Jewish Clinton, 1920–1952:
"Well to the Fore among Toronto Schools"

In the fall of 1917, the *Toronto Star Weekly* commissioned a well-known Toronto journalist, W.A. Craik, to write a feature article profiling Clinton Street Public School. Craik was well-prepared for the assignment. Over a two-year period during the First World War he had reported on some sixty-four public schools in Toronto, so by the time he visited Clinton, Craik had a solid basis for comparing and judging.[1] Clinton did well by Craik. It is an "excellent" school, the article concluded, with "a record of solid achievement … that places it well to the fore among Toronto schools." Why the high marks? The school had been blessed with consistently strong leadership since its creation in 1888, and a brand-new physical plant made it "spacious, bright and airy"; but most of all Clinton profited from the community in which it was embedded:

> The Clinton Street School district is both compact and homogeneous. It forms an almost exact square, extending north and south from Bloor to College, and east and west from Palmerston to Crawford. The population is describable as solid middle-class, including artisans and business and professional men, with their families. As yet the district has not been affected to any important extent by the influx of foreign-born population, and the percentage of Hebrew boys and girls in attendance at the school is not more than seven.[2]

Craik's comment that the Clinton community did not have to deal with an "influx of foreign-born population" seems curious at first. After all, while many in the Clinton community had deep roots in Canada, almost 40 per cent of Clinton parents at the time had been born in Britain, not Canada. But anyone reading the *Toronto Star Weekly* that day would have understood that Craik was not speaking of these British-Canadian immigrants when he spoke of the "foreign-born." Like many others, he used the expression as code to describe the growing number – the "influx" he called it – of immigrants to Toronto who were neither British by origin, middle class by status, nor Protestant or Anglican by belief. And no one – as the punch line of Craik's summary suggests – fitted the description of "foreign-born" better than the 7 per cent of Clinton students who were Jewish.

And then, in the blink of a demographer's eye, Clinton Street Public School changed. It went from being the solidly British and Protestant school Craik profiled in 1917 into a school that served as a gateway to Canadian society for the "foreign-born," especially Jews (see figure 2.1). Morley Safer, Clinton class of 1946 and well-known television journalist, described his school as a "patchwork

Figure 2.1 Clinton Street School – Religion by Family – 1920–1980

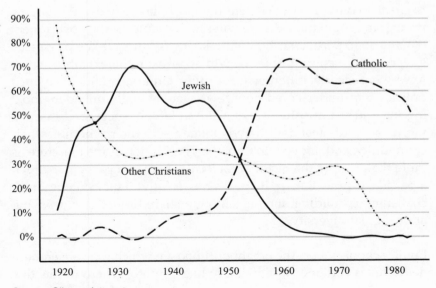

Source: Clinton data set

quilt" of ethnic groups – Jewish, Ukrainian, Scots, Irish, English, and Italian.[3] And so it was; but within this quilt the Jewish pattern (if you will) stood out. Recall Craik's figures. In 1917, at best 7 per cent of the school's population was Jewish. By the mid-1920s, 40 per cent of the student body was Jewish, and from that point forward until the mid-1950s, the proportion of Jewish students at Clinton never dipped below 40 per cent and sometimes rose above 70 per cent. In other words, for almost three decades Clinton was a largely Jewish school in a public education system whose officially stated aim was to prepare children "to live in a democratic society" based "upon the Christian ideal" and that sought "to bring home to the pupils ... the fundamental truths of Christianity."[4]

The next two chapters tell the story of what I call Jewish Clinton: how the school, its students, and their parents made a largely Jewish school work within an educational system created in the image of Protestant Ontario. In one respect the story of Jewish Clinton is a small piece of local educational history that will resonate most meaningfully, I suspect, with those who lived it or whose school experience was in some ways comparable to it. But the story of Jewish Clinton, I want to argue, has much broader implications, for Jewish Clinton was in effect an early experiment in how (and how not) to create a community of citizens out of a religiously diverse, largely immigrant population. As we will see in chapter 3, the government of Ontario in particular did not make it easy. Indeed, the provincial government went out of its way to accentuate the extent to which Jews were clearly different from other Ontarians and developed policies that underscored how Jews were actually outsiders looking in. And yet in spite of this, Clinton largely succeeded in making its students feel as if they belonged – to their school, to their community, and, indeed, to Canada. The Clinton story, therefore, is more than simply the history of a local school in a particular city at a particular time. Rather, it speaks powerfully to the contemporary challenge of building and sustaining a shared sense of citizenship amidst great diversity.

Public schools reflect the neighbourhoods in which they are embedded. This is certainly true in a city like Toronto, where to this day the rules governing school enrolment are set by comparatively rigid "catchment" boundaries that define who is eligible (or not) to attend a given school. So to understand the transformation of Clinton in the 1920s (and beyond), we need first to understand the transformation of the west end neighbourhood that feeds it. Who lived there? What did they do? What did they bring to the community?

Begin with the big picture. The wave of immigration that settled much of western Canada at the turn of the twentieth century also transformed Toronto's Jewish population. According to census data, the Jewish population in Toronto grew explosively in the decade between 1901 and 1911 – from 3,090 to 18,237. By 1921 (and despite the First World War, which effectively froze immigration from Europe), the number of Jews in Toronto almost doubled again – yielding a total of nearly 35,000.[5] By far the greatest number of these new immigrants came from eastern Europe, especially Poland, Russia, Ukraine, Lithuania, and Rumania, where religious persecution through the system of pogroms was harshest. As Gerald Tulchinsky has noted, "at higher levels, government officials publicly manifested sympathy for Jewish suffering." Indeed, speaking at a public meeting in 1906, organized to protest Russian pogroms, Prime Minister Laurier "offered refugees 'a hearty welcome' in Canada."[6] The net effect of Jewish immigration on Toronto's demographic profile was significant. According to census figures, in 1901 only 1.5 per cent of Torontonians were Jewish.[7] By 1921, this had risen to 6.6 per cent and by 1931 to 7.2 per cent.[8] This made Jews the largest non-Anglo/Celtic ethnic community in the city – by a considerable margin.

Many of these newly arrived immigrants settled initially in the downtown area known as The Ward. It was cheap and close to the garment district – both Eaton's and Simpson's had factories nearby – but it was also infamously squalid and increasingly an embarrassment to Toronto's political elite.[9] The result is that the immigrant communities that settled there were at once "pushed" out of The Ward by the city and "pulled" to more congenial and salubrious neighbourhoods by their own desire to build a better life for themselves. For many Jews, this meant looking west to Spadina Avenue (by this point "a principal centre of Toronto's clothing industry"),[10] Kensington Market, or beyond Bathurst Street into the Clinton area – to streets like Markham, Palmerston, Euclid, Manning, Clinton, and Grace, both north and south of College Street. According to Daniel Hiebert, whose demographic analysis of Jewish Toronto in this era remains the gold standard, the geographical area that corresponds roughly to the Clinton catchment area basically doubled in population between 1915 and 1931.[11] Most of this increase came from Jewish families moving in, which explains the sudden growth in the number of Jewish students at Clinton.

Why the west end? First and foremost, the area was close to the garment industry on Spadina Avenue. This was hugely important because about 40 per cent of working Jews in Toronto in the 1920s, 1930s, and 1940s were employed in the garment industry in one way or another;[12] the percentage was even higher in the Clinton area.[13] Many were tailors. Beyond this there were cutters and designers, furriers and hat makers, all of whom circulated in and around the small garment factories on Spadina. As Hiebert and others have pointed out, many of these garment workers gravitated to, and were radicalized by, the labour movement.[14] They worked long hours in dreadful conditions, were paid little, and were receptive to calls for collective action to improve working conditions. The garment industry became a flashpoint for union activity because the business was at once highly competitive (which kept wages low) and extraordinarily volatile (which made work unpredictable). Workers bore the brunt of both and "actively protested against low pay, seasonal layoffs, piecework rates, unsanitary shops, and employers' aggressive union-busting tactics."[15]

Yet as Hiebert also notes, one of the striking things about the garment industry on Spadina was the steady growth of Jewish ownership over the years. He estimates that, by the 1930s, between one-third and one-half of the garment industry was controlled by Jews.[16] Tip Top Tailors, a firm which creatively exploited a mid-range price gap in the clothing market, is the classic example.[17] So when Jewish garment workers protested the conditions under which they worked, the object of their protest was often Jewish factory owners who were also their neighbours. Employers found the Clinton district an attractive place to live for the same reason that it appealed to their employees: it was close to work. According to Hiebert's analysis of assessment rolls from the 1930s, while just over 50 per cent of heads of households in the Clinton area were blue-collar workers (mostly garment workers), 10 per cent were factory owners and another 11 per cent worked in white-collar positions.[18] Add to this mix those residents who were self-employed – butchers, bakers, window washers, taxi drivers, scrap dealers, and the occasional bookie – and the socio-economic picture of the Clinton area becomes still more heterogeneous and more resistant to easy description. It is tempting, as some have done, to call the Clinton district a working-class neighbourhood. This is too simple. Between the 1920s and the 1940s, it became a mixed socio-economic community, in which workers and owners, the self-employed and factory workers, professionals and semi-skilled labourers rubbed shoulders as they lived on the same or adjacent streets. Their economic interests and political commitments may have been starkly different, but they walked the same streets – and sent their children to the same schools.

Toronto's west end was attractive as well because it had ample, late-model housing. The Clinton area opened up only after the College streetcar line was extended beyond Bathurst Street in 1880. Even in the 1890s, however, the area was still patchy in its development, so when these Jewish families were in the market for a place to live in the 1920s, the housing stock west of Bathurst must have seemed attractive – and relatively affordable. By 1931, almost three-quarters of the houses in the Clinton area were occupied by their owners, the highest concentration in Jewish Toronto.[19] To be sure, the high rate of home ownership had something to do with the relatively large number of wealthy families living on streets like Palmerston Boulevard, distinguished by its entrance gates and elegant light standards. And it probably also underestimates the extent to which a family-owned dwelling housed several branches of the same family or boarders – one family to a floor. Still, it is remarkable that almost two-thirds of blue-collar workers in Toronto's downtown Jewish core lived in a family-owned house of some sort;[20] others had the peace of mind that came from long-term rental agreements.

This fact underscores another defining characteristic of the Clinton community – its relative stability. Whatever their class status,

Figure 2.2 Destination of Graduates – 1932–1940

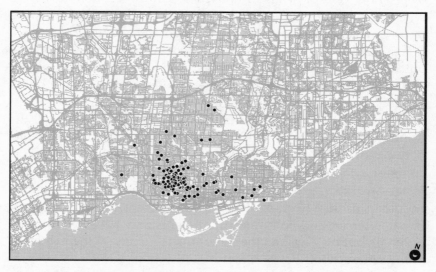

Sources: Clinton data set and open-source maps

these families weren't moving any time soon. In part, this stability reflects economic necessity. Even if families aspired to own a larger house in a tonier suburban neighbourhood – and no doubt many did – the one-two punch of the Depression and the Second World War severely limited their mobility. As figure 2.2 shows clearly, most Clinton graduates in the 1930s stayed in the neighbourhood when they graduated from grade 8, and most of those who left the school before grade 8 moved to another school in the same neighbourhood. The exodus "up the hill" to suburban Bathurst Heights occurred later, made possible by the economic prosperity that followed the war.

Economic considerations aside, families flocked to the west end and stayed there because it connected them to a vibrant Jewish life – in its many religious, cultural, and political forms. Here again it is diversity that stands out. For observant Jews it was important to be close enough to synagogues to be able to walk to and from services, and the Clinton area was near enough to established synagogues, like the ones on McCaul Street and Cecil Street, to fit these ambulatory criteria. Once a critical population mass was reached closer to home, small, "storefront" synagogues (many bearing the name of a particular town or locale in Poland or Russia) began popping up in the Clinton neighbourhood itself,[21] and more than a few Clinton boys preparing for their bar mitzvah attended after-school Hebrew lessons at a local *chader* (Hebrew school) – like the one on Manning Avenue directly across the street from the school or, slightly farther afield, at the Talmud Torah on Brunswick Avenue just north of College. There were kosher butchers and Jewish bakeries; the director of the famous Toronto Jewish Folk Choir (a Clinton parent) made music out of his house on Palmerston Boulevard; and in the 1940s Canada's first Jewish Boy Scout Troop, the 54thB, met weekly at Clinton. For those more interested in politically centred activities, the possibilities were almost endless. Jerry Gray (and several of his Clinton friends) attended meetings and activities sponsored by the United Jewish Peoples' Order (UJPO) – the leading left-wing organization. It was there, at the UJPO summer camp *Naivelt* (or New World), that his celebrated folk group, The Travellers, was born. The *Arbeiter Ring*, or Workman's Circle, was UJPO's social democratic counterpart (or rival), and many of the unions, especially those affiliated with the garment industry, provided social services, organized rallies, and sponsored lectures. All of these activities nurtured a rich and diverse associational life in downtown Toronto.

As this sketch of the area's subculture suggests, downtown Toronto had something that most other parts of the city – most other parts of Canada, actually – lacked: a colourful, even raucous, political scene energized by an electorally competitive Left. Consider, for example, electoral politics at the provincial level. Clinton was located in the provincial riding of Bellwoods, a long, narrow slice of a constituency that ran from Lake Ontario in the south to St Clair Avenue in the north, and from about Bathurst on the east to Dovercourt on the west. Its neighbour to the east, St Andrews, was similarly configured, stretching from the lake to St Clair Avenue, and from Spadina to Bathurst. Between them, Bellwoods and St Andrews constituted the heart and soul of Jewish Toronto. In the 1920s and 1930s, the constituencies alternated between Liberal and Conservative representatives. But in the elections of 1943, 1945, and 1948, they returned Ontario's only Labour Progressives – the "re-branded" name of the outlawed Communist Party. St Andrews was held by the much-beloved Joe Salsberg.[22] Voters in Bellwoods elected the fiery Cape Bretoner A.A. MacLeod (whose daughter attended Clinton). In all three of MacLeod's victories, the Conservative candidate finished second. And in all three, MacLeod won because of his popularity in the Clinton catchment area. In the election of 1945, for example, MacLeod won a hard-fought, four-way election in which he prevailed with just over one-third of the vote. But on the streets that fed Clinton Street School he polled almost twenty points higher, capturing more than half of all votes cast.[23] Salsberg did even better on the one street in his constituency that overlapped Clinton's catchment area.[24]

Working side by side, MacLeod and Salsberg became a dynamic tag team at Queen's Park and a constant thorn in the side of Premier George Drew. For Drew the challenge represented by this "pair of rats" went beyond conventional partisan differences. "'Rat' is the only word to use," Drew maintained, "because they are gnawing away at the foundation of our free society."[25] For many of his constituents on the other hand, including a significant number of Clinton parents, MacLeod and Salsberg – and the principles they represented – were nearly heroic. Jack Quarter, who came from a communist family, recalled visiting his grandfather, who lived a few blocks away: "I was maybe eleven years old when Joe Stalin died. I came to my … grandparents' place on Lippincott to visit, with my dad, and my grandfather was standing over this … big radio … listening to the news with tears in his eyes. And I remember around the same time when the Rosenbergs were put to death in Sing Sing Prison in New York, I remember vividly the look of horror on my father's face."[26]

The Left's strength – but also the electorate's polarization – affected the school board as well. Throughout the 1930s and 1940s, voters in the local ward in which Clinton was situated, Ward 5, had a penchant for electing school board trustees with radically different views of the world. On the Right, the most strident was Harold Menzies, who was virulently anti-communist and who used every possible opportunity over the course of several terms on the school board to protect Toronto's students from communism.[27] On the Left were trustees like Rose Henderson (a maverick CCF trustee in the 1930s),[28] well-known for her advocacy on behalf of disadvantaged students; Edna Ryerson (in the 1940s), who wore her communist colours proudly; and John Boyd (another Labour Progressive). Rose Henderson, in fact, almost became a household name at Clinton. When she died suddenly in 1937, a motion was floated at the school board to re-name Clinton the Rose Henderson Public School. In the event, the proposal was scuppered by the Conservative-dominated school board, with editorial assistance from the *Toronto Telegram*.[29] Clinton it was; Clinton it remained.

Ethnically heterogeneous, economically mixed, demographically stable, culturally diverse, and politically charged, from the early 1920s through the 1940s Clinton's neighbourhood was a far cry from the "compact and homogeneous" British-Canadian community Craik had described for his *Star Weekly* readers in 1917. And yet, for all its kaleidoscopic human variety, there was one thing on which just about everyone in the Clinton orbit agreed: school mattered. Left or Right, worker or boss, owner or renter, religious or secular, among residents there was a powerful consensus that education was the key to a better life; and that the school and its teachers were there, in one well-known graduate's words, "to kick us up the social ladder."[30] Some parents were actively engaged with their children's education (especially those mothers who ran the Home and School Association); more were not (especially those fathers who worked long, long hours). But it really wasn't active participation that counted. Almost without exception, the graduates I interviewed recalled that their parents thought their job was to reinforce, forcefully and usually uncritically, the basic rule that their children should do what their teachers told them to do. Punctuality was enforced, good marks were expected, and a phone call from the school to explain a child's detention brought shame. In this world, Home and School was more than the name of the organization that met once a month; it was a mutually supportive Axis of Good that worked to deliver a sound education.

The home-school nexus no doubt drew strength from the fact that the partners – parents and teachers – spoke the same language, literally as well as figuratively. This is noteworthy. Louis Rosenberg, the outstanding demographer of Canadian Jewry, pointed out many years ago that the facility and speed with which first-generation Jewish immigrants learned English was quite remarkable. According to the 1931 census data that Rosenberg analysed, almost 95 per cent of foreign-born Jews over the age of ten were able to speak English.[31] Apart from immigrants from Scandinavian countries, no other first-generation immigrant community commanded such proficiency in English at the time. These data are consistent with my interviews. Many of the graduates spoke warmly about Yiddish language and culture, and a good number told me that Yiddish remained vital in their homes – especially when grandparents visited or lived with them. Still, for almost of all of them, English was the *lingua franca* at home, as it was at school.

What was spoken was also read, and many of the graduates recalled the importance of books in their family's life. For one a subscription to a daily newspaper, typically the *Toronto Star*, provoked lively dinner-time conversations and nurtured a life-long interest in current events. The parents of another, who couldn't afford books, much less a newspaper subscription, nevertheless scrimped and saved to buy a multi-volume set of *Compton's Encyclopedia* for their children. A third showed me her mother's book collection, in Yiddish and English, lovingly preserved to this day. But the prize for greatest dedication to reading surely must go to Howard Moscoe, later a well-known city councillor, who attended Women's Christian Temperance Union (WCTU) meetings held at the school just so that he could receive the free books that were awarded at the end of the term.[32] To be sure, it is dangerous to draw direct connections between the presence of books and academic performance. As one astute graduate noted, he came away from his childhood with a love of reading; his two brothers, who lived in the same home, did not. Still, in galvanizing the connection between home and school, it can't have hurt to have lived in an environment where reading was valued.

Clinton Street Public School was central to the lives of these families. What was it like? In many ways, Clinton was a rather typical Toronto school, and was probably not so different from many urban schools in

Canada at the time. Like other Toronto schools, the Clinton experience began with kindergarten. Thanks to the advocacy of James L. Hughes, Toronto's inspector of schools from 1874 to 1913,[33] the city had been well ahead of the curve in developing pre-school programs. And since kindergarten was thought to be particularly valuable in socializing downtown, immigrant, and working-class children, it comes as no surprise that Clinton was among the first to establish a regular pre-school program. Eva (or Evelyn) Woolley began teaching kindergarten at Clinton in 1898, a post she held for more than thirty years. Her room, furnished with a piano and adorned with a stained-glass window, was the place where many a Clinton student was introduced to formal education. In fact, kindergarten was also sometimes surprisingly informal. Indeed, one student who entered kindergarten in 1928 recalled vividly how Miss Woolley, now in the twilight of her career, would get down on the floor to lead her young charges in games.

What began in kindergarten ended, nine years later, in the senior fourth form – what came to be known after 1937 as grade 8. (This configuration remained until 1958, when, under escalating enrolment pressures, Clinton scaled back its operations to grade 6.) In an era in which most students did not attend school beyond grade 8,[34] the kindergarten-to-grade-8 school took on special importance. For many students this was the only formal schooling they would receive. For those who did pursue their studies beyond grade 8, the junior and senior public school experience provided both the rudder to steer their passage and the materials and skills they needed to realize their aspirations.

Steering took the form of sorting – and sometimes actively segregating – students according to certain "innate" or immutable characteristics.[35] One such characteristic was gender. As almost every graduate I interviewed reminded me, Clinton (like other schools of its era) had separate entrances for boys and girls – and separate playgrounds besides.[36] (One graduate I spoke with, accused of bothering his female classmates, was punished by being consigned to playing in the girls' playground for a week. To this day, he wonders what purpose was served by this punishment.) Gender also clearly governed instruction in the "useful" sciences. Girls attended classes in household science (aka home economics); boys went to manual training (for much of this period "shop" classes were located at neighbouring King Edward School). Interestingly, household science still generates strong views. As one graduate put it sardonically, "I remember Miss Anglin, our household science teacher, who made most of the girls vow never to become homemakers."[37] Another remembered how "ridiculous" it was to come away from these classes having learned only how to make hot chocolate and slice grapefruit. A third, though, attributed her lifelong love of sewing and beading to the instruction she was given as a student at Clinton. About the boys' training in "shop" I heard much less, save for recollections of tie racks constructed and a much-disliked teacher at King Edward who enforced discipline by rapping students on the knuckles with a solid metal pipe.

Academic streaming was another form of sorting. Toronto schools did not institute "gifted" programs until after the Second World War, but in the 1920s and 1930s they found other ways to identify and create special programs for "bright," academically inclined students. One technique was to accelerate capable students collectively. For most of the interwar and immediate post-war period, the school created a class that completed three years of academic work in two. The group typically began together in grade 3, and after two years together they were promoted to grade 6. How and why the program began is unclear. It is quite likely that class acceleration was as much a strategy to overcome overcrowding as it was a way to acknowledge individual intellectual capacity, and to this day most of the graduates I spoke with have no clear idea why they had been selected to accelerate. Still, whatever the mysteries surrounding it, this sort of collective acceleration was an important part – and not always a happy part – of the Clinton experience for a considerable number of students.

About the criteria for assigning students to what were called auxiliary (later re-named "opportunity") classes more is known. Like many North American school boards in the 1920s, the Toronto Board of Education (TBE) was taken with the arguments of Lewis Terman, whose treatise *The Intelligence of Schoolchildren* became the go-to guide for educational administrators in Toronto and beyond.[38] Terman maintained that "innate differences in intelligence" were "chiefly responsible" for "the school laggard,"[39] and he developed the Stan-ford-Binet test – popularly known as the IQ (intelligence quotient) test – to capture these innate differences. Toronto's educational leadership understood perfectly well the profound implications that followed from Terman's theory and from the use of IQ tests. Indeed, one of the city's most prominent educators hailed intelligence tests as "the greatest single contribution to the field of education in our time."[40] If intelligence was really inborn, then it would be "wasting energy" to hold "mentally slow and defective children up to a level of progress which is normal to the average child, or superior child." Under the circumstances, it would be "wiser to take account of the inequalities of children in original endowment and to differentiate the course of study" according to IQ.[41] Moreover, if intelligence was fixed by "original endowment," then the potential for cognitive growth was radically limited. Once IQ became the critical measure of intelligence and educational potential, other potentially "fixable" factors in a student's life – like a family's socio-economic position, or linguistic ability, or illness – came to matter less or not at all.[42]

Both implications – that intelligence is innate and that it is fixed – led in the same direction: to the creation of a special stream for those students who were deemed "subnormal," typically defined as those who scored between fifty and seventy-five on the school-administered IQ test.[43] In 1920 there was a single auxiliary class in Toronto; by the end of the 1920–1 school year there were thirteen, and by 1930–1 the number had grown to fifty-three.[44] As with the establishment of kindergarten classes, Clinton was close to the leading edge of this educational experiment. It created its first auxiliary class in 1922, and for the next three decades the school assigned one teacher to an auxiliary class of approximately twenty students.[45] One graduate's poignant memory perhaps stands in for many: "I believe that I befriended one member of the (auxiliary) class ... He, like his classmates, was not well treated by the so-called normal students. His mother was a friend of my mother, and I suppose my mother made me realize that he deserved understanding and not mistreatment. He was a gentle soul and, I thought, not severely disabled. But, generally, the auxiliary class students were separated from the others."

The final example of academic sorting at Clinton, deaf education, is also the most distinctive. When, in 1924, the TBE decided to establish specialized day school instruction for "totally deaf" students, Clinton was designated the board's magnet school. First established for deaf children in the early grades, deaf education classes subsequently expanded to provide instruction for older students as well, and the school remained the centre for deaf education in the public school system until 1953.[46] The TBE (and therefore Clinton) was committed to what was known as the "oralist" approach to deaf education, which stressed lip reading (rather than signing) and the acquisition of speech through imitation. Like many of the other forms of special education that relied on sorting students, oralism was embraced as a progressive school reform that attempted to meet the needs of an increasingly diverse body of students. On the one hand, oralism was a method that tailored instruction to the specific needs of deaf students. On the other, it provided both the tools and the hope that these students would ultimately be able to join the social mainstream. As Toronto's director of education put it, the goal of oralism was to overcome the "antiquated belief that 'if a child were deaf, he must also be dumb.'"[47] This reliance on "strict" oralist techniques, however, was controversial at the time – and remains so. David Peikoff, one of the harshest critics of the TBE's commitment to oralism, put it this way: "Beneath all the glitter and glamour of prepared public demonstrations, the Clinton Street day school has not been able to equip the greatest number of their [deaf] graduates with a truly liberal education."[48] Indeed, he continued, Clinton deaf students had been "mentally warped for life."[49] One doesn't have to go quite that far to appreciate just how isolating life at Clinton must have been for these students. A small number of the graduates I spoke with said they did try to communicate with deaf students on occasion, and the deaf students occasionally participated in school-wide activities and events.[50] But most students on either side of the divide had little contact with each other for one very practical reason: the classrooms for the deaf students were located in the original (now rather dilapidated) school, and the students entered and exited from a completely different set of doors – out of sight and out of mind.

Sorting – by gender, ability, or deafness – was central to Clinton as it was to other urban schools in North America at the time. But there was another, related practice that touched many students more directly. The auxiliary classes, after all, only accounted for about 2 or 3 per cent of Clinton's total enrolment; this hardly exhausted the supply of students who faced academic or personal challenges, or who lived at the school's margins. What stood out for a number of graduates, I discovered, was less the process of sorting that led to special treatment than the apparent indifference to individual students in the "regular" stream who for a variety of reasons didn't quite fit in. Doreen Kronick, who went on to become a leading authority on learning disabilities,[51] noted that those who struggled academically "just sat around class till they turned sixteen and somebody gave them a lunch bucket and they went off to work." She remembers those students "not getting very much understanding" at school.[52] Indeed, school officials tended to describe, label, and blame such students for being "annoying," "disruptive," and, perhaps most damning of all, "a general nuisance."[53] Nor was the emphasis on conformity restricted to regulating unruly behaviour. One student vividly recalled being hounded by the school's principal because he was left-handed. The student resisted the pressure to change his writing hand, but the uninvited initiative to change still rankles some seventy years later. Alan Borovoy dedicated his memoir to his school chum, Louis Goldstein, who had been orphaned as a young child and who wore a brace on his leg as the result of childhood polio. Borovoy writes:

Louis Goldstein was probably my oldest friend ... For some reason, he began to confide in me at an early age. For long periods of time, therefore, I was seeing the world through his eyes. He keenly felt his differentness. And it hurt ... One aspect of Louis's differentness was the school's insistence on calling him by the name with which he had been born rather than that of the family with whom he lived. In view of the way I was identifying with him, I grew up angry at the school authorities. Indeed, during a television interview years later I ventilated my indignation over his treatment. On television, I called the educators of that era, "insensitive bastards." In talking about that period in our lives, I felt myself actually reliving much of the experience.[54]

For Borovoy, lifelong civil libertarian and gadfly, this was not Clinton's finest hour.

Once a child had been sorted, streamed, and normalized, what was it like to be a student? What did students learn and how did they learn it? Historians who have posed these questions about public schools in the interwar years have produced two quite different pictures of what school was like. Both, actually, resonate with the Clinton experience. One view, most clearly identified with Neil Sutherland, emphasizes the formalism of instruction and the premium placed on discipline:

> Whether pupils attended school cheerfully or apprehensively or in a state of fear, curriculum, teaching methods, and the pattern of school discipline combined to press them into the formal mode of learning. Its system was based on teachers talking and pupils listening, a system that discouraged independent thought, a system that provided little opportunity to be creative, a system that blamed rather than praised, a system that made no direct or purposed effort to build a sense of self-worth. Even those who enjoyed it then now recall a system that put its rigour into the rote learning of times tables, of spelling words, of the "Lady of the Lake," of the capes and bays of Canada, of "the twelve adverbial modifiers (of place, of reason, of time ...)," and of the Kings and Queens.[55]

As Sutherland points out, teachers can hardly be blamed for employing formal methods. Most urban Canadian schools in the interwar period, including Clinton, assigned forty (or more) students to a class. Sheer size "made other forms of teaching and learning impossible."[56] But formalism was more than a strategy of necessity. Educators embraced formalism both because they thought it was the best way for students to learn skills of numeracy and literacy and because they believed it was an efficient way for students to master particular, and actually quite demanding, bodies of knowledge.[57] One of Toronto's school inspectors, reporting on the state of teaching methods in schools in 1932, noted with satisfaction that Toronto teachers were placing more emphasis on the usefulness of drill. "More stress," he noted, "is laid on the *drill* and the *review* lessons.

Young teachers usually overlook the value of drill and review until they hold their first tests."[58]

For some students the formal method worked well. One graduate recalled rather fondly the rat-a-tat-tat of Miss Alexander's conductor's baton as she walked down the aisle, leading her students as they recited the times tables in unison. He was a bright enough kid, he thought, but teachers like Miss Alexander instilled habits of self-discipline that proved extremely useful later on. Others chafed under it. As one graduate put it, "I'm proud of having gone to Clinton. I think it gave me a good grounding," but "I didn't like the rigid discipline." For others formalism was synonymous with boredom. A particularly evocative description comes from a student who went to school in Montreal, but her account is consistent with what I heard from some Clinton grads as well: "The girls' school I attended for some three years was dreadful. In all that time I was taught as much Latin as one can pick up in less than a term at college. I also learned some geometry, and one English teacher taught us how to compose a précis, which is a very useful skill. The rest of the teachers just stood in front of us and read the textbook out loud. What I really learned was the meaning of boredom, and I learned that so well I have never been bored since then."[59]

Nor were the opportunities for drill, discipline, and self-control confined to the classroom. Like many other Canadian schools, Clinton organized a cadet corps both before and during the Second World War. As the teacher in charge explained, the goal was not to recruit students into the army. It was, rather, "to teach you to talk properly, to stand properly, to control yourself. Instead of feeling apprehensive that one so young is being asked to think and act in a military manner, think of it rather as an opportunity to develop muscular control."[60] Looking back, these lessons in the principles of kinesiology were not top of mind for the former cadets I interviewed. Some remembered the endless marching in formation up and down the Clinton playground (and occasionally farther afield when asked to participate in larger rallies with other cadets). What lingered for others were memories of the ill-fitting red tunics, which, by all accounts, had been retrieved from a collection left over from the First World War. And from one I learned that the basement of the old building had been turned into a rifle range where the young cadets were taught how to shoot with 0.22-calibre rifles on loan from Ottawa.

Formalism aimed to instil moral as well as intellectual and physical discipline, and to this end Clinton developed a rich system of carrots and sticks, incentives and punishments. The incentives were sometimes informal and classroom-specific; several graduates recalled the "honour" of being chosen to clean the blackboard or deliver messages to the main office. Others were formal and school-wide, like the honours certificate (and sometimes a medal) awarded annually, from the late 1920s until 1949, to those students who behaved well, had spotless attendance records, and were consistently punctual. According to my data, an average of 9 per cent of Clinton students received an honours certificate annually during the interwar years. Three trends emerge from these data. The first is that there was almost no gender bias in the awarding of honours certificates; boys were as likely to earn honours certificates as girls. The second is that immigrant status mattered. Second-generation immigrants – that is, those students who were born in Canada to parents born elsewhere – were far more likely to receive honours certificates than either first-generation immigrants or students whose families had been in Canada for at least three generations. Here is one way in which the Axis of Good – the entente between immigrant parents and the school – paid dividends. And, finally, if memory is any measure of significance, then it is unclear how important the honour certificate was in students' lives. Only a few of the former students I interviewed mentioned them; still fewer had kept them amidst their memorabilia.

If honour certificates were meant to build compliance by appealing to a student's vanity or pride, punishment was meant to induce compliance through fear. Here the memories are vivid, not vague. One graduate remembered the first and only time a teacher spanked her. Another recalled a teacher in the 1930s – her aunt, as it happens – who dealt with children who spoke out of turn by tying a kerchief around their mouths. Others recalled the role played by student monitors, older students who "joined teachers and principals in the task of teaching and maintaining appropriate standards, especially among the younger children."[61] The position of monitor was another honorific, framed as an exercise in democratic self-control. In fact, according to one student, the monitors who patrolled the playground were like "prison guards and would turn you in for the slightest infraction of school rules. Monitors could be more brutal than the most demanding of teachers. A lesson perhaps in the corrupting nature of power."[62]

But it is the punishment of last resort – the strap – that tells the most interesting story. The strap was used routinely to punish students in Toronto schools until 1971;[63] everyone from Jewish Clinton remembered it, including those who had no personal experience with it. The data I've compiled on its use at the school reveal several patterns.[64] The first is that corporal punishment, unlike honour certificates, was deeply gendered – in two ways. On the one hand, the strap was administered almost exclusively to boys; only 5 per cent of those strapped between 1931 and 1971 were girls. On the other, one of the punishable offences that appears time and again in the official records involves boys hitting (and occasionally hitting on) girls. One boy was given eight "slaps" for "punching a girl," another for slapping a girl in class, and a third got it for "indecent action with a girl." Second, the frequency of corporal punishment varies widely from year to year. In 1932–3, one of the first years for which we have reliable data, a total of 236 strappings occurred over the course of the school year at Clinton. This is astonishing. It means that the school used corporal punishment frequently enough to be able to redden the palms of roughly one-fifth of the student body over the course of a single academic year.[65] The frequency of strapping then receded quickly from this high point, and from the mid-1930s until after the Second World War there were typically fifty strappings per year.[66] When a new principal arrived on the scene in 1950–1, a new policy of restraint seems to have arrived with him. Where in the 1940s (under Principal Austin) corporal punishment was administered on average close to fifty times per year, in the 1950s (under Principal Pollard) its use dropped dramatically, to an average of ten times a year. As Figure 2.3 shows, a similar decline appears if one calculates the number of "slaps" administered.

What offences were punishable by the strap at Clinton? Here the school seems to have been pretty much free to define its own

Figure 2.3 Corporal Punishment – 1932–1970

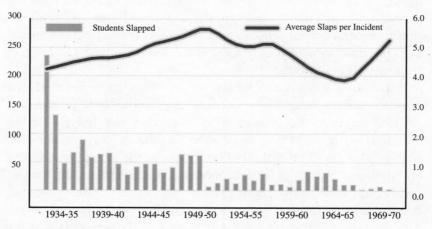

Source: Clinton data set

criteria and rule book for corporal punishment. During the interwar years there were no specific board-wide guidelines, and the only provincial standard was hopelessly vague: teachers were expected "to practice such discipline as would be exercised by a kind, firm, and judicious parent."[67] Still, it is possible to organize most of the punishable offences into four basic categories.[68] First and most frequently reported are cases of defiance to authority and/or breaking the rules. "Sauciness and disobedience," "non-conformity to rules," "insubordination," and "defiant incitement of others to disobey" all merited the strap. So did uttering an "anti-British remark" during wartime. A second category involved what lawyers who advertise on late-night television call personal injury. The list of offences is colourful and a tad scary: "fighting" of course, but also "cruelty," "biting a little girl's arm," "gangster tactics," "slashing with a knife," "putting glue on a boy's face," and "turning a boy upside down in the hall." Perhaps most interesting here is that the term "bullying" – physical intimidation – appears frequently and explicitly as a punishable offence as early as 1933. Third, the school dealt swiftly with wilful damage to property. "Destroying school property," "malicious destruction," and stealing "a watch from a teacher's desk" all turn up on the lists of offences; but then so does "picking the flowers." And, fourth, corporal punishment was sometimes used to show a teacher's disapproval of behaviour that betrayed what teachers considered to be a lack of self-discipline. "Chronic lateness," "continued laziness," "repeated truancy," and "carelessness" all merited several slaps. Beyond this, there are cases in which the punishment seems to say more about the teacher's exasperation than the student's crime. How else to explain strapping the boy who was caught "singing during my absence," the miscreant who was "hoo-hooing," or the boy whose offence was "grinning"?

In his account of pedagogical formalism, Neil Sutherland comments that "even those who enjoyed it then now recall a system that put its rigour into ... rote learning"[69] and routinized punishment. But this is precisely the point. Many students *did* enjoy their school experience, enough of them to make me wonder whether Sutherland's description of unrelenting formalism isn't somewhat overdrawn. The fact is that many students enjoyed their Clinton experience because they liked (and often admired) their teachers. To be sure, there were some teachers (and principals) who didn't make the Top Ten. Mr Austin, who served as principal through most of the 1940s, was not well liked by many students who found him "severe," "austere," and "sanctimonious." Another student, from the 1930s, left this mixed review of the teachers she knew: "Miss Kemp, tough but great; Mr McFarlane, rough but great; Miss Meek, as her name implies; Mr Berry, a friend indeed."[70] One of the shop teachers was singled out for his particularly harsh discipline. And from the other end of the historical period I call Jewish Clinton, the early 1950s, I heard about some of the upper-year, male teachers who were described as "screamers." One, in particular, "was very quick to grab kids by the hair if he didn't like what you were doing, or what you were saying ... I remember turning myself into a skinhead because of that class."

But these are the exceptions. When one looks at what former students have said about their teachers at Clinton, it is hard not to be struck by how positive their assessments are. Mr Scholfield, who served as principal in the 1930s, received generally high marks. One graduate wrote that he was "a wonderful, compassionate, charming man"; another that he "was the most wonderful principal and man I have ever met."[71] In the interviews I conducted, most responded to my invitation to assess their Clinton teachers by describing them as "caring," "warm," "compassionate," and "nurturing." One recalled how his teacher visited him in the hospital as he recovered from an appendectomy. Another recalled seeing a teacher wipe a tear from her eye as her charges dispersed at the end of the school year. A third recalled how pleased he was that his teacher attended his bar mitzvah. Yet another remembered how the school had defended him against an irate neighbour who claimed that the student had damaged his property. And a surprisingly large number of the graduates either kept in contact with their teachers or reconnected with them as adults.[72] As one graduate put it, his teachers – especially women teachers and especially in the early grades – were "mother figures."

Nor was the curriculum quite as dull, repetitive, and uniform as some have portrayed it. Former students recall all sorts of assignments and activities – spelling bees, science experiments, speaking contests, dramatic performances, imperial celebrations – all of which enlivened (and provided some relief from) the bookish, repetitive methods of teaching and learning that otherwise dominated. Some of those activities were clearly designed to draw students into the larger world beyond Clinton's walls. One student who attended in the late 1920s recalled how "Mr Hooker led us through Gordon Sinclair's motor trip through India with a map on the wall and the *Daily Star* columns read daily in class."[73] Coronations and royal visits were a big deal. And, of course, students followed the ups and downs of the Second World War with care. Morley Safer recalls that "in class we had to study Aircraft Identification in which the silhouettes of various German, American and British planes were displayed on charts. It was perhaps the only subject I excelled in ... and [I] can still tell the difference between a Heinkel and a Lancaster."[74]

A handful of students with good voices – among them Sam Sniderman (well known by his adult nickname, Sam the Record Man) and Jerry Gray (of The Travellers folk group) – were invited to represent Clinton in the annual Toronto schools concert at Massey Hall. Another student still remembered the time his grade 8 teacher,

Mr Timpson, took the class to see Sir Ernest MacMillan conduct the Toronto Symphony Orchestra playing the *Peer Gynt Suite*. An aspiring journalist hung out patiently at Maple Leaf Gardens until he scored an interview for the school paper with Teeder Kennedy, one of the hockey idols of the day. Students participated in all sorts of school-sponsored activities during the Second World War, including collecting the aluminum liners from cigarette packages, building penny collections used to purchase treats for Canadian troops overseas, and planting a Victory Garden adjacent to the school. One former student even recalled reciting the patriotic ditty she had composed at a Toronto-wide school contest organized to promote the sale of war bonds. Nor did the end of the war put an end to Clinton's anglophilia. The coronation of Queen Elizabeth II generated an opportunity for students to create large scrapbooks to commemorate the occasion. One graduate admitted that he became so absorbed in the exercise that he actually thought the class was going to travel to England to witness the event.

And then, of course, there were extra-curricular sporting activities. By our standards, the number and range of organized sports teams were limited. This reflects both the absence of a real gymnasium and the forbidding nature of the playground outdoors (first covered in wooden planks, then concrete). As a result, most of the sports at Clinton developed organically and without official authorization – various forms of pick-up handball, baseball, roof ball, and the favourite, "Buck, Buck, How Many Fingers Up," among them. Still, the school regularly recruited players for the school's hockey team, won the city-wide championship in baseball in 1939, and sent its best track-and-field athletes to the city championship in the spring. All of these activities enlivened school life.

There is an ongoing debate among historians of education about the extent to which the principles of "progressive education" displaced "formalism" in North American schools in the early to mid-decades of the twentieth century. Though there are several different versions of this debate, the core controversy turns on whether, in these years, the curriculum was adapted to the needs of the individual child (progressivism) or whether the individual child was compelled to adapt to the curriculum (formalism). But for those who taught at Jewish Clinton, as well as those who attended, this bright-line distinction between formalism and progressivism would surely pose a false dichotomy. To be sure, there were teachers at Clinton, as elsewhere, "who offered no more than rigid adherence to dull routine and tedious drill." Yet by the same token, "as teachers became more experienced, more at ease and in command of their classrooms, instruction was likely to become more imaginative, and methods more varied."[75] And Clinton's teachers were nothing if not experienced.[76] They may not have fully or self-consciously embraced progressive principles in their teaching, but the evidence suggests that Clinton teachers nevertheless managed to accomplish the most important thing, namely to feed an enduring "curiosity about how this world works."[77]

Paul Axelrod's analysis of Ontario schools at mid-century fits the Clinton case rather well: "Thus it is not a case of progressive *or* traditional education, as the theorists and polemicists would have it. School policy was an amalgam in which educators were using available and emerging tools to address the perceived instructional needs of a ballooning population. They employed what they thought worked. But they did so within the political culture and dominant values of the province and the times."[78]

And work it did. When W.A. Craik reported on his tour of Toronto schools during the First World War, he lamented that in most schools enrolment took the form of a "pyramid."[79] Classes in the lower grades were brimming with students, he said, but enrolments thinned seriously in the higher grades because many students left school to find employment as soon as they were permitted. School attendance in Toronto (and Ontario) improved during the interwar years. Still, even after the Second World War only two-thirds of students qualified for secondary school, only 61 per cent of the school-aged population actually enrolled in high school, and only 46 per cent remained in school past the age of sixteen.[80] Clinton was quite different, perhaps even exceptional. Parents and teachers alike simply assumed that most of the school's graduates would continue their formal education and, indeed, that most of them would wade into the academic stream at the neighbourhood high school, Harbord Collegiate. As Principal Scholfield put it in his final address to the students in the Class of 1942, "It will not be long now before our Grade VIII pupils will be eagerly planning their secondary school courses ... We are justly proud of the success we have had in establishing a high standard of scholarship in this school. Year after year, the secondary schools give splendid reports of our graduates."[81] The principal was no doubt gilding the lily to some extent, but what is so striking about his comment is that he simply assumed – quite accurately it turns out – that most graduates would go on to high school.[82] In the end, Clinton sustained Craik's positive evaluation; it remained "an excellent school" with "a record of solid achievement that places it well to the fore of Toronto schools."[83] Far from dragging the school down as Craik and others seemed to fear, the "foreign-born population" that had come to dominate the Clinton community in the interwar years actually pulled it up. Moreover, as we will see in chapter 3, the presence of so many Jewish students accomplished something still more important: it forced the school for the first time to face up to the challenge of diversity.

3

At Clinton You're a Somebody: Religion and the Idea of Citizenship

Paul Axelrod's statement that public schools in Ontario reflected the "political culture and dominant values of the province and the times"[1] reminds us that in one respect Clinton was anything but typical: it was largely Jewish. To recall: from the mid-1920s until the early 1950s, at least 40 per cent of the student population at Clinton was Jewish, and often it was as high as 70 per cent. How did a largely Jewish school like Clinton find its way in the Anglo-Protestant cultural milieu that was interwar Toronto? How did educators respond to the goal set out for them by the Ontario Department of Education "to bring home to the pupils, as far as their capacity allows, the fundamental principles of Christianity and their bearing on human life and thought"?[2] And what can we learn from the Clinton experience about the place of religious education in a diverse community?

The British essayist Jan Morris described the Toronto of 1926 as "a city of 500,000, growing fast and very pleased with itself."[3] Torontonians, she says, "were mostly of Scottish extraction, and on the face of it the city was still very British – with Union Jacks all over the place, the *Toronto Globe* reverberatingly imperialist, the Lieutenant-Governor's mansion rigid with formality." Yet as she goes on to argue, there was some "falseness" about Toronto's colonial self-image in the 1920s for "behind the façade of imperial loyalty there was a strongly nationalist impulse." It was "a city of the Americas ... a self-made city, built on grab and enterprise."[4] It was also, increasingly, a city of immigrants, and beneath the calm, British-Canadian surface there was deep anxiety about whether these "foreign-born" newcomers – like Jews – fitted the mould of the "new" Canada that was being built. In this context, it became respectable to argue that being Jewish and being Canadian were simply incompatible, a project doomed to failure from the outset. This was evidently the view of the daily *Toronto Telegram*, which editorialized in 1924 that "an influx of Jews puts a worm next the kernel of every fair city where they get a hold. These people have no national tradition … They are not the material out of which to shape a people holding a national spirit. They remain cosmopolitan, while war drains the blood of the solid citizens of a nation."[5] It was the view of immigration officials, like C.A. Blair, who made it virtually impossible for Jews fleeing Europe in the 1930s to emigrate to Canada.[6] And it was the practice of many others – from university professors to landlords to thugs – at least to tolerate systematic discrimination and to create forms of mistreatment that targeted Jews.[7]

Virtually all of the Clinton grads I interviewed had experienced anti-Semitism at first hand whilst growing up. One sailed through the interview for what would have been her first part-time job only to lose the position when she told the employer she was Jewish. Some could remember being taunted and beaten up; others honed their sprinting skills running from thugs. One alumna related how, when travelling on the St Clair streetcar to Hebrew school, she concealed her Hebrew books. Yet another volunteered that he really wanted to become an engineer but that it was understood that this profession was essentially closed to Jews. And everyone lived in the shadow of the infamous Christie Pits riot of August 1933, in which "hundreds of Jewish youths, assisted by a small number of Italians and Ukrainians, battled the Pit Gang, a crew with a long tradition of harassing minorities in Toronto's lower west end." The riot took place following a baseball game between local Jewish and church teams, precipitated when "the Gang had unfurled a large banner bearing a swastika to well-orchestrated choruses of 'Hail Hitler.' Jewish players and spectators had tried to tear the banner down. Within minutes, axe handles, lead pipes, chains, and other weapons were wielded with terrible effect by both sides."[8]

For Jewish kids (and their parents), incidents like the riot at Christie Pits reinforced a keen sense of Jewish Toronto geography, and they distinguished areas that were safe to roam from those that were perilous. One said that his mother carried with her a mental map of where her son was permitted to travel. It was, he said, as if she were talking about present-day Israel. South of College was like Egypt, north of Bloor Lebanon, east of Yonge Syria and west of Grace a vast sea of potential danger. Clinton kids themselves came equipped with their own internal GPS systems. Zipping about the neighbourhood on their bikes when it was warm or looking for shortcuts to and from school when it was cold, they measured safety and danger street by street, sometimes even house by house. Euclid and Manning were largely Jewish and safe. Clinton was more mixed ethnically, so travel there depended on whether you had Italian and Ukrainian friends (as many did).[9] Two streets to the west, Grace was again friendly territory, and Beatrice next to it was passable but close to the boundary that separated friendly territory from unknown trouble. The problem was with Jersey Avenue, which lay between Clinton and Grace. Jersey Avenue provided the perfect shortcut from Grace Street (and points west) to the school, but it was also home to the "Jersey boys" – older boys from Anglo families, equipped with brass knuckles, who regularly taunted and terrorized Jewish kids in the neighbourhood. The Jersey boys, as one grad put it, were "Jew haters," always spoiling for a fight, as if to extend the Christie Pits riot to extra innings.

Perhaps inevitably, the Clinton schoolyard provided a venue – and an audience – for these fights. Berko Devor's account of a fight that broke out in the Clinton yard in the late 1930s is particularly evocative:

> It was understood in the late '30's that Jewish kids kept to the Manning Avenue side of the boys' schoolyard. The word was out at afternoon recess that Izzie Stepak, the Jewish gladiator, and Woodsy, representing the WASPs, would bare-fist it out in a widening of the alley half-way between Clinton and Manning at the back of the boys' schoolyard. I watched over the heads of their followers who formed the encompassing boundary of a ring.
>
> Suddenly a hush descended. The circle opened. Mr Richards, the Junior Fourth teacher, entered the ring. The two combatants did not drop

their guard. He motioned them to continue. More punishing blows to Izzie's ribs and then a trickle of blood from Woodsy's lip. A left-right combination landed firmly and blood flowed from Woodsy's nose. A fully accepted signal from Mr Richards ended the fight.

Woodsy started for his home on Jersey Avenue. "We know who won!" his supporters called. Izzie refused to admit any pain from his battered ribs. He left for his home on Grace Street. "Izzie won!" his followers shouted. I say Izzie Stepak won. But then, I am a Jew.[10]

There were many other such fights on (or near) the Clinton schoolyard in the 1930s. Curiously enough, the atmosphere seems to have calmed and become more pacific during wartime and in the immediate post-war years. A possible reason, one grad suggested, is deliciously ironic: these sorts of fights stopped when the Jersey boys moved out of the neighbourhood, which occurred when most of them joined the armed forces to fight for Canada against Hitler.

The territory beyond Clinton, on the other hand, was still potentially dangerous. Ralph Halbert was a very young student when the fight described by Berko Devor occurred. By the time he had become a member of Clinton's bantam hockey team, the war was on. Yet Christie Pits remained a danger zone and the Pits Gang a genuine threat. He told me about a particularly memorable game that he played at the rink used for school games at the bottom of the Pits:

> I played hockey and I played right wing for the Bantams, the Clinton Street School (team). We played (Essex Public School) ... and around the boards outside of the rink were fifteen-, sixteen-year-olds who should have graduated from public school by that time and they were standing there with chunks of wood. And it so happened that I scored the winning goal. And our coach was Mr Lowrie. In the second half of the two periods he became the referee and before he dropped the puck he said when the final whistle blows get out of here and I understood what that meant. So [I] ran to the corner of the rink where I had my rubber boots.[11]

And with that, he gathered up his boots and hockey stick and ran "up the hill to Bloor and down Grace still in my skates" all the way home – ahead of the plank-wielding thugs.

One of the interesting aspects of these accounts is the part played by the teacher-referees, Mr Richards and Mr Lowrie. No one knows (or at least remembers) exactly what possessed them to act as they did. What we do know, however, is that individual teachers were important players in the process of making first- and second-generation immigrant Jewish kids feel comfortable in their downtown school. Or sometimes not. One graduate recalled her grade 5 teacher, who began a lesson with the statement: "The problem with you Jews is ..." A generation earlier, in Montreal, a similar statement provoked a wildcat strike among students.[12] At Clinton, it provoked a swift and effective complaint to the principal by the girl's mother, who happened to be a pillar of the parent council.

More frequently, teachers distinguished themselves by their sensitivity. When one of the Jewish teachers at Clinton in the 1930s (and there weren't many) was transferred to neighbouring King Edward School, some of the teachers began to worry that she would feel like an outsider in the new staffroom. Taking matters into their own hands, a number of the Clinton teachers regularly walked to King Edward to give Miss Mirochnick friendly company for lunch.[13] Mr Timpson, who taught the senior grades at Clinton for more than twenty years, once built a menorah out of hula hoops so that his Jewish students would be able to celebrate Hanukkah at school, then took his creation home and displayed it in his front window.[14] The most touching story, though, comes from Fred Weinberg, class of 1932, who went on to become a well-known paediatrician. He recounted that he had stood at the top of his class in grade 8, for which achievement he was awarded a book prize. And what book did his teacher choose? A Hebrew Bible, which, Weinberg said, he cherished and used his entire adult life.[15]

Of course, such individual acts of kindness and unkindness did not occur in an institutional vacuum. Happily, the perspective of the TBE on "the foreign-born" differed from the editorial stance taken by the *Toronto Evening Telegram*. Where the *Telegram* saw unremitting threat, the TBE saw considerable promise. Where the *Telegram* saw corrosion, the TBE saw malleability. Where the *Telegram* directed its venom at adults, the TBE directed its energies at children. And where the *Telegram* measured the "foreign-born" by their (in)capacity to assimilate to Canadian life, the TBE developed policies to instruct and "mould" students into good Canadians.

As the statement on the front cover of all TBE report cards put it, school wasn't just about learning to read and do math; it was equally about developing "some of the qualities of a good citizen"[16] – good middle-class virtues like healthy habits, reliability, self-control, cooperation, courtesy, and industry. And what was the moral foundation of these "personal qualities"? Christianity. The famous Grey Book, the provincial statement of educational philosophy published in 1937, made the linkage between citizenship and Christianity both explicit and authoritative: "(t)he schools of Ontario exist for the purpose of preparing children to live in a democratic society which bases its life upon the Christian ideal." To achieve this goal "the school must seek to lead the child to choose and accept as his own those ideals of conduct and endeavour which a Christian and democratic society approves." So while "the curriculum ... does not prescribe a course in morals nor include religion as a separate subject, [a school's curriculum] should be pervaded by the spirit of religion."[17]

How, in practice, was this "spirit of religion" embedded in the curriculum if not through a separate subject? And where did this leave the Jewish students of Clinton? The short answer is that Christianity directly insinuated itself into the day-to-day life at Clinton in three ways and at three moments: the daily recitation of the Lord's Prayer, regular Bible readings, and the celebration of major Christian holidays, especially Christmas. The precise protocol that governed these religious exercises seems to have varied, especially since they were typically classroom-based. The Lord's Prayer was *de rigueur* throughout the school and throughout the interwar years; the graduates I interviewed all remembered that this is how the day began. Bible readings and some hymns, selected from a menu approved by the Department of Education, made less of a lasting impression, perhaps because some of the teachers chose readings from the Old Testament, like Psalms. And the core Christian celebrations, especially Christmas, were marked with gusto. Several graduates recalled that each classroom had its own Christmas tree and nativity pageant, a re-enactment of the Christmas story featuring a largely Jewish cast and crew.

Reactions to these explicitly Christian, indeed Protestant, religious exercises varied as well. Among the graduates I interviewed, a small number said they found the religious exercises offensive both then and now, and a few at the other end of the spectrum said that they (and their parents) were largely indifferent to them. In their view, participating in these religious exercises was a relatively small price to pay to join the mainstream of Canadian society – especially when religious exercises at school were counterbalanced by Jewish education at home. For most, though, it is clear that compulsory religious exercises caused enough discomfort to produce a set of creative strategies to remove their sting. One student said she dealt with the Lord's Prayer by keeping her eyes open while reciting it, as if this would somehow reduce the sinfulness of having recited a Christian prayer. Another said that he and his friends came up with creative ways to avoid uttering words that were simply too Christian for any self-respecting Jewish student to repeat. Mumbling worked well, as did long, strategic silences. A third said he and his friends mouthed the words but didn't actually voice them. But my favourite example demonstrates the usefulness of self-delusion. One Clinton graduate recalled how she heard and interpreted the 23rd Psalm in a way that was both consoling and comprehensible to her young mind: "For years after," she recalled, "I thought that 'Shirley,' 'Goodness' and 'Mercy' were the names of three angels who were going to follow me the rest of my days."[18] One student summed it up by saying that, in the end, religious exercises at Clinton were "not a huge deal" for him or his family. As long as these explicitly Christian exercises were limited to the Lord's Prayer, intermittent Bible readings, and a Christmas pageant, most students and most parents found them tolerable.

All of this changed in 1944 when Ontario's Conservative government, led by George Drew, introduced compulsory religious instruction in all Ontario public schools. The new rules required that all students in grades 1 through 8 receive religious education for two half-hour periods per week during the regular school day – over and above the time allocated to the conventional religious exercises. According to the regulations, instruction would follow guidelines set by provincial authorities, in part to ensure that instruction avoided "issues of a controversial or sectarian nature."[19] Should an individual school board desire, it could invite members of the clergy or lay people to provide instruction rather than teachers (something that occurred, as it turns out, with some frequency in the higher grades). And, to accommodate dissenters, the regulations provided an exemption clause. "No pupil," it read, "shall be required to take part in any religious exercises or be subject to any instruction in Religious Education to which objection is raised by his parent or guardian."[20]

In one stroke, the "Drew Regulations" (as they became known) transformed the relationship between religion and public education in Ontario. It is certainly true, as we have seen, that previous provincial governments did not shy away from framing the purposes of education in terms of "the Christian ideal." It is true, as well, that schools were permitted to invite clergy to give religious classes before the school day began or after it ended. And it is even true, as Robert Stamp has noted, that in 1940–1 as many as 10 per cent of Ontario's schools had successfully finessed the rules in ways that blurred the boundary between voluntary and compulsory, intra- and extra-curricular.[21] Still, until 1944, religious instruction was legally, and in practice largely, an extra-curricular, voluntary activity in Ontario public schools. The Drew government departed from longstanding practice by folding religious instruction into the regular school day. It broke trail in a direction that neither Ontario – nor indeed any province or state – had explored by making the teaching of Christianity a core, compulsory subject in every public school. Its teaching, in the words of the manual that accompanied the new regulations, was to be "as thorough and serious as that which the teacher gives to Social Studies or to Science."[22]

Why did Drew act, and why at that moment? In many ways, the Drew Regulations grew out of a sense of moral crisis and weakness among mainstream Protestant churches, not moral superiority and strength. As several historians have shown, the Depression and the Second World War had left Protestant churches "feeling besieged."[23] They faced shrinking congregations, declining Sunday school attendance, and the scars left by the divisive interdenominational debate that had created the United Church of Canada. Martin Sable summarizes the position of the churches nicely: "With both empty pews and empty coffers, churches were desperate to find a cheap and effective way to reach Ontario's children with the message of Christ and, equally important, implant the value of regular church attendance."[24] But it wasn't just a matter of institutional self-interest. There was also a real sense of moral decline in the air in the interwar era as citizens watched unwelcome social trends – juvenile delinquency, lack of parental control, and other forms of moral malaise – take hold. One minister from Brantford lamented, in the depths of the Depression, that the youth of the day did not follow Jesus; instead, "they choose for their heroes Napoleon Bonaparte, Babe Ruth, John Dillinger, or Mae West."[25] Nor did the war ease their concerns. True, freedom and democracy would ultimately triumph against Nazism, but it was a close call that sorely tested and exposed the thinness of the moral fibre of Canadian youth. Robert Charles Wallace, the principal of Queen's University, drew out the evident policy implications in a speech to educators in 1941: the future of democracy, he said, turned on "Protestants putting religion into the education system."[26]

The Drew Regulations did their best to do just that. George Drew became premier in August 1943, following an election in which his Conservatives won a minority government. In addition to his duties as premier, Drew chose to serve as minister of education to signal the importance of his youth agenda. His government's Speech from the Throne in February 1944 announced the intention of introducing religious education into the schools, albeit with few details. By August 1944 the regulations were in place, a teaching manual that set out the basic curricular building blocks had been distributed, and detailed teaching guides had been published for every grade. Implementation – and note that this religious education was now a compulsory subject – began in September 1944.[27]

It's worth making two points about this sketch of a timeline. The first is that the new rules were implemented so quickly in part because the government encountered little opposition to them. The Liberals moved a vote of non-confidence in the Ontario legislature in March 1944 on the issue, but the CCF was divided and the vote failed. Teachers who were uncomfortable at the prospect of instructing their students in religion remained silent as they did not want to jeopardize their relationship with Premier Drew. (The teachers' federation was grateful to him for legislation that had significantly strengthened their legal status as a professional organization.) The Protestant churches stood squarely behind the changes, and the Catholic church remained on the sidelines during the debate, tantalized by the precedent for greater public support for religion yet leery of getting too close to a project so closely identified with the Protestant churches. Among those who occupied positions of religious authority, only a few, like Rabbi Abraham Feinberg of Holy Blossom Temple in Toronto, spoke out against the new regulations.[28] Feinberg, whose views on the place of religion in liberal society we will examine in greater detail in a moment, objected to the regulations in part because they advanced the very sort of sectarian instruction they claimed to avoid. What the regulations called "Religious Instruction" was, in his view, clearly "Christian Instruction."[29] His concerns were quickly dismissed. Dr J.G. Althouse, Drew's deputy minister of education, advised the Premier simply to ignore Feinberg: "It's my view that you've already considered Rabbi Feinberg's point of view and rejected it in favour of the theory that this government is committed to the support of Christianity."[30]

The second implication of fast-tracking religious instruction is that it "placed a heavy burden on classroom teachers."[31] Almost overnight, teachers in Ontario, regardless of their faith, were now expected to provide two half-hour periods per week of religious education – a subject for which very few of them were trained. The Drew government must have understood that these new regulations put teachers in a tight spot because the Department of Education went out of its way, over the summer of 1944, to generate materials to help teachers meet their new curricular responsibilities. Working with the Inter Church Council (an organization that brought together clergy and other representatives from a range of Protestant and Anglican churches), the department adapted British curricular materials for the Ontario system. The teaching guides, one per grade, became a sort of *Coles Notes* for teachers faced with the challenge of teaching religion for the first time. Each was divided into between thirty and thirty-five different lessons, organized around the explication of a scriptural passage or story. Each guide provided ideas for extending the lesson through related, age-appropriate activities (dramatization or memorization or craftwork), and most contained background notes and modern illustrations to show the relevance of the Bible's teaching. Of course, "the best lessons are undoubtedly the result of personal preparation by each teacher, with his own class in mind." But given "the increasing pressure on the timetable," it made sense to provide teachers with ready-made lesson outlines and practical class work. Think of these guides, the editor announced slightly defensively, not as a crutch but as a pedagogical walking-stick that would allow teachers and students to explore religious terrain together. Originally, the idea had been to import the guides directly from Britain, but when officials discovered they were in short supply the department authorized Ryerson Press (the publishing arm of the United Church) to publish a Canadian version. And publish they did. Ultimately, some 50,000 guides were distributed to Ontario schools in the first year alone.[32]

Three basic themes run through all six guides, none of them friendly to Jews and Judaism. First, not surprisingly, the guides centred on telling and explicating the specifically Christian story. The titles of the various guides telegraph this emphasis clearly: *Stories of God and Jesus* in grade 2, *Jesus and His Friends* in grade 3, and *Jesus and the Kingdom* in grade 6. This does not mean that the guides ignored Old Testament stories and characters altogether. In fact, the suggested lessons contained plenty of examples that were drawn from the pre-Christian era. But the approach to understanding these stories was entirely Christian. As one of the guides put it, children would find it useful to learn about the Old Testament because those were the stories and lessons that Jesus must have grown up with and loved.[33] Old Testament stories thus made it easier to appreciate the life of Jesus, the environment in which he moved, and the religious education he would have received. The Old Testament was essentially instrumental. It served as a platform for understanding the New.

Old Testament knowledge was useful for another reason; it allowed teachers and students to see clearly the moral superiority of

Christianity over what had preceded it – Judaism. Here is a sample. Among Jews in Palestine, "rules of hygiene were unknown" and "sanitary conditions were appalling"; by contrast, Jesus possessed "a robust wholesome body, with a mind that was clear and sane" (I: 67). Among Jews, "religious observance and the rules for daily living were reduced to a system" (III: 109) that was rigid, static, and closed to discussion; this was "absolutely contrary to the teaching of Jesus" (III: 110), which was supple, dynamic, and open. To the exponents of Judaic law, "outcasts were outcasts" (III: 115); to Jesus, outcasts, like the tax-collector Zaccheaus, were objects of his friendship and love (III: 114). Jews were "serious-minded people, and games had little place in their social life" (I: 56), but Jesus was fun-loving. (I: 54–5). In sum, Jesus was completely different from "the ordinary religious teachers" of the day. Unlike the rigid, rule-driven rabbis, "He knew all about ordinary people's work and difficulties, and seemed to understand how hard it was for them to keep the little rules by which the religious teachers set so much store. There was something so fresh, so human, so appealing about this new Teacher and His ideas of religion" (IV: 3–4). At just about every turn, the guides found ways to contrast old and new, rigid and supple, exclusive and inclusive – in short, Jews versus Jesus.

The very starkness of the contrast set up the guides' spine-tingling retelling of the Passion story. To understand the drama of Holy Week, the students needed to ponder one fundamental question: "Why did the Jewish authorities wish to put Jesus to death?" (VI: 43). The guides provided a straightforward narrative answer: as news of Jesus' teaching and healing spread, "the Jewish rulers" felt increasingly threatened. His decision to spend the week of Passover in Jerusalem served as a declaration of "war between the rulers and Jesus – they dogged His footsteps and interrupted His teaching" (VI: 37). When attempts to silence him failed, the "Jewish priests" manufactured charges against him, condemned him in their religious court and, "bent on murder" (IV: 92), delivered him to Pontius Pilate, the Roman governor. Pilate was actually "convinced of the innocence of Jesus" (VI: 40), but he was "goaded beyond endurance by the Jewish leaders. They had ... aroused the blood-lust of the mob, and had egged them on to threaten to report the governor to Caesar" (IV: 93). Ultimately, "Pilate gave in to the crowd and condemned an innocent man to death" (VI: 40). Meanwhile, "their hate satisfied, the rulers scoffed at Jesus, mocking him with words that were a noble tribute – 'He saved others, Himself He cannot save'" (VI: 41). Or, to distil the guides' version of the Passion story into one pithy sentence: Jews killed Jesus.

One perceptive reader pointed out that, when the guides spoke about those who surrounded Jesus, the authors invariably referred to *individuals* – James and John, Martha and Mary, and so on. When talking about Jesus' enemies, on the other hand, the authors usually referred to them in the *collective* – the "Jewish rulers" or the "Jewish priests" or, as in the passage just cited, simply "the mob."[34] This penchant for generalization almost certainly made it easier for teachers and students to connect the dots between the biblical story related by the guides and the Jewish students in their class. Whatever the exact causes, the Canadian Jewish Congress began to collect disturbing reports from Jewish parents of anti-Semitic incidents in local schools. A parent in Brantford wrote, in 1945, to complain that "anti-Semitism was being spread in the minds of youngsters during their religious teaching periods." In this case, the parent believed there was a direct connection between the textbook that claimed "Jews were eager to have Jesus killed" and the beating his seven-year-old daughter had received on the playground because "she was a rotten Jew."[35] Harry Arthurs, who went on to become the president of York University, remembers vividly being beaten up in the playground at Regal Road Public School in Toronto following a religious class in which a minister from the local United Church "addressed a school assembly on the crucifixion of Christ by the Jews."[36] Another Regal Road graduate, who also went on to become a distinguished legal academic, remembers how the Christian friend he walked to and from school with every day suddenly disappeared after discovering that he was Jewish. And at Palmerston Public School, Clinton's neighbour just north of Bloor Street, a nine-year-old student reported that his teachers had "mentioned that it was 'the Jews who killed Christ'"; the student "was quite disturbed at this, anticipating that the rest of the children would take it out on him after the class."[37]

Most of these incidents occurred in schools in which Jewish students were a clear minority. This was certainly true of the smaller centres, like Brantford and St Catharines and Kitchener, where vigilant parents had reported their concerns about anti-Semitism in the classroom and on the playground. But it was also true at most Toronto schools. According to a 1944 census of Jewish students at Toronto schools produced by the Canadian Jewish Congress (CJC), there were only about fifty Jewish students at Regal Road, and, even at Palmerston, where the Jewish population was considerably larger, it still did not come close to 50 per cent of the school's population.[38] But what of the downtown schools – like Lansdowne, King Edward, and Clinton – where Jewish students were in the majority?[39] How did religious education play out there? Did they teach to the Guide? Did Jewish students apply for exemptions from religious education? After several years of experience with the new rules about religious education and with enough anecdotal evidence to register concern, the CJC, in 1952, approached the superintendent of schools for permission to undertake a fact-finding survey to determine how religious education was conducted in Toronto schools. The superintendent, Zach Phimister, told the CJC delegation that no Jewish parents had applied for exemptions from religious instruction in the downtown core, at least not since an "initial flurry," and that "as for non-Jewish students, no exemptions had ever been asked for." The delegation "indicated surprise that parents belonging to the many sectarian groups with strong convictions had not expressed their exception to the teaching by way of requesting exemption. It was also interesting that there were 4,500 Catholic pupils in the Toronto schools and that no such request had come from their parents either."[40] The Toronto schools used the same provincially sanctioned teachers' guides that everyone else did. Perhaps, the superintendent suggested, the low rate of exemptions reflected the "general atmosphere and broadness of outlook in the Toronto schools" and "a heavy measure of discretion and sensitivity on the part of the teachers."[41]

In the event, the request to undertake a fact-finding survey was denied on the grounds that the TBE does not allow external organizations to study the internal operation of its schools. Undaunted, the

CJC moved to Plan B, contacting Jewish teachers at each of the three largest Jewish schools (Clinton, King Edward, and Lansdowne) and asking them to describe how compulsory religious education, the Drew initiative, worked at their schools. The teachers answered as if one. The approach to religious education at their schools was indeed "tempered by a heavy measure of discretion and sensitivity." In fact, the schools basically went a step further and didn't teach religion at all. The Jewish teacher from King Edward said that "when the regulations had first come into effect there had been such a storm of protest and applications for exemption that the principal had decided to drop the whole matter. To conform with the regulations the subject is duly noted down on the time-table and then tacitly ignored." "There was," he explained, "a 'gentleman's agreement' or 'unwritten code' between the various levels of authority to leave the whole question lie." At Lansdowne, the teacher said that he "obeys the letter of the law by giving readings from the Old Testament and by conducting the class in the Lord's prayer" but that there was "no religious instruction" beyond that. And at Clinton, the "whole program has been so soft-pedaled and watered down that the parents have evidently felt no cause for complaint."[42]

The reference to parents is telling. Miss Vellis, the Clinton teacher, said that "the regulations are not strictly enforced here, largely because (the school population is predominantly Jewish) and because the Jewish parents are evidently very active in the Home and School Association." As her colleague from King Edward put it, "the school was not prepared to cope with the furore that would inevitably result if such a program were introduced." This probably explains why, when I asked Jewish graduates from immediate post-war Clinton about religious instruction, none could recall it. It also explains why the implementation of religious education never appears as an agenda item at Parent Council meetings of the time. Instead, parents were invited to hear presentations on such things as the Springfield Plan – an integrated educational program of anti-discrimination materials developed in Springfield, Massachusetts.[43] The decision to take a pass on religious instruction was an act of local resistance, inspired by parents and carried out by teachers. Clinton was not part of some Anglo-Ontarian assimilationist juggernaut but an institution that worked together with parents to find what worked for its community of students and parents. As the saying goes, Clinton parents and teachers were on the same page, but it was not a page drawn from the official teacher guide to religion in Ontario schools. Clinton's reaction to the Drew Regulations thus underscores one of the basic ideas of this book: that while public education is a fundamental, and largely unchallenged, state or governmental responsibility, it is not invariably a "top down" exercise in which the central authority leads and local schools follow. At least sometimes, power emanates from the bottom up.[44]

Clinton's resistance to religious instruction in the schools is part of a larger story – actually several stories – about social and political change in Toronto and Canada during the twentieth century. One story is about the decline of Protestant churches and the concurrent rise of religious diversity. As numerous scholars of religion have noted, "the sixties, broadly defined, resulted in a catastrophic exodus from the institutional churches" both in Canada and abroad.[45] I can speak to the decline of church membership personally. My father was the minister of a large United Church in Regina, Saskatchewan, in the early 1960s. At the time, the church held two Sunday services and ran a Sunday school for 1,000 children. When he returned in the mid-1980s as a guest minister, there was only one service, and no more than 100 children were enrolled in the church Sunday school. The point is not necessarily that those who used to attend Protestant churches lost religious belief entirely. Rather, it is that they didn't want their religion tied up with an institution like the church – or the school, presumably. At the same time, as a result of the liberalization of Canada's immigration laws, the country – especially in large cities like Toronto – became far more religiously diverse than it was when George Drew promulgated his regulations.

The size of the non-Christian population in Canada has basically doubled in each of the past three decades. Whereas in Drew's era Judaism was the only non-Christian religion to enjoy what in census terms was a critical mass, it is now one of many non-Christian religions to have significant representation in the census. And several of these – Islam, Hinduism, Sikhism, and Buddhism – now have communities that are larger than the Jewish population. Given these demographic trends, an explicitly Protestant, or even Christian, instructional framework simply did not fit the new social reality in Canada. When these two trends – declining religiosity and increasing diversity – met, they created a perfect storm for the Drew Regulations. And sure enough, beginning in the 1960s, more school boards began to request board-wide exemptions from religious instruction, more schools simply ignored the regulations, and more government commissions came to criticize religious instruction in public schools on both pragmatic and philosophical grounds.[46] As Heather Laing suggests, what was left (and it was not a trivial left-over)[47] was the idea that Christianity forms an important part of Canada's cultural heritage.[48]

The problem, however, with telling the story of the decline of religious instruction in Ontario schools in terms of these broad social trends is that the story line tends to become flat and linear, as if there was a smooth and steady decline of religiosity over the years. This is not the case. Religious instruction did indeed recede, but the process that led it there was "prolonged" and "contested,"[49] not quick and smooth. Indeed, it may surprise readers to learn that the Drew Regulations remained in force in Ontario schools until 1990, and even then their departure was not voluntary. Rather, they were "ousted"[50] only when the Ontario Court of Appeal ruled that compulsory religious instruction was inconsistent with the Charter of Rights and Freedoms.[51]

This second, legal story is usually told in the context of growing rights consciousness. Before the charter came along, most of the discussions about religious education in the schools were "really discussions about democracy: particularly about how an education system works in a democracy and what democratic rights are held by parents, schools, and the state."[52] The editor of the *United Church Observer* drew out the majoritarian logic of this democratic argument in a particularly unvarnished fashion: "Atheists and agnostics, Jews and Unitarians are at some disadvantage in a society the majority of whose members profess Christianity; so are Christians in Jerusalem, Mecca and Moscow. But can't they be reasonable about this, instead of demanding that our children be deprived of what the majority believes is good."[53] Besides, as defenders of the Drew rules were fond of pointing out, the regulations included an exemption for any student or teacher who found Christian teaching offensive. What could be more "reasonable" than that?

The evident problem with this formulation is that to be secure, individual rights cannot be defined and protected by the very majority that is most likely to disregard them. This is Charter of Rights logic 101, and it helps to explain why the Drew Regulations were not jettisoned until the charter came into effect. The opponents of the Drew rules had pursued several legal arguments before the charter existed, largely unsuccessfully. The charter changed the rules of the game by flipping the simple majoritarian logic on its head. If someone claims that her rights of religion and conscience have been violated, courts don't typically ask (as the *United Church Observer* did) whether *she* has been reasonable. Rather, they put the onus on *governments* to demonstrate that *they* have been reasonable in limiting individual rights. In this case, the Ontario Court of Appeal held that compulsory religious education did indeed violate freedom of religion because it was a form of indoctrination that even the exemption clause could not save as a "reasonable limitation."

But viewing the controversy over religious education in Ontario schools simply as a question of rights and justice about how religious minorities should be treated misses an important element in the story. That element is citizenship, and what it means to be a citizen in a diverse, polyethnic, global community like Toronto. By citizenship I mean two related things. First is the sense, privately felt and publicly acknowledged, that one is part of and identifies meaningfully with a larger political community. Here citizenship means sharing a common civic identity that creates mutual concern, loyalty, and fellow feeling. This is the *self* in self-government. The second is that citizenship entails participation in the creation and receipt of public goods. Here citizenship means sharing burdens and benefits. This is the *government* in self-government. While the rights story focuses on protecting individual differences against uniformity, citizenship focuses on fostering what we have in common with others despite our differences. The civic challenge – knitting a diverse group of human beings into a self-governing community – is one of the most pressing challenges that global cities face. To meet the challenge, we need to develop an idea of citizenship that will foster, not pre-empt or undermine, self-government.

Here is where the story of religious education in Ontario is helpful. The Drew government's decision to require religious instruction in public schools (and the controversy it engendered) turned into something of a natural experiment in how to think about citizenship in a fundamentally heterogeneous political community. Many at the time believed, in the words of one Clinton principal, that a "NEW ORDER" was being created in the world that would place new demands on individual citizens and that would require the cultivation of those sorts of "personal qualities" enumerated on report cards.[54] How did this bear on citizenship? Think about the art of cooking. Preparing a delicious meal requires more than just throwing together a random assortment of ingredients. Good cooks will start with a recipe from a tried-and-true source. They will ensure that they have all of the ingredients the recipe calls for and that they are of the highest quality. They will prepare them properly and then combine them in the right order. For the Drew government, making citizens fit for self-government was a bit like following a good recipe, where education was like "prepping" the ingredients. Students needed to possess reliability, self-control, industry, and the like, added, stirred, and mixed in just the right proportions. The problem is that one of the essential ingredients in this recipe for self-government was Christianity, so trying to make democratic citizens out of Jewish students was inherently problematic. It was like trying to prepare a recipe in which one of the basic ingredients was missing. The recipe might still work, more or less, but everyone would notice that something was missing and complain that the dish didn't taste as good as it had the last time it was served. Jewish-Canadians could be citizens. They could vote and run for elected office and hold property and pay taxes and enlist to fight for their country in times of war and do whatever else citizens can or must do. But other members of the community would understand that, in one crucial respect, they weren't quite full citizens. In an educational system that was trying to prepare students to live "in a democracy which bases itself upon the Christian ideal," Jewish students were missing one key ingredient. They were citizens-minus.[55]

As citizens-minus, Jews were outsiders. Indeed, for anyone who took advantage of the exemption from religious education, this outsider status was not just symbolic but direct and literal: students exempted from the Drew Regulations stood outside the room while their classmates received religious instruction. Worse, if Jews were citizens-minus, those who enjoyed full citizenship could justify all manner of quotas, restrictions, and verbal epithets – the sort of everyday anti-Semitism that every Jewish kid experienced at some point or other. To the extent that Jews lacked a key quality of full citizenship, they could also be denied its full benefits.

The opportunity to criticize this idea of qualified citizenship arose when the Drew government, in 1945, created the Hope Commission to study the public education system. The commission had a broad remit to put the system under the microscope and to recommend "changes that would better equip the province's young people for the modern world."[56] In the course of its public hearings, the commission attracted a number of briefs that centred on the place of religious education in the schools, including one from a committee of the Canadian Jewish Congress (CJC) chaired by Abraham Feinberg, the rabbi of Holy Blossom Temple in Toronto. The committee's brief was uncompromising in its criticism of compulsory religious instruction: "We wish to voice our strong protest," it began, "against a situation which, inadvertently, divides Canadians into a superior grade, consisting of those of a standardized creed and origin, and an inferior grade, obliged to uphold a different conviction."[57] According to Rabbi Feinberg and the CJC, the essential vice of religious education in the schools is that it weakens the sense of shared citizenship – "the bond of Canadianism"[58] – among students. The public school thus draws attention to "differences in religious belief" when it should be "the place where the children of all Canadians may come together, and implement their unity and equality of citizenship."[59] Here is the basic weakness of the recipe-like definition of citizenship that makes religious belief one of the key ingredients. It divides rather than unites, which is why it is especially unsuitable for diverse societies.

What was the alternative? Rabbi Feinberg was obviously not opposed to religion as such. He began his oral presentation to the

Hope Commission by stating his belief that "religion, as taught by genuine Christianity and true Judaism, is the spiritual core of democracy" because it "sanctifies the dignity of *all human beings* as children of God."[60] And he continued by noting his own belief that "*character training* is the inescapable task of every educational institution, including the public schools. This duty becomes supremely challenging in an age which has mastered, through the atom, the inmost secret of cosmic energy."[61] But, in his view, mixing religion and the state by bringing religious instruction into the schools was bad both for religion and for the state. It was bad for religion because "*the absolute division of authority between Church and State*"[62] was the only sure protection for individual religious freedom. It was bad for the state because it undercut the "common ground" that made it possible for people of "all creeds and diverse origins" to "learn to live and work and play together" in their "amalgam of Canadianism."[63] This was the key. "The non-sectarian public school," Feinberg argued, "is the most successful tool yet devised for preparing all people, of every grade and group, to assume the duties and prerogatives of democratic citizenship. Religious instruction, by emphasizing *differences*, cannot fail to fan the embers of intolerance wherever a minority exists."[64] Keeping church and state separate, therefore, is the foundation of liberal democracy. Giving the majority religion "the resources of the State to propagate its own doctrine ... approaches perilously close to the totalitarian method."[65]

The challenge Feinberg threw down to the Hope Commission was to reform public education according to liberal principles. In Feinberg's liberal schema, the distinction between private belief and public power was fundamental. Feinberg himself was American born and trained, and it is easy enough to hear echoes of Thomas Jefferson's "wall of separation" playing in the background. One could criticize Feinberg for this, arguing that he didn't understand that Canada had never signed on to the First Amendment and that his prescriptions, as a result, didn't fit the Canadian case. How, for instance, can one make sense of publicly funded Catholic schools using an American constitutional vocabulary? Did he not understand that Canada was established on the basis of "cooperation" between church and state, not their separation? But focusing on

Feinberg's mastery (or lack of mastery) of Canadian history misses the point. In George Drew's world, Jews really had two options. One was to deny their Jewishness so that they could assimilate fully into Canadian society. The other was to retain their Jewishness but at the cost of remaining citizens-minus. Rabbi Feinberg, on the other hand, believed that there were other ways to combine Jewish and Canadian identities. His important contribution to the debate is that he outlined a conception of citizenship that made it possible for Jewish Canadians (and by extension other religious minorities) to think of themselves both as Jewish *and* as full-fledged Canadians rather than citizens-minus.

The idea that Jews should not have to make a stark choice between their (private) religious beliefs and their (public) citizenship resonated powerfully. When Lynne Marks interviewed Jewish women who had attended Harbord Collegiate in the 1920s and 1930s, she found remarkably consistent patterns "of both acculturation and continuity among the first Canadian-born generation. Young women adopted Canadian ways, while retaining a strong sense of themselves as Jews."[66] If anything, Feinberg's vision of liberal citizenship spoke even more powerfully to the second generation of students who attended Clinton just before and during the Second World War. As one graduate put it to me, his family's view was that Jewish-Canadians were like coffee cream – "half-and-half." They could be as variously Jewish as they chose to be in their private lives and as deeply connected to Canada as they chose (or were compelled) to be in their public lives. As long as Canadianization did not directly threaten their Jewishness – as Drew-style religious instruction clearly did – most parents did not see any insuperable conflict in reconciling their private and public lives.

In fact, some students also embraced this sort of liberal citizenship because it provided something – like psychological security – that their Jewishness by itself could not provide. One Clinton graduate explained the added value that Canadian identity carried with it when she recalled a class visit during the war. The new principal, the imperious Mr Austin, singled out one of the boys and asked him pointedly, "What are you?" The boy was non-plused by the question, but gathered himself and replied, "I'm Jewish." To which the principal rejoined, "I didn't ask you that. I didn't ask you that at all, why are you telling me you're Jewish … So then he says, 'Aren't you a Canadian?' … He said you should be proud to be a Canadian 'cause that's what you are and I didn't ask your religion." Seventy years later, the incident remained vivid in this graduate's mind. At a time when Jews were the most vulnerable population in the world, she said, it gave her great comfort to know that the Jewish identity she wore proudly was not the only identity she had. It was reassuring to know, she said, that she was both Jewish *and* Canadian.[67]

Not every family at Clinton measured the threat to their Jewishness with the same ruler or drew the line between public and private in exactly the same way. Second-generation immigrants combined the Canadian and Jewish parts of their life differently from first-generation students. Rabbi Feinberg, who took strong objection to the singing of Christmas carols in public schools,[68] certainly did not speak for all Jews, nor even all rabbis, on the question.[69] Still, the basic point holds: the liberal idea of citizenship was widely embraced because it provided a way – many ways, actually – to combine diversity with citizenship. If one could keep religion and the state from getting tangled up with each other, all would be well.

Rabbi Feinberg's testimony before the Hope Commission in 1945 was remarkably prescient. His argument that there is a difference between teaching religion and teaching *about* religion, his insistence that religious education endangered the principles of equality and neutrality, and his commitment to the "absolute division of authority between Church and State"[70] all anticipated the contours of subsequent political debates and constitutional doctrines. Reading Feinberg's testimony now, however, in the context of current controversies about the relationship between religion and the state, exposes a deep ambiguity in his argument. Feinberg was interested, first and foremost, in protecting individual religious freedom from state power: unless there is an "absolute division between Church and State," the "rights of conscience" will be vulnerable to majority pressure. But what if we invert the logic? Could one not say, using the same principles, that the "absolute" separation between church and state is necessary to protect the secular state from contamination by religious belief? That is, after all, basically the foundation of what is called *laicité* in France, and it is the basis of the Quebec Charter of Values that was introduced (but ultimately not enacted into law) by the government of Quebec in 2013. The Quebec Charter would have prohibited public officers of any sort from wearing or displaying "ostentatious" religious symbols because to do so would, in the government's view, undermine the "values of separation of religions and State and the religious neutrality and the secular nature of the State."[71] Separation, in other words, works both ways. If it prevents the state from using schools to teach religion, it should also compel religious believers to check their religious symbols at the public door – in the name of secular equality.

Clearly, this is not the sort of "absolute division of authority between Church and State" that Rabbi Feinberg had in mind or even anticipated. So how does his approach to religion and citizenship differ and depart from the approach promoted by the government of Quebec? Feinberg didn't develop his idea of equal citizenship at length, but we can extract a couple of its main elements from his endorsement of the Springfield Plan. The Springfield Plan – which, as I mentioned earlier, had been the subject of a presentation for Clinton School parents in 1945 – was a multi-layered curricular initiative that had been used in the schools of Springfield, Massachusetts, to expose and combat racial discrimination. The Springfield Plan attracted a lot of attention in progressive American educational circles at the end of the Second World War. What excited Feinberg was that the Springfield curriculum provided a toolkit of "positive techniques" that could and should be "adapted for public school use, in order to implant and encourage the growth of mutual understanding and respect among children of the numerous ethnic and religious groups which dwell together in Ontario."[72]

What Feinberg wanted to say, I think, is that you need to judge the rules that govern how schools work not just by whether they protect religious freedom (which had been his starting point) but by their capacity to build a community of citizens, to forge "the bond of Canadianism"[73] among students, especially immigrant students. Put slightly differently, the larger issues raised by the Drew Regulations were not just about freedom of religion but about equal citizenship. Feinberg didn't develop the point fully, but the political theorist Bernard Yack has done so in a recent book entitled *Nationalism and the Moral Psychology of Community*. Yack defines community as "a group of individuals who imagine themselves connected to each other as objects of special concern and loyalty by something that they share."[74] As he explains, "communities rest on a combination of objective and subjective factors, something shared and something felt." The things individuals share are many and various – "a belief, a territory, a purpose, an activity, or merely the lack of a quality that some other group is thought to possess."[75] It is in this (objective) sense that we speak of a gay community (where the shared quality is sexual orientation) or an urban community (where the shared thing is a densely inhabited area). But sharing a quality is not sufficient on its own to create community. "In addition to sharing something ... the members of each of these groups are connected by feelings of social friendship that dispose them to devote special attention to each other's well-being."[76] This idea of social friendship is key. Friends feel connected to each other in a way that disposes them to want to pay special attention to each other, take care of each other, and display loyalty to each other. Community, in this sense, provides a way to extend the basic dynamic of friendship "beyond the relatively narrow confines of personal affection and familiarity."[77]

Community in this sense – fellow feeling based on shared traits – is a much undervalued moral resource. "Communities encourage people to identify with the experiences of the people to whom they are connected by ties of mutual concern and loyalty, to treat them with special pride and sympathy."[78] But that connection, once created on the basis of what we share, also provides a window from which we can begin to appreciate what we don't share. Here again the analogy to everyday friendship is instructive. Strong friendships often begin in the workplace where individuals share the challenges and frustrations of working together. But such friendships routinely develop beyond complaining about a boss or gossiping about a client; they dispose friends to learn about, and gain a greater appreciation of, other aspects of their colleagues' lives that aren't shared – religious practices, family rituals, and cultural customs, for instance. Community that is built on social friendship works the same way. It provides a way to attend to the needs of others in a way "that bridges, rather than erases"[79] individual differences. In a place and at a moment when we are surrounded by a multitude of human differences, this ability to bridge is hugely helpful.

Yack's analysis of community is attractive in part because it helps to make sense of the long, slow demise of religious education in Ontario. The fact is that the Drew Regulations failed because they were based on a characteristic or trait – Protestant Christianity – that was never shared by all Ontarians and that, over the years, came to be shared by fewer and fewer of them. George Drew championed religious education because he thought it would be a galvanizing force in building the new Ontario by waking the province's youth from their agnostic slumber. About this he was simply mistaken. He anticipated neither the massive exodus from Protestant churches nor the growing religious diversity of Canadian society. But Yack's analysis is attractive as well because it exposes the error of trying to build strong communities and engaged citizens on a foundation of self-preference. Drew's regulations followed his (and his supporters') preference to establish Protestantism as the gold standard for religious education. In so doing, he passed over a real opportunity to create a stronger community by bridging religious differences rather than isolating, hardening, and devaluing them. And while the context is somewhat different, one can detect the same flaw in the debate over religious symbols in Quebec or the more recent controversy that was provoked when the Harper government tried to prevent a Muslim woman from wearing a niqab at her citizenship ceremony. One of the reasons these initiatives became so divisive is that they represented a strategy to create a shared view of the world that depends on concealing or denying differences rather than bridging them. And that is no way to build a strong community either, because it tries to build on characteristics that some of its members don't share rather than cultivating those they do.

Here lies the real lesson of Jewish Clinton, a lesson that connects past, present, and future. Jewish Clinton was, I have argued, something of a natural experiment in building community and making citizens out of a diverse population. What the school's leadership (by which I include principals, teachers, and parents) understood is that a school, like any well-functioning community, is only as strong as the traits it shares and the special concern and loyalty that this shared quality generates. Clinton's neighbour-hood was heterogeneous in terms of class, ethnicity, and political preferences – a not-quite-random assortment of people thrown together by the accident that they happened to live within the school's catchment boundaries. And the school's staff, which was drawn from and mirrored Protestant Ontario, was quite differ-ent again. What they shared, despite their differences, was a keen desire for students to succeed and "get kicked up the social lad-der."[80] And from that shared desire developed the Axis of Good that connected home and school and that generated a bond of trust and loyalty between them.

This does not mean that everyone agreed about everything or that there were not clear differences in power or that the community was as inclusive as it might have been. Indeed, the importance of conventional academic achievement to this shared vision probably reinforced the sense that students with disabilities were somehow outsiders. But it does mean that, for those students in the regular academic stream, the school worked as a community because it pro-vided a site for nurturing the feelings of mutual concern that charac-terize friendships large and small. When Clinton teachers went out of their way to care for their students – through the gift of a Hebrew Bible or a visit in the hospital or protection from an irate neighbour or the creation of a homemade menorah – their acts of kindness were anything but random. They were small acts of friendship that reflected the teachers' feelings that they shared something with their students' families, namely the desire to impart and acquire the education that would allow them to succeed.

One of the most popular advertising jingles of the late 1960s and 1970s was sponsored by a muffler company that promoted its ser-vice with the phrase "At Speedy You're a Somebody." The slogan is evocative, not just because it was coined by someone who (briefly) attended Clinton.[81] It captures the sense that I heard time and again from graduates that they felt as if Clinton School had taken them seriously, that they were somebodies. They felt as if they really belonged, that they had what Judith Shklar called "standing"[82] in

Figure 3.1 Destination of Graduates – 1948–1956

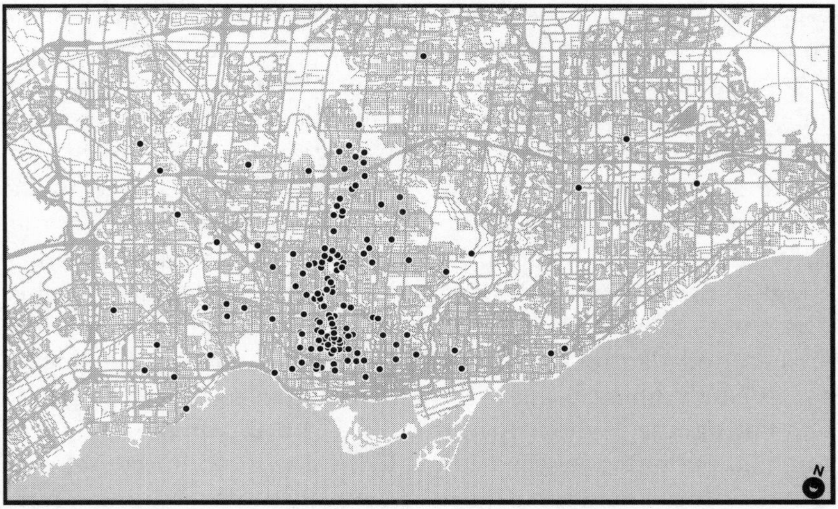

Sources: Clinton data set and open-source maps

the school community; they were citizens, not citizens-minus. They would soon enough have to deal with universities that put quotas on their admission and professional associations that limited their participation, but for the moment the opportunity to make their way in the world was pretty much available to any Clinton kid who wanted to seize it. The Drew government used Ontario schools to rank religions in ways that drew attention to the differences among them. Clinton School took the opposite approach. It found a basis for community – for belonging – that bridged religious differences rather than deepening them. In so doing, it created a community that was identified with a religion precisely because it did not make religion the basis of community.

Communities based on shared characteristics are inherently dynamic; they don't stand still. Certainly this was true of the Clinton community, which changed massively and suddenly in the mid-1950s. In the 1920s and 1930s, students who graduated from Clinton typically stayed in the neighbourhood to attend secondary school – usually Harbord Collegiate, Central Technical School, or Central Commerce. This pattern changed dramatically in the 1940s, especially following the Second World War. What happened, of course, is that Clinton's Jewish population moved "up the hill" to take advantage of the post-war prosperity that had produced new suburbs, modern infrastructure, and middle-class comforts unavailable during the Depression and the war years. As one can see from figure 3.1 (above), students who once would have stayed in the neighbourhood to attend secondary school now created a trail up Bathurst Street – stopping along the way at high schools like Vaughan Road, Forest Hill, Sandford Fleming, and Bathurst Heights. The homes they left behind did not remain vacant, however. The area around Clinton soon became what was (and remains) known as Little Italy, home to a new wave of immigrants – especially Italian and Portuguese – who helped to build and maintain the infrastructure that permitted Jewish Clinton to head to the suburbs. Yet with that new population came the need to reconstitute the Clinton community, to find and nurture a shared goal that would sustain their educational life together. How Clinton School reinvented itself in light of this challenge is the subject of the next two chapters.

4

European Clinton, 1950–1965: "Ruth beside the Alien Corn"

In October 1965, the Clinton community gathered to lay the cornerstone for the "new" Clinton Street Public School. Dignitaries spoke, a school trustee planted a time capsule, the school choir sang, and the assembled guests were invited to join voices in the nineteenth-century Protestant hymn "Christ is made the sure foundation, Christ the head and corner stone."[1] So much for the tolerant ecumenism that characterized Jewish Clinton. But nothing symbolized the new Clinton more evocatively than the presence of the Rev. Alex Zeidman, a Presbyterian minister and director of the Scott Mission, who offered a prayer of dedication for the new building. Zeidman carried on the work begun by his father, Morris, a Polish Jew who immigrated to Toronto before the First World War, converted to Christianity, experienced a "dramatic" calling to the ministry, and subsequently spent his career building the Scott Mission – where he provided aid to needy immigrants and the poor.[2]

The new Clinton Street School was like the Zeidmans: it had its own dramatic conversion experience, which entailed a break with its Jewish past. And like the Zeidmans, Clinton found a new calling. Its new mission, one might say, was to serve a new, and diametrically different, population of immigrants in need. As many of Clinton's Jewish families left the downtown core for the comfort and amenities of the northern suburbs, the neighbourhood became home to a new wave of immigrants – this time overwhelmingly from Italy, Portugal, and central Europe. As Jewish Clinton

Figure 4.1 Religion by Family, 1945–1970

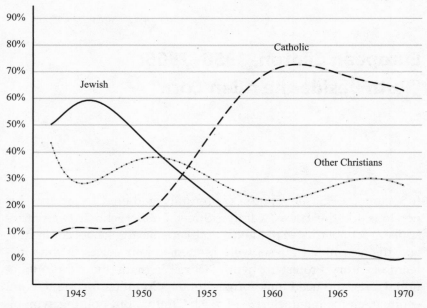

Source: Clinton data set

dissolved, European Clinton formed. The question of citizenship – how to integrate immigrants into Canadian society – remained front and centre, but now the diversity focus shifted away from religion to language and culture. The next two chapters chronicle the growth of what I call European Clinton and the ideas of citizenship that accompanied it. Chapter 4 concentrates on Clinton's makeover in the 1950s and early 1960s and explains the school's dilemmas in responding to the influx of New Canadians. Chapter 5 picks up the story from the moment the new school building opened in 1966 and shows how, over the next decade, these dilemmas continued to play out at the school.

The basic demographic facts with which I ended the previous chapter bear repeating here as they provide a sense of the speed and intensity with which Jewish Clinton morphed into European

Figure 4.2 Ethnicity by Father's Birthplace, 1950–1975

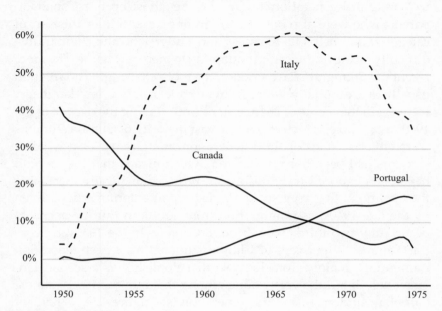

Source: Clinton data set

Clinton. In 1953, just over 30 per cent of incoming students at Clinton were Jewish, and an equal number were Catholic; by 1960, only 5 per cent of incoming students were Jewish while 75 per cent were Catholic (see figure 4.1).

That is how quickly the neighbourhood changed. The same story of dramatic change emerges if we focus on ethnicity rather than religion. In the late 1940s, roughly 5 per cent of Clinton students came from Italian families, and by the early 1950s, about a quarter were of Italian descent. By the early 1960s, a decade on, at least half of the students entering Clinton were Italian in origin, and by the time the new school opened in 1966, fully 60 per cent of the students had a parent born in Italy (see figure 4.2).

As a third way to gauge the extent of demographic change, consider immigrant status. It is common practice to distinguish between first-generation (i.e., those born abroad), second-generation (i.e., those born in Canada to parents who were born in another country), and third-generation immigrants (i.e., those born in Canada to parents who were also born here). Among other things, this sort of categorization helps us to assess and understand the comparative difficulty facing immigrants in adapting to their new home. The more recent the immigration experience, the more challenging adaptation usually is – especially when it involves learning a new language. Here again the theme of change stands out. Taking the decade of the 1940s as a whole, it is clear that the vast majority of Clinton students were either second- or third-generation immigrants. That is, most students had been born in Canada, which means that they would have been exposed to English from birth, dramatically increasing the likelihood that they spoke English upon entering school. Even by the late 1940s, as immigration from southern Europe began to occur, fully two-thirds were born in Canada. In the 1950s, by contrast, almost 60 per cent of Clinton students were first-generation immigrants, mainly from Italy, so that English was a second language for all but the very young among them. In the 1960s, almost half of all students were first generation (see figure 4.3).[3] Whatever the frame of reference – religion, ethnicity, or immigration status – the story is essentially the same: the 1950s and early 1960s brought sudden, swift, and seismic change to the Clinton community.

What produced these changes? And what were the consequences for Clinton Street School?

The Second World War stands as a watershed event of the twentieth century. It transformed global politics and put in place the dramatis personae of the Cold War. It also produced momentum for assertions of national autonomy, ranging from the passage of the Citizenship Act (1946) in Canada to decolonization in Africa, and it led directly to the creation of the United Nations and the Declaration of Human Rights. In its wake Europe was rebuilt, and countries like Canada experienced an era of unprecedented economic prosperity – all the while producing babies to enjoy it. It is notable, amidst this massive social, economic, and political change, that Canada's immigration policy changed almost not at all. It remained committed, as it was between the wars, to controlling the number and type of immigrants allowed to enter Canada by excluding whole swathes of

Figure 4.3 Immigration Status by Decade

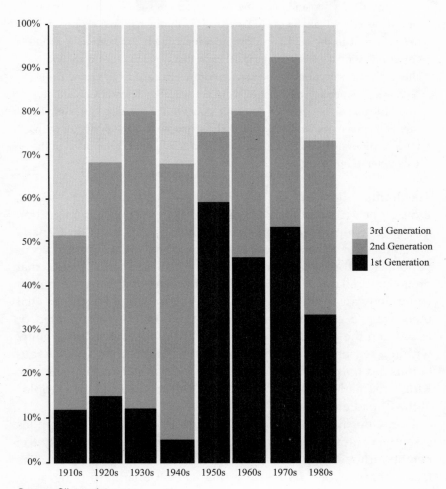

Source: Clinton data set

potential citizens based on race, ethnicity, and geographic origin. As Prime Minister Mackenzie King put it to Parliament in 1947:

The policy of the government is to foster the growth of the population of Canada by the encouragement of immigration. The government will

seek, by legislation, regulation, and vigorous administration, to ensure
the careful selection and permanent settlement of such numbers of immigrants as can advantageously be absorbed in our national economy ...
With regard to the selection of immigrants, much has been said about
discrimination. I wish to make quite clear that Canada is perfectly within
her rights in selecting the persons whom we regard as desirable future
citizens. It is not a "fundamental right" of any alien to enter Canada. It is
a privilege. It is a matter of domestic policy ... There will, I am sure, be
general agreement with the view that the people of Canada do not wish,
as a result of mass immigration, to make a fundamental alteration in the
character of our people.[4]

The Immigration Act of 1952 essentially codified King's views.
Indeed, the act gave broad discretion to the minister of immigration
and citizenship to deny prospective immigrants entry to Canada
on account of their "nationality, citizenship, ethnic group, occu-
pation, class, or geographical origin." And lest anyone escape that
broad umbrella of restrictions, the act added that the government
could deny an application if an immigration officer concluded that
there was "a probable inability to become readily assimilated or
to assume the duties and responsibilities of Canadian citizenship,
within a reasonable time after admission."[5] What the Drew Regulations did for protecting Anglo-Protestantism in Ontario's schools,
King's regulations did for protecting "the character of our people"
at the Canadian border.

I provide this brief piece of policy history because it supplies
essential context for understanding just who settled in the Clinton
neighbourhood, where they came from, and in what numbers. The
fact is that, beyond its moral repugnancy, Canadian immigration
policy in the immediate post-war era generated a real dilemma for
Ottawa. On the one hand, the government's official policy was to
encourage immigration to stoke the growing economy. There were
roads to build, houses to construct, cars to assemble, and a growing
menu of financial and social services to provide. Canadian employers needed workers, and as the boom continued it became clear that
the demand for labour would continue for some time to come. On
the other hand, the government's long list of exclusions severely

restricted the number of sources from which it could draw the immigrants to fill these jobs. Most potential immigrants from Asia, Africa, and the Middle East were ineligible because they weren't white. (The government created an exception for non-whites from some Commonwealth countries, but hard and fast quotas severely limited the flow.) With Europe newly divided by the "Iron Curtain," most potential immigrants in eastern Europe were now unable to emigrate, and the chill associated with the Cold War meant that Canadian officials were quick to weed out those who strayed too far from the political mainstream. Even after and despite the Holocaust, Jews were viewed with suspicion.[6]

Where, then, to look? Immigrants from Britain and northern Europe were in high demand, but the fact is that, by the early 1950s, most of the Brits and northern Europeans who wanted to emigrate (like war brides from Britain and farmers from the Netherlands) had already arrived or were just as likely to settle in the United States, Australia, or New Zealand. Another possibility was to recruit immigrants from the displaced persons (or DP) camps that housed refugees from war-torn Europe. This was no grand humanitarian program, no "United Way campaign. It was a labour-importation scheme, pure and simple," and Canada cherry-picked those – Estonians, Latvians, and Lithuanians – who were "highly prized as hard working 'Nordic types.'"[7] A third group of potential immigrants was produced by civil unrest in eastern Europe. Following the Hungarian uprising of 1956, for instance, Canada seized the opportunity to fast-track admission to Hungarian refugees. In the end, about 37,000 Hungarians settled in Canada,[8] many of them in Toronto, and many of those in the west end near Clinton Street School. Still, the federal government's post-war approach to immigration was, in its own terms, highly "selective." As Franca Iacovetta has concluded, Canadian immigration policy "was rooted in the basic premise that northern Europeans had a greater proclivity to orderly society and free parliamentary institutions, or at least shared the same complexion, mores, and religion as English Canadians, and thus were the most easily assimilated."[9]

The problem with this "selective" approach was that it simply couldn't meet the labour shortage that had become acute by 1950.

The need, therefore, to stretch the definition of eligibility became increasingly urgent. As a result, government officials began to think about Canada as a "product of a 'mixture' of white European nationalities"[10] that was more diverse, complex, and open-ended than usually imagined. In the words of one leading public intellectual turned government pamphleteer, "none of our national groups from Europe is really alien to the rest of us."[11] This was a crucial move. For once "Italians, Slavs, Jews, and Greeks, among others, came to be viewed as legitimate Canadians officially on par with their Anglo- and French-Canadian counterparts" it became possible to cast the immigration net much farther afield.[12]

The most impressive example of this change in attitude – and the one that bears most directly on Clinton – was the new (and quite sudden) openness to immigration from Italy. The first step was to remove Italy from the enemy aliens list, which occurred in January 1947. Then, in the fall of 1950, Ottawa established immigration offices throughout Europe and "entered into a bilateral agreement with Italy to foster and process large-scale immigration to Canada."[13] Not surprisingly in light of the intellectual context I've described, Canada preferred immigrants from northern Italy. Equally unsurprisingly, most of those who applied and were pre-approved by the Italian government were from the south. Where Canada's economy enjoyed a post-war boom, the economy of southern Italy stagnated under the weight of chronic unemployment, poor land management, deep geographical and class divisions, a high birth rate, and pent-up demand for emigration. In a word, many Italians wanted to escape what was simply called *la miseria*, and Canada held out the promise of a better life. The effects, both on Canada and Italy, were transformative. In 1949, the Commissioner for Overseas Immigration, Laval Fortier, wrote that "the Italian South peasant is not the type we are looking for in Canada. His standard of living, his way of life, even his civilization seem so different that I doubt if he could ever become an asset to our country."[14] Two years later, the same man, Laval Fortier, now deputy minister of citizenship and immigration, oversaw the newly renovated program of immigration that opened the door wide to Italian immigration. In all, more than 240,000 Italians immigrated to Canada in the first wave between

1951 and 1961. By 1971, that number had almost doubled, of which three out of every five, *pace* Fortier, hailed from the south.[15]

"Canada has become a new home for many people from all over the world. They do not all come to Toronto." So began a 1960 curriculum guide to accompany a grade 3 social studies unit entitled "New Neighbours from Other Lands."[16] One can perhaps forgive students and teachers alike for the misimpression that all immigrants were bound for Toronto because, indeed, the city was a magnet for newcomers, especially from Italy. Between 1951 and 1961, 40 per cent of all Italian immigrants to Canada settled in Toronto.[17] Jobs were plentiful, there was already an Italian population to ease the transition, and, once the first wave of immigrants had settled, chain migration led other family members and *paesani* (co-villagers) to settle nearby. "Nearby" is, of course, wonderfully imprecise, but for the first generation of post-war Italian immigrants to Toronto, the area surrounding the intersection of College and Grace Streets in the west end was the epicentre of the community.

Like the Jewish community before it, Italians found Toronto's west end congenial for a whole variety of reasons. For one thing, there was already a critical mass of Italian families living in the neighbourhood. John Zucchi estimates that, by 1935, there were about 16,000 residents of Italian origin living in Toronto.[18] Like Jews, many Italian immigrants had moved away from the parlous conditions of The Ward and towards the west end because it was close to the industrial web of factories that provided steady employment.[19] This meant that post-war immigrants were in many cases already connected to the west end through family or village relationships. Beyond this, housing was relatively affordable and, perhaps more important, was readily available and versatile. Single boarders could be taken in, families could live together, and ingenious forms of community-based financing meant that financial equity could be established reasonably quickly.[20] Proximity to the College streetcar, and from there to the new subway system, was crucial for men who worked in construction and had either to travel to plants located in one of the industrial suburbs or to move from site to site. It was no less important for the growing number of women who worked, often shift work, downtown. Social clubs and mutual aid societies were established in the area, and there were churches to provide for spiritual needs. St Agnes Church (a short distance away at the corner of Grace and Dundas) had been designated as an Italian parish in 1913.[21] By 1958 it was so overwhelmed by new parishioners that it was offering ten masses every Sunday, in Italian and English.[22] There were several other Catholic churches in the west end, and a range of other non-Catholic churches, including a small but thriving Italian United Church (Canada's largest Protestant denomination).

Another way to understand the attraction of Little Italy is that it was a good neighbourhood in which to raise children. Studies of life in Toronto's Little Italy are plentiful, but, curiously, almost none of them talk about the experiences and place of children, though they were central to the neighbourhood's life. Most of the immigrants who arrived in the first wave in the 1950s were young. Some had recently been married in Italy and arrived in Canada as couples (sometimes already with a child or two); others were married and arrived alone, but with the intention to make enough money to bring the rest of the family from Italy; and still others arrived single and met their spouses here. One way or another, building families and providing for them was a central goal. According to the records at St Agnes Church, in 1958 alone priests performed 763 baptisms and 310 weddings – more than two baptisms and almost one wedding every day.[23] Thus did the school-aged population grow. The census tracts that provide local demographic snapshots of the country every ten years almost perfectly match the catchment zone of Clinton Street School,[24] so it is possible to follow population shifts in the community that fed Clinton with considerable accuracy. Between 1951 and 1961, the total population in the Clinton catchment area increased by 14 per cent (about 1,500 people). But the number of children thirteen years old and younger increased by a whopping 65 per cent – from just over 2,000 to more than 3,300, an increase of 1,300 school-aged (or soon to become school-aged) children.[25] They all needed schools and teachers – and they needed them immediately.

How did Clinton deal with these dramatic demographic changes? The school's first challenge was to find the physical capacity to accommodate the explosion, a problem not peculiar to Clinton. As R.D. Gidney notes, Ontario's population as a whole increased by 50 per cent between 1946 and 1961, and its elementary school population increased by 116 per cent.[26] This increase in school enrolments – greater than in any other fifteen-year period in Canadian history[27] – was driven by a combination of intense immigration and the baby boom. But these explosive enrolments also reflected the growing consensus – especially in urban Ontario – that school · should begin earlier and end later. On the one hand, the Toronto school board embraced the principles of early intervention, with the result that Clinton, in 1948, became one of the first city schools to mount regular junior kindergarten classes for four-year-olds (in addition to senior kindergarten for five-year-olds). On the other hand, both educators and the public were warming to the new idea that most teenagers, not just the academically inclined minority, should expect to complete high school.[28] The confluence of these factors created a perfect storm, and the sharp increase in enrolment that ensued put enormous strain on aging physical plants, teaching capacity, and the ingenuity of those who administered public education. As C.C. Goldring, Toronto's long-serving director of education put it, "When we consider the future of public education in Ontario, we are aware of many problems. In my opinion, problem number one is the need for more money. The reason for this requirement is that our school enrolment is increasing. We need more teachers and we need more buildings."[29]

As the 1950s progressed, Clinton (like many other schools) began to feel the pinch of overcrowding. In 1950 the school had twenty-eight regular classes. By 1957, as the neighbourhood's youthful population swelled, the school had to find room for thirty-two classes – not an easy task in an elegant but aging building. One quick and reasonably painless fix entailed capping the school at grade 6 and re-assigning the students from grades 7 and 8 to another "intermediate" (or middle) school. The venerable King Edward School, Clinton's closest neighbour to the east, had been razed and recently rebuilt, in part to provide better facilities for intermediate students, so the administrative decision to redefine Clinton as a "junior" public school that ended at grade 6 was straightforward. One can detect a hint of regret in the principal's message to the school following the change, but the transition seems to have gone smoothly enough over the spring and summer of 1958. And Clinton did gain a modicum of breathing room as a result.

A second more ambitious and more expensive strategy to deal with sudden overcrowding was to build new elementary schools to meet the enrolment boom, and "local trustees throughout the province, assisted by the Ontario government, embarked on a vast program of renewing the physical infrastructure of education."[30] Low-rise, cinder-block, ranch-style schools equipped with state-of-the-art equipment popped up all over the province. Set amidst turn-of-the-century homes in downtown Toronto, these new schools seemed particularly incongruous and out of place. Never mind, they were needed. To reduce the enrolment pressures on Clinton in particular, a new school, Montrose, was constructed a few streets to the west. It was designed to serve the western half of Little Italy, which included streets formerly part of Clinton's catchment. In the end, about 200 Clinton students transferred to Montrose.[31]

As the creation of Montrose suggests, the TBE wasn't just concerned about physical space, but also with the quality of the educational environment and with giving students access to up-to-date facilities and equipment. By the early 1960s it became clear that "old" Clinton was on its last legs despite efforts to spruce it up, repair the electrical system, and replace the heating system. The school had some beautiful features – elegant stone entrances, a grand wooden staircase, distinctive doorknobs, gorgeous stained glass, and bathrooms done in marble. But there was no gymnasium to speak of, nor a library; the mechanical systems were outdated; and, according to the local school trustee, the school's playground was one of the smallest in the city.[32] After considering renovation, the TBE concluded that it made more sense to demolish the old school and to replace it with a building fully equipped with modern gadgets and a vastly expanded outdoor space. That decision was universally lamented by those I interviewed; one said that the day the demolition crew arrived "was the saddest day of my life." Jack Quarter, who attended Clinton in the early 1950s and returned to tour the school as a professor of education twenty-five years later, wasn't quite as nostalgic about the education he received in the old school, but he too regretted the loss of the old building: "After my visit, I was convinced that the new Clinton School was a great improvement over the one I attended. But I did wish that the old building, faulty heating system and all, hadn't been torn down."[33]

Oddly enough, the planners seem to have been so spellbound by the opportunity to create "splendid facilities"[34] that they lost sight of the rising enrolment trajectory. The first design for a new building was approved by the school board in April 1964; it called for the creation of twenty-four standard classrooms (supplemented by kindergarten rooms, a library, and a general-purpose auditorium/ gymnasium). Thinking their enrolment projections were too high, a second, revised plan was submitted a few months later, in September 1964, which recommended that the structure be downsized and the number of classrooms reduced from twenty-four to twenty-one.[35] But as the planners continued to pore over the data, they came to the inescapable conclusion not just that they had over-corrected, but that even the first version of the plan could not meet existing student demand. As a result, the architects and engineers assigned to the project scrambled, at the very moment construction was beginning, to modify the original design to include a partial third floor with additional classrooms, yielding a total of twenty-eight standard classrooms.[36] Even this was not enough. For the first few years after the school opened in 1966, a portion of its new, expanded playground had to be sacrificed to accommodate a handful of portable classrooms. So in the end, Clinton got its new school. Amazingly enough, in light of the moving enrolment targets, it even had room for almost all of its students.

The final form of relief from intense enrolment pressure came from a source over which the TBE had no control whatsoever – the system of separate or Catholic schools. The history of Catholic education in Ontario is long, complex, and contentious.[37] For our purposes, the important thing to understand is that Catholic parents enjoyed what we now refer to as school choice. They could send their elementary-aged children to a school like Clinton in the secular, public system, or they could direct them around the corner to St Francis of Assisi or across the street to St Lucy's, which were also publicly funded for kindergarten and grades 1 through 8, taught the Ontario curriculum, and provided religious instruction as well. As I noted earlier, by 1960 fully 75 per cent of Clinton students came from Catholic families, so the separate school system was clearly not for everyone. Some of those I interviewed thought that the decision to attend Clinton was simply a matter of convenience; Clinton was closer, their parents reasoned, or didn't involve crossing a busy street. Others said they went to public school because their families wanted to maintain a healthy distance between church and school. And a few parents told me, bluntly, that they embraced the public system because they resented being told what to do by "the priests." Yet, just as clearly, Catholic school was an attractive alternative for many parents and, despite chronic underfunding, the Catholic school system in Toronto grew extraordinarily quickly during the period.[38] The fact is that, in an area like west end Toronto, Catholic schools, which had enrolments equal to and sometimes exceeding their public counterparts, were life-savers. Without them, the existing public schools – already struggling to cope with sharply increased enrolments – would have been overwhelmed.

One final, related safety valve for the pressures of high enrolment deserves mention. The terms "public" and "separate" suggest educational systems that are parallel rather than intersecting. They are different both in inspiration and operation; students choose one or the other and stay put. This is not, in fact, how many students (and their families) saw (or see) it. A significant number of the students I interviewed attended both Catholic and public schools over the course of their school lives – a public elementary school, followed by a Catholic high school (or vice versa), and sometimes back again. For them educational border-crossing was routine and unexceptional. But what surprised me was just how early and often the systems intersected in European Clinton. When students returned to school from their summer vacation there would always be a few classmates who had mysteriously disappeared from the school, having transferred over the summer to a Catholic school. Indeed, over 15 per cent of all transfers from Clinton involved a move not out of district but to a Catholic school in the area. And while I spoke with graduates of nearby St Lucy's Catholic School who said they longed to attend Clinton because it had the reputation for being a "better" school with more relaxed discipline, there were fewer transfers into Clinton from the Catholic system than out.[39] It was never easy to predict exactly how many students would defect from one system to the other. This complicated enrolment planning enormously, as the several revisions to the Clinton building plan attest. Yet, on balance, these mid-course corrections provided another means of relieving enrolment pressures on Clinton.

How to reconfigure old schools, build new schools, and coexist with intersecting schools: these were the major challenges that pre-occupied school leaders struggling to cope with the swelling enrol-ments that followed swift and dramatic demographic change in the 1950s and early 1960s. Yet where physical expansion was dynamic and forward-looking, the in-school experience was suffused with a "moderate conservatism"[40] that was more resistant to change. It may be that the two phenomena are related: school officials were perhaps so preoccupied with physical expansion that they had nei-ther the time nor the energy to devote to pedagogical reform. Per-haps. But the relative absence of attention to what was taught and how it was taught also reflected a certain (somewhat smug) satis-faction with the state of elementary education in Ontario. As C.C. Goldring put it to an assembly of school trustees in 1955, "It is my opinion that, speaking generally, the children in Grades I to VI in the typical Ontario school receive as good an education as is available in any publicly supported school system in the world."[41] Goldring found certain developments in the higher grades worrisome, but "our work in the first six grades is done very well."[42] If the system ain't broke, in other words, don't fix it.

The upshot is that, within the school itself, the typical classroom experience in European Clinton was not so different from that in Jewish Clinton before it. What did this mean in practice? Two ele-ments of continuity between one era and the next stand out. One is the sort of flexible formalism that guided pedagogy; the other is an emphasis on order and discipline.

The essence of formalism, as we saw earlier, is the idea that teach-ers should talk and students should listen:[43] that the curriculum consists of an ordered body of knowledge and that the job of the student is to master it – usually through repetition and memorization. One teacher who taught grade 2 at Clinton in the early to mid-1950s explained how this worked in her classroom. Responsible for teaching a class of forty students, she first sorted them by ability – either into groups (bearing cheerful names like chickadees and robins) or by row (the "row by the window" was some teachers' code for those who struggled academically). After the sorting, she would proceed to instruct one group while the others either did seat work or worked at the board. Then it would be time for the next group to gather round her desk as the first group returned to their seats to complete exercises that applied what they had just learned, and so on. The result of this attempt to customize instruction by level or ability meant that most students most of the time completed endless exercises on their own. Principal McArthur captured the spirit of formalism nicely in this almost confessional note to students in the 1961 edition of the *Clinton Chronicle*, the school's annual literary magazine: "You, the pupils, learn to read, spell, write and many other skills in your classrooms. Much of the work, for the most part, is merely composed of exercises which the teachers have assigned. Sometimes it must seem boring and of little use."[44]

But this formalism was leavened, in European as in Jewish Clinton, by a variety of intra- and extra-curricular activities that both built on, and served as something of an antidote to, the more monotonous routines of everyday classroom life. *The Chronicle*, Principal McArthur went on to say, "presents an excellent medium for making use of your school learnings. The creation of art, stories, poems and anecdotes enables you to put to use the subjects which you study in school."[45] Not surprisingly, it is these more creative activities, not the repetitious classroom lessons, that graduates tend to remember. Miss Waddell, who taught the accelerated 3/4/5 class, used her artistic gifts to keep the walls bright and lessons fresh. She kept hamsters in the class, featured current events on the bulletin board, and subscribed to a commercially produced "step" reading system that permitted students to develop their reading skills at their own pace. Nancy MacDonald, who became a legendary music teacher at Clinton, began her career in 1958 as a grade 2 teacher. She somehow managed to procure tickets so that she could take groups of students to the O'Keefe Centre (the new concert hall/theatre in town) on Saturday afternoons to see the production *du jour*. Local field trips, to the children's library or the provincial legislature at Queen's Park or to CBC television for taping of the children's show *Razzle Dazzle*, were common. But so, too, were more adventurous outings, including a regular trip to Niagara Falls (by way of General Brock's monument, erected to commemorate his gallantry in the War of 1812) and overnight camp at the board's newly repurposed natural science school on Toronto Island – a highlight then and a regular part of the school experience for most elementary school students in Toronto to this day.

The school's leadership clearly wanted to impress parents with the wide range of extra-curricular activities available to their children. The Home and School *Bulletin*, published monthly during the 1950s, included a regular column entitled "The Voice of Clinton," written by one of the senior teachers. The column typically provided an account of the many current extra-curricular activities at the school – of choirs at different levels, the Dramatic Club, talent shows, chess club, intra-mural sports, school teams in various sports, charitable campaigns organized by groups like the Junior Red Cross, and so on. As Glenna Davis, one of the teachers who wrote the column, put it, "The Voice of Clinton has attempted to bring you a picture of the full life we lead here at school this term and every term."[46] At the beginning of the next school year, Miss Davis framed the school's program as a form of citizenship training: "Clinton teachers are interested in developing well-rounded citizens with varied interests. To that end a full programme of extra-curricular activities has been planned for the year."[47] In short, Clinton may have been ruled by pedagogical formalism, but it was a flexible formalism.

An equally essential goal of the education of these "well-rounded citizens" in training was to demonstrate the importance of social order. As I noted in chapter 2, this quest for social order was represented in Jewish Clinton by the use of corporal punishment. Those who received "slaps" not only misbehaved; in an important sense their punishment was meant to convey the clear message that they had placed themselves outside the moral community that was Clinton. Noel Pollard, who served as Clinton's principal through the 1950s, was clearly much more reluctant than his predecessors to use corporal punishment. Where in the 1940s the punishment ledger books record an average of forty-seven strappings per year, under Pollard the number of reported instances of corporal punishment declined in the 1950s to sixteen per year. This does not mean that teachers were any less devoted to enforcing discipline and maintaining order. One graduate told me that several of the male teachers, especially those who had returned from military duty in the Second World War, were "screamers" who became apoplectic with rage when students disobeyed their instructions. Another told me, in detail, about his grade 6 teacher, a Mrs M., who picked him up by the scruff of the neck and pinned him to the wall until he was left gasping for breath. This teacher seems to have been particularly "mean," especially because students noticed that she tended to single out immigrant students for punishment, but her approach was not atypical. And when the fear of punishment did not work, there was always humiliation. Clinton students in the early years of this period who violated the rules were sometimes consigned to the back of the class, dunce hats on their heads. Others remembered being forced to write lines – interminably. In one case, the punishment for talking out of turn meant spending a whole weekend copying out every entry under the letter "A" from the dictionary.

To be sure, many graduates fondly remembered teachers for their nurturing qualities – especially women teachers in the early grades, and especially in the later years of the period under consideration here. But what remains for many, especially those who had a rebellious streak, was just how "austere" the school seemed. Lloyd Dennis, who rose to fame a decade later as a school reformer, once described schools in post-war Ontario as "pickle factories."[48] The metaphor nicely captures the sourness that accompanied the emphasis on discipline.

The need for social order characterized the school's enduring moral climate; the need to promote hard work characterized its more variable weather. Through the 1930s, 1940s, and early 1950s, the alliance between parents and teachers that I call the Axis of Good kept students' feet to the academic fire. But then, by the late 1950s, something had changed. Principal Pollard was concerned enough about academic slippage that he made it one of the themes of his farewell address to students in 1960. "Scholarship worries me somewhat," he said:

> Our standard of achievement has fallen off in the last few years. We still have many excellent students but we have too many whose progress is not as rapid as it should be. Some of these are good workers who have language difficulties and I know that they will give a good account of themselves as soon as they have mastered English. Unfortunately, though, there are others for whom there is not much excuse. I wish we could convince these latter pupils that education and willingness to work are two keys to success in this Canada of ours.[49]

One of his vice-principals, Miss Farley, was blunter still. She used her column in the 1959 edition of the *Chronicle* to draw attention to "those pupils who do not do their best work, those who have the ability which they lose through sheer laziness or lack of desire." But where punishing rule-breakers provided at least the illusion of maintaining social order, Miss Farley had no quick remedy for lack of motivation. She was left to wonder: "Let us each set ourselves a goal and work steadily and consistently toward that goal, and some day who knows but we may surprise even ourselves. Perhaps a magic formula would help the lazy ones to become industrious, and the disinterested to become interested. Who knows?"[50]

How to manage a classroom; what to teach and how to teach it; and how to motivate students. These are perennial questions for teachers, and Clinton's take on them in the 1950s and early 1960s was well within the mainstream of what large organizations now like to call "best practices." But Principal Pollard's farewell statement, quoted above, also referred to one feature of Clinton's life that set it apart from most other schools in Toronto, namely the number of students for whom English was a second language. One can infer from the fact that, already by the early 1950s, more than half of the students entering Clinton were born abroad that for most students English was either a second language, not spoken at home, or both. This linguistic fact posed an enormous, fundamental challenge to a school that delivered its program in English. Where did Clinton's leadership look for guidance? And how did they meet the challenge?

Franca Iacovetta has argued that post-war Canada deployed a whole "army" of "gatekeepers" who conspired to inculcate middle-class values and weed out threats to national security among newly arrived immigrants.[51] Government officials, courts, voluntary associations, social workers, filmmakers, popular experts – "all pitched in to contain or eradicate alleged 'threats' or 'enemies within' who might contaminate the wider society."[52] Yet immigrant students at Toronto schools received nothing like this sort of attention. Indeed, what is striking is just how indifferent educators at various levels were to the needs of first-generation students – especially those unable to function well in English.

Under other circumstances, Clinton's leadership might have looked to the Hope Commission for guidance and inspiration. Given a broad mandate to map out the future of public education in the province, the commission provided a promising opportunity to consider the implications of broad social and economic change for education, including the integration of immigrant students. Several things militated against its usefulness, however. One was timing. The Hope Commission reported in 1950, but most of its work was completed by 1948 – that is, before the door to immigration opened decisively. Indeed, the commission included but one passing reference to "conditions that are now favourable for selective immigration."[53] Obviously, the commissioners didn't – and perhaps couldn't – see the immigration train hurtling down the track towards them. Yet even if they had foreseen the spike in European immigration, it is not clear that Hope would have dealt seriously with the challenges it posed on the ground. The commission's final report was long on abstract philosophical principles and the nitty-gritty of administrative organization, but with respect to the social context of schools it had tin ears. Besides, the commission was seriously divided over the issue of separate schools, and taking social diversity more seriously would have deepened the divide still further. As a guide to education amidst rapidly increasing diversity, Hope was of no help.[54]

A more likely source of intellectual leadership was C.C. Goldring, the director of the Toronto Board of Education. Goldring was ideally positioned to shape the contours of public debate about educating immigrant students. On the one hand, he had home field advantage; as the head of Toronto schools he could see the changes occurring under his administrative nose. On the other, Goldring had an abiding intellectual interest in questions of citizenship. He had written an intermediate textbook on the subject in 1948 and, throughout the 1950s, lectured widely, indeed internationally, on the challenges of fitting education to citizenship in a changing world. And yet, for some reason, Goldring rarely spoke about the role of schools in integrating large numbers of immigrant children into Canadian society. It is not as if he was unaware of the global dynamics of change and the pivotal role schools must play to ensure positive results as borders become more porous. In a 1950 broadcast, for instance, he explained to his radio audience how "the aeroplane has brought all parts of the world close together ... Parts of certain continents, formerly thought of as undeveloped, are changing rapidly. In the future, young Canadians will get jobs in distant parts of the world, and probably will accept them quite casually. A life of adventure awaits many a Canadian boy and girl now in school."[55] It seems not to have occurred to him, however, that this travel might be two-way and that children from these "distant parts of the world" were potential Canadian citizens.

Loren Lind, whose 1974 book *The Learning Machine* provides a scathing indictment of Toronto schools on the question of diversity, had this to say about Goldring's approach:

> Cecil Charles Goldring, director of education, studied the "immigrant problem" in 1951, only to find that his school principals found these strangers were timid, they clung tenaciously to native customs, they had trouble forming friendships, they were distressed ... Goldring ... seemed determined not to overreact. He ended his report by quoting the principal who said, "I think the less fuss about the matter the better. They should merge with the general population as soon as possible."[56]

In another speech, this time in 1955, Goldring enunciated the progressive principle that "we should aim to educate, in terms of their needs, all of the children of all the people." This would be a challenge, he went on, because there are so many needs to meet: gifted children, special classes for "slow learners," evening classes for youth who work, special programs for the physically handicapped, and teachers for children who are home-bound or hospitalized. But among the special needs he lists, the one that jumps off the page in the Clinton context is "*adult* education for new citizens." "We have a duty," he continued, "to provide evening classes for the adults to teach them the English language as quickly as possible and to give them some knowledge of Canadian ways of life, traditions, and beliefs."[57] So even when Goldring acknowledged the special needs of recent immigrants, it was largely to adults that he referred. About the needs of immigrant children he had far less to say.

If not by the provincial government or Toronto's director of education, could leadership be provided by organizations one step removed from, but committed to, the public educational system – universities, for example? *Design for Learning*, edited and introduced by Northrop Frye, was a book-length study that distilled a series of discussions, begun in 1960, between Toronto school teachers and University of Toronto professors on topics "of common interest." This was a unique collaboration. As Frye pointed out in his introduction, it was perhaps "the first time in Toronto's history that the University and the Board of Education had really talked to each other about education."[58] So here was an opportunity for professors to learn about, and suggest ways to approach, the challenges faced by teachers on the ground in English, the social sciences, and the physical sciences. The committee was stocked with academic heavyweights. In addition to Frye, the University of Toronto contingent included C.B. Macpherson (political economy), Jack Saywell (history), and Donald Ivey (physics), among others. The teachers included Lloyd Dennis (who later rose to fame as co-author of the Hall-Dennis Report) and J. Edward Parsons, a Clinton teacher. Parsons was a pioneer of ESL training at Clinton and yet, despite his presence on the English working group, *Design for Learning* simply assumed that students come fully equipped with English-language skills. The central question for the committee to grapple with might have been, "How can universities help schools teach the subjects of a liberal education?" – a question that might have opened up the discussion to the social reality that English is not the first language for many students. Instead, the committee chose to organize its discussions around a quite different question: "Does teaching in the schools ... reflect contemporary conceptions of the subjects being taught?"[59] This led, predictably enough, to the conclusion that schools were out of touch with the most recent scholarly theories. For teachers (like Parsons) facing a classroom of students struggling to understand lessons in English, this abstract and clearly academic approach offered little to take away.

In the 1940s, Jewish Clinton adroitly sidestepped compulsory religious education by finding a way *not* to teach what the provincial government thought it (and every other Ontario school) should teach. In the 1950s, by contrast, European Clinton was in the position of having to create ESL programs where none existed and where neither the provincial government nor the TBE had shown any great interest in mounting them. And where the 1940s required local resistance to an existing policy, the 1950s depended on local innovation in an intellectual and curricular vacuum.

Actually, it's not entirely fair to say that the TBE did nothing to provide language training for newly arrived immigrant students. When children from the displaced persons camps in Europe began to arrive after the Second World War, the Toronto board designated Ryerson Public School as its magnet school. Here newly arrived students attended an English-language "boot camp" for a few months, received a workbook and textbook in Basic English, then transferred to the neighbourhood school closest to their homes. (In January 1949, for instance, nineteen of these students attended Clinton – spread across all the grades.)[60] Once in their local schools, students were assigned to a regular classroom and grade that was "considerably below [their] intellectual level of maturation" but corresponded with their fluency in English. As a result, children who were ten or eleven were often placed in grade 2 on the theory that "it is more than discouraging to assign the pupil to too high a grade and then have to demote him."[61] The obvious problem is that this created a yawning mismatch between age and grade, a mismatch only deepened by the fact that many of the newly arrived students were well ahead of their age peers in subjects like mathematics. Nor was this easy for teachers, who had to devise "methods of instructing two or three non-English pupils in addition to [their] regular class."[62] Just the same, the number of children from DP camps was actually quite small, and the system could absorb them without any major reallocation of intellectual or financial resources. However, once first-generation immigrant students came to make up half of the school's population – which happened as early as 1952 at Clinton – such a piecemeal approach simply could not work.

This massive transformation of Clinton's student population clearly required a more comprehensive approach with more dedicated resources. Precisely how Clinton developed dedicated ESL teaching remains slightly hazy. Whether the school's leadership seized an opportunity presented by the board to build a pilot program or whether Clinton simply took the initiative on its own to reallocate resources in a way that would free up one of its teachers is difficult to know. What we do know is that between the principal, Noel Pollard, and a teacher, J. Edward Parsons, Clinton established its first dedicated ESL class in September 1951 – long before the Toronto board recognized the need for ESL instruction more generally.

By the time he took over the ESL file at Clinton, Parsons was a seasoned teacher who, by the early 1950s, was one of the longest-serving staff members at the school – and one of the most respected. As one of his colleagues put it to me, "he was way up there, on a pedestal." Students remember that he had a genuine presence: a big man with a flair for the dramatic, unmistakable then and memorable now. Parsons experimented with two models for teaching English as a second language. He described what became known as the "withdrawal" method for the Home and School *Bulletin* this way:

> When new Canadian boys and girls come to Clinton Street School for the first time, they are put through a screening process to determine whether or not they should attend regular grade-class or be enrolled in Room 14. The latter is done if their knowledge of English is non-existent or too inadequate to permit them to learn in regular grades with children of their own ages. On the other hand, if the child is not more than seven years of age he would be happier in the Kindergarten or Grade 1, and is so placed.

A year ago September [i.e., 1951], Room 14 was first pressed into service for this purpose. During the first ten months, seventy-one children ranging in age from seven to seventeen were enrolled in the special class, though the total number at any one time never exceeded thirty ...

Room 14 works on an apparently complicated but actually fairly smooth-running time-table, different for each child, which permits him to take intensive instruction in basic English at the same time as he is learning all the other subjects of the curriculum in whatever grade suits his age and capacity. Far from suffering from isolation as a new Canadian, he is deliberately thrown into an area of far wider social situations and social contacts than is normally the lot of the native Canadian child. Another advantage is that promotion can readily take place at any time during the school year.[63]

This was intensive, time-limited ESL training, obtained in the company of other immigrant students.

Later on, Parsons and Clinton as a whole came to favour a more integrative approach, in which New Canadian students spent part of the day together doing intensive English, then returned to their age-appropriate classes "to learn mathematics, arts, music and so on." The great advantage of this approach, according to school officials interviewed by *The Telegram* in 1961, was the "rapid integration of New Canadian children into the system," with the result that "they have felt at home much earlier than if they had been segregated for the entire school day."[64]

The ESL system that evolved over the 1950s and early 1960s at Clinton was far from perfect. Most kids lost at least a year in making the transition from Europe to Clinton; others were held back for a second year of (senior) kindergarten. Moreover, even with Clinton's revolving door approach, not every student who might have benefited from intensive English instruction could be accommodated. Still, the results were impressive. By 1961, a decade after the introduction of ESL classes, more than 600 students had received intensive English-language instruction.[65]

ESL was not simply about developing linguistic skills, however. As the term "New Canadians" suggests, learning the language was a vehicle for learning what it meant to be Canadian. C.C. Goldring made the connection between language, culture, and citizenship explicit:

> We have received into this country during recent years, tens of thousands of people from Europe with little understanding of the English language or Canadian ways and ideals. Most of them wish to become good Canadians. We have a duty to provide evening classes for the adults to teach them the English language as quickly as possible and to give them some knowledge of Canadian ways of life, traditions, and beliefs.[66]

Principal Pollard made essentially the same connection, only this time for children, in his farewell address in 1960: "We are especially proud ... because our pupils come from many lands and a great many of them are just learning *our* language and *our* ways."[67] Pollard's pride in Clinton's ahead-of-the-curve efforts to integrate immigrant students was apt enough, but as others have pointed out, the goal of programs like ESL remained knotted to the mast of assimilation. Writing in 1974, cultural critic and journalist Loren Lind argued that the post-war educational rhetoric around citizenship really embodied "the secret wish that immigrants, if they must come, would silently grow up to be like us."[68] He continued: "Toronto's programs for immigrant children have the basic aim of adapting these new arrivals to the language and culture of Anglo-Saxon Toronto. It has taken a variety of forms, from neo-progressive to straight-out traditional, but never has it gone beyond a rather crude version of cultural assimilation."[69] Jane Gaskell and Ben Levin, though speaking with greater academic restraint, came to the same conclusion when they surveyed Toronto schools during the 1950s and 1960s: "The overall goals articulated by the board," they argue, "were to assimilate immigrants, improve the educational standing of the poor, and socialize all children according to the norms of the Anglo-Saxon elite."[70]

Why was assimilation such an important goal for school administrators? And what did it entail in the school setting? One answer is that assimilation served as a kind of civic credit rating that could be used to establish an individual or group's fitness for Canadian citizenship. In this sense assimilation was not just a way of describing what authorities hoped immigrants would eventually become – that is, like the rest of "us." Rather, assimilation was a precondition or qualification that made immigrants eligible for full citizenship. It wasn't a consequence of becoming Canadian; it was a precondition. C.C. Goldring, whose 1948 intermediate textbook was entitled *Canadian Citizenship*, explained why formal citizenship was not offered to immigrants immediately upon their arrival in Canada: "There must be time for the newcomer to prove his worth, to learn Canadian ways, to develop a desire to become a good, loyal Canadian citizen, and then to renounce the citizenship of his former country."[71] Assimilation by this account is a demanding process, and one in which much of the hard work falls to the immigrants themselves. Newcomers must "learn," "develop," and "prove" *before* they become citizens. Notice how categorical Goldring's account is. Immigrants must "renounce" their former citizenship; they must shed their previous (civic) identity in order to acquire a new one. To this day, demographers use the term "conversion" to describe the process of becoming the citizen of a new country. The term is suggestive. Assimilation is a bit like religious conversion. It is possible – recall the example of the Zeidmans who left Judaism to become Christians – but it is a demanding, serious, and often wrenching project to leave one community and join another.

If assimilation is a tall order, then it is a task best begun early, and what better vehicle for the hard work of making citizens in the Anglo-Canadian image than schools? The experience of assimilation at schools like European Clinton was often difficult, coercive, and invasive, and many of the most striking examples involve language. Steve vividly recalled completing a written exercise – perhaps about Christopher Columbus – which included a reference to the Italian city of Genova. His teacher immediately crossed it out and replaced it with Genoa. When Steve said that he had seen the alternative spelling in an Italian book, the teacher simply told him he was wrong. It's Genoa in English, so Genoa it remained. Other graduates remembered teachers on the playground reprimanding students who spoke Italian rather than English at recess. And another remembered her parents receiving a call from the school to exhort them to speak English at home so that their children would master English more quickly.

And then there was the question of names. As Harold Troper has noted, "school teachers and administrators, thinking they were liberating immigrant children from narrow Old-World parochialism or protecting them from the schoolyard bully, took liberties with many an immigrant child's most personal possession – his or her name. Gabriella became Gail, Luigi became Louis, Olga became Alice, and Hershel became Harold."[72] Anglicizing names certainly occurred at Clinton. Take as one example among many the experience of eleven-year-old Giuseppe. Because his parents both worked, Giuseppe made his way to Clinton on his own on the first day of school in September, 1958. When he identified himself as a new student, the school secretary asked him what his name was. "Giuseppe," he answered brightly, but the name that appears on his official registration card is Gios – the best Anglo-friendly facsimile the school official could produce on the spot. So Giuseppe officially became Gios – a name that stuck for the rest of his years as a student and most of his adult life.

But assimilation wasn't just about language and names, and the pressure to fit in was not applied solely by school officials. Just as virtually all of the members of Jewish Clinton with whom I spoke had experienced some form of anti-Semitism at first hand, so virtually all of the members of European Clinton with whom I spoke knew at first hand what it felt like not to "fit in." The student who felt embarrassed because her family ate lasagna rather than turkey for Thanksgiving dinner, the girl envious of her "Canadian" classmate whose family had formal sit-down dinners and discussed current events, the boy homesick for the rural life he had been forced to leave behind – the emotional costs of assimilation were a recurrent theme in my interviews. These psycho-social challenges were also front and centre in one of the most popular children's books written about the era – *The Sandwich*.[73] The book tells the story of a grade 2 boy, Vincenzo Ferrante, who struggles to be accepted at school. The back cover blurb explains his dilemma: "Vincenzo is different from his friends. They bring peanut butter and jelly sandwiches. He has a mortadella and provolone cheese sandwich. Everyone laughs at him and says, 'Vincenzo eats stinky meat.' Can Vincenzo solve his problem and still eat the lunch he wants?" *The Sandwich* attracted considerable attention from the media, in part because its plot line captured the experience of many an immigrant student. When Ian Wallace, the book's co-author, promoted the book in schools across Canada, he was struck by the number of students who identified with Vincenzo and who related their own, often painful, stories of difference and exclusion. And where was *The Sandwich* set? Clinton Street School.[74]

Assimilation – building a civic credit rating to qualify as a "real" Canadian – was certainly an important part of the environment at a school like Clinton in the 1950s and early 1960s, but it wasn't *always* as coercive as the accounts and the examples above suggest. In many cases, it didn't have to be: some students were in fact more than eager to "fit in." For many of the families who came to Toronto after spending time in displaced persons camps, for instance, Canada represented a remarkable opportunity to begin afresh; what they left behind – both personally and politically – did not exactly evoke warm, fuzzy feelings. As one graduate told me, his family used to joke that DP stood for "Delayed Pioneer," an allusion that nicely captures his parents' sense that they were turning over a new leaf. Indeed, assimilation was deeply attractive to many of the Italians who arrived in the west end. One woman recalled how envious she was of her teacher's dainty watercress sandwich, which she thought was far more appealing than the eggplant on crusty bread that her own mother had packed for her. Another told me that she thinks of her childhood self as one of the characters in *The Sandwich* who aspired to the peanut-butter-and-jelly-sandwich lunch. She and her best Anglo-Canadian friend used to spend Sunday evenings together. One week she would go to her friend's house for roast beef dinner, the next week her friend would come to her place for homemade pizza – each preferring the other's cuisine. All of these social and gastronomical rituals revolved around a trademark assimilation experience – watching the *Disney Hour* together on television.

Nor was the assimilation exercise always as crude or as complete as Loren Lind and others imply. Indeed, what is striking is the extent to which New Canadians often resisted and limited "Canadian" ways of thinking by creating clear boundaries to protect their culturally distinctive private spheres. In chapter 3, I noted that one of the defects of the Drew Regulations was that Premier Drew's aggressive commitment to religious (read: Protestant) instruction in schools violated an implicit social contract. Most Jewish Canadians were quite willing to become "Canadian" in public so long as they could remain Jewish in private. To recall one graduate's formulation, they were like coffee cream – half and half. This was a basic liberal promise, and the Drew Regulations violated it.

European Clinton was not so different. By choosing a public school for their children, most of the immigrant families who filled Clinton in the 1950s and early 1960s had opened themselves to what Principal Pollard called "our values and our ways." But this was not a blank cheque, and some parents erected high barriers to protect what was important to them from the homogenizing thrust of assimilation. One woman told me that she was not allowed to participate in extra-curricular activities because her mother insisted she return home immediately after school. The rule was usually framed in terms of the mother's need for help with housework, but the daughter fully understood that her mother also wanted to limit contact with "English" kids at school. Another mother went a step further by banning all non-essential English books from the house. From her perspective, books (especially novels) were potentially threatening or subversive, and since she did not have a sufficient command of English to be able to distinguish harmful from healthy she banned them all. As Dolores astutely noted, her mother was like those parents who sharply limit their children's use of computers because they fear the unknown dangers lurking on the Internet. To defend something valuable from a perceived threat is not irrational, but it can often breed isolation.

Book banning was an extreme reaction, but its motivation – to preserve a sphere that was insulated from Anglo-Canadian "values and ways" – was widely shared at European Clinton. Most families seem to have accepted (and some even welcomed) the school's assimilationist mission, but only within clearly defined limits that left space for linguistic, cultural, and religious diversity. For such a system to work, however, it was important to have some sort of broker who could patrol the boundary between school and home to maintain the integrity of each sphere. Better yet was to find a person or an institution that could promote a conversation between the school and its parents. At European Clinton, that task fell largely to two groups: teachers and the Home and School Association.

Most of the graduates I spoke with are parents of, or closely related to, children who have been through public elementary schools, and several have become teachers themselves. Almost all of them noted how much more directly involved they (and other parents) are in their children's education than their parents were in theirs. There are several explanations for this generational difference. Many European Clinton parents couldn't really help with homework because they didn't read and understand English well enough to be helpful. Long, exhausting shifts at work – often for both parents – cut into the amount of discretionary time parents had to spend with their children in the evening. Entrenched gender norms in the 1950s meant that most of the responsibility for monitoring school progress fell exclusively to mothers – except, perhaps, for administering the punishments that followed from misbehaving at school.[75] Besides, homework was for students to tackle on their own. In an era before helicopter parents had been invented, homework was not meant to be a team sport.

In this context, the ability of teachers to reach out and translate (sometimes literally) the school's expectations and norms was crucial. For both students and parents, teachers spoke with authority about what it meant to be Canadian. The complexity and importance of this assignment was driven home when I spoke with Imogene Walker. Raised in Edmonton, Ms Walker arrived in Toronto in 1956 having spent the previous year backpacking around Europe with a group of friends. She was "wet behind the ears,"[76] she admitted, but knew that she wanted to teach in an inner-city school, and ended up teaching grade 5 at Clinton.

Ms Walker took up her position just at the moment that Jewish families were leaving the neighbourhood and Italian families were taking their place. As she noted, one of her classes had eight Jewish kids and one Scots Presbyterian; the rest, in a class of forty, were

Italian. Ms Walker was not above acting as one of those "gatekeep-ers"[77] who took it upon themselves to tutor students in "Canadian" ways. On one occasion, she noticed that "the classroom was a bit smelly and I said, you know what, I'm giving you homework this week. I want everybody to make sure that they have a bath and get their ears really clean this time … that's your homework for this weekend. I said, I know it's hard but see if you can't squeeze it in sometime."[78] But she also reached out to the parents in a way that defies the usual characterization of assimilation. One particularly evocative example returns to the theme of religious education. By the late 1950s, Clinton had knuckled under to provincial regulations and had begun to teach religion as part of the regular curriculum. For Ms Walker, this presented a dilemma. Loyal member of the United Church as she was, she thought that religious education was important. But she had no desire to turn her classroom into a Sunday school, and she was keenly aware that the version of the Bible she was required to teach would be either foreign or offensive to many of her students. Her solution was to approach the "class mothers" and explain her approach. "I said you know, there's a problem that the Bible we use is a Gideon Bible, and I know that's not the Catholic Bible and I know that this is not the Torah. But what I'll do is teach it as a story and then when they get to high school and they have Ruth beside the alien corn, at least they'll know who Ruth was"[79] – a particularly evocative example in light of the students' experience as immigrants.[80] From Ms Walker's perspective, the important thing was that she had done what the school required in a way that was "respectful" of the traditions of her students. And from the parents came the response, "We trust you."[81]

The other institution charged with the task of cultural transla-tion was the Home and School Association. Robert Putnam has famously argued that civic engagement through voluntary associa-tions enriches and improves democratic life, and he has argued that the1950s (at least in the United States) was the golden age of civic engagement in which citizens "bonded" and "bridged" with one another through every which kind of civic organization, Home and School Associations prominently among them.[82] The Clinton Home and School Association is an example of the importance of Putnam's civic engagement. It met monthly through the school year. Each class had a volunteer "school mother" (or group of mothers) to work with and build interest among parents. Parents could join the association for thirty-five cents per year, and as an incentive to prod parents into attending the monthly meeting, a prize was awarded to the class that generated the highest turnout. The meetings themselves were typically organized around a guest presentation, with topics ranging from self-help ("If your child isn't doing well at school" and "Where does happiness come from?"), to new technologies ("Television comes to Home and School"). There was an annual "Kindergarten Tea" for new parents, a "Father's Night" that aimed to increase the participation of men, and at least one school concert per year.[83] Impressively organized and supported by a robust volunteer infrastructure, the Home and School meetings drew extremely well. Thanks to the detailed notes left behind by one of the presidents, we know that in 1957–8 Home and School meetings attracted an average of 250 parents and teachers each month – about ten times the number that attend such meetings nowadays.[84]

But the importance of the Home and School Association goes beyond its capacity to mobilize parent interest. Perhaps more than any other Clinton institution, the Home and School Association was on the front lines, managing the interface between school and home, teachers and parents, assimilation and diversity. Its approach reveals the tension and ambiguity that informed and defined the first decade and a half of European Clinton. In a letter sent to Clinton parents to advertise the Home and School Christmas party in December 1957, the president, Mrs Cecchini, stated her hope that "our Christmas party will bring together parents from across the world and help in welding them together as good Canadian citizens."[85] That is strong stuff – to *weld* these multinational parents into "good Canadian citizens." But having brandished the civic welder's torch, Mrs Cecchini went on to highlight that the party's dessert table "will be representative of every nationality in the school and will be the best known and most palatable baked goods of each country."[86] Nor was this an isolated gesture. In announcing the schedule of the year's meetings, Mrs Cecchini made a point of saying that the executive had been scrupulous in ensuring that none of the meeting dates conflicted with religious holidays. When the topic turned to recruiting members, she commented that it would be easy to prepare a letter to parents in Italian if this would make them more comfortable, and at one of the first monthly meetings she invited parents to get involved in Home and School, "whether you speak English fluently or not."[87] All of these actions betray sensitivity to diversity in a way that hardly fits the tidy contours of "assimilation."

Mrs Cecchini personified the deep ambiguity that informed European Clinton's approach to, and understanding of, citizenship. She embraced both assimilation ("welding good Canadian citizens") and diversity (showing sensitivity to the cultural and religious pluralism of her community). Fine. But what was the relationship between them? Was linguistic and cultural diversity something to be preserved and celebrated? Or was it something of a necessary and temporary evil, a way-station on the road to full assimilation? Did Clinton practice represent a type of partial assimilation that would become more complete over time or was it a prototype for what later became known as multiculturalism? By the time the new Clinton opened in 1966, the school had spent well over a decade feeling its way – with little guidance from others – through these questions. In the next decade, as we shall soon see, greater guidance and a clearer set of answers emerged to these questions.

5

European Clinton, 1965–1975:
From Mungie Cakes to Multiculturalism

In the life of a school, nothing shouts "change" quite like moving into a brand-new building. At least so it was for the "new" Clinton, which welcomed its first class of students in September 1966. Writing about the newly constructed school, a reporter from the *Toronto Star* gushed over Clinton's state-of-the-art facilities: "The 1,300 children there have the most modern teaching aids while at classes and all the fun of the fair at recess. And a hedged-courtyard full of all the toy shop goodies youngsters dream about is available for the four kindergarten classes – monkey-bars and tricycles, scooters and cuddly toys. The auditorium-cum-gymnasium has a full-size stage, fancy lighting and dressing rooms. Children in kindergarten to Grade 6 can experiment with plays and concerts that sometimes attract audiences of more than a thousand." The library in a modern school such as Clinton "is now called a 'resource centre' because it's loaded with electronic information gadgets as well as books."[1]

In truth, the journalist over-reported the number of students enrolled in Clinton that first year, and his account of the pedagogical bells and whistles seems charmingly dated in retrospect. But he got one crucial thing right: the new school had been built in and for a moment of educational change. And, indeed, there were changes aplenty in the decade that followed: in the composition of the school's community; in basic challenges to how and what was taught; and in new ways of thinking about citizenship and diversity that were filtering down to schools like Clinton from "above."

Among these notions none was as important – or ultimately as dominant – as the emerging idea of multiculturalism. It is only slightly too simple to say that, just as the old idea of assimilation had been the default position that governed thinking during the first decade of European Clinton, new theories of integration and multiculturalism ruled the second. What multiculturalism meant, the extent to which it took hold, and whether it made a difference at Clinton is the subject of this chapter.

As we saw in chapter 4, massive immigration into downtown Toronto in the 1950s reshaped the Clinton community in two related ways. On the one hand, the population tsunami dramatically increased the area's school-age population. The boom put enormous pressure on the physical infrastructure and on the ingenuity of school officials, who had to find classroom space for many more students than the schools in the area were meant to accommodate. On the other hand, the surge of new immigrants into the area meant that there were far more children who either did not speak English when they arrived at Clinton (typically, first-generation immigrants) or didn't speak English at home (typically, second-generation immigrants). Taken together, first- and second-generation immigrant kids accounted for the vast majority of Clinton students – over 80 per cent in the first half of the 1960s – a basic demographic fact that made the school distinctive and fuelled its commitment to deliver programs that would "Canadianize" its students.

Then the neighbourhood began to change again. As Jordan Stanger-Ross has demonstrated, Little Italy remained (and to this day remains) a gathering place where Toronto's Italian community celebrates important events both sacred (the annual Good Friday procession from St Francis of Assisi Church)[2] and profane (the World Cup). But already by the mid-1960s the neighbourhood that fed Clinton Street School was losing its character as an "Italian residential enclave."[3] What Stanger-Ross shows in detail is that many Italian families left downtown for the near suburbs – pushed by difficult living conditions in which two or three large families often shared a single house and pulled by affordable property beyond the core. Just as the Jewish population in the west end had moved "up the hill" in the late 1940s and 1950s to suburban neighbourhoods, so the

Italian population created its own path to the suburbs two decades later. This dispersion was gradual but relentless. Using census figures as benchmarks, Stanger-Ross reports that at its high-water mark in 1961, 35 per cent of Little Italy's residents reported Italian origins; by 1991 only 13 per cent did.[4] Because the parents of young, growing families were especially eager to have a place of their own, the effect on Clinton was both more pronounced and more sudden. When the new school opened in 1966, more than half of all incoming students had a parent born in Italy; by 1975, just a decade later, only 15 per cent of incoming students came from a home in which one of the parents was born in Italy.

Yet for all this population shifting, European Clinton remained European. For one thing, Italian students had a presence at the school often greater than their numbers alone might suggest. In conducting interviews, I typically asked former students from the late 1960s and early 1970s to estimate what proportion of their class and school was Italian. Almost invariably the answers overestimated, often dramatically, the actual number of Italian students who attended the "new" Clinton. Even at its post-1966 height, the school was never 70 to 80 per cent Italian as some of them thought, but it is entirely plausible that it felt that way on the playground. Certainly the "mungie cakes"* I interviewed – the mildly pejorative label used by southern Europeans in Toronto to describe Anglo-Canadians – thought so. And the Toronto Board of Education (TBE) noticed the larger-than-life presence of Italians in schools like Clinton as well. "It has reached the point," one TBE report noted, "where there are Greeks learning Italian so that they can get along in Toronto."[5]

More importantly, European Clinton remained European because as, the Italian population dispersed, the next wave of European immigrants began to arrive, especially from Portugal. The same

---

* Literally, "cake eater." The origin of the term, commonly used in Toronto, is obscure. Joe Pantalone, former city councillor and deputy mayor, furnished one plausible genealogy. The Italian immigrants who came to Toronto in the 1950s were mystified, he says, by the Anglo taste for sandwiches made with slices of Wonder bread or its equivalent – thin, white, slightly sweet, and largely flavourless. For people used to thick, crusty, flavourful loaves, this was not bread, it was more like a white cake. Hence, Anglos became known as "cake eaters," those who *mangia* cake.

basic market dynamics that explain Italian immigration to Canada in the 1950s drove Portuguese immigration in the late 1960s and 1970s. There was still strong demand for labour, most of it unskilled and semi-skilled, to build the country's infrastructure, and the need for construction workers and allied trades was especially acute in Toronto, which became overwhelmingly the centre of Canada's Portuguese community. On the other side of the market equation, Portugal had a ready supply of potential immigrants. A combination of grinding poverty and disasters both natural (periodic volcanoes) and human (the Salazar presidency) made emigration attractive for many Portuguese, especially from the Azorean islands. Though the scale of Portuguese immigration was hardly comparable to the wave of Italian immigration in the 1950s, it was still significant. In the 1960s, some 60,000 Portuguese immigrants settled in Canada. In the 1970s, another 80,000 arrived, many of whom settled in downtown Toronto.[6]

Kensington Market and Alexandra Park became "ports of entry" for many Portuguese immigrants because housing there was affordable, proximity to transportation made employment accessible, and, once a critical mass was reached, these neighbourhoods quickly became hubs for Portuguese associational life.[7] As the community grew, it drifted westwards beyond Bathurst Street and into Clinton's ethnically mixed catchment. The growing presence of Portuguese students at Clinton tracks this migration remarkably closely. In the late 1950s and early 1960s, Clinton had only a handful of Portuguese students. By the time the new school opened in 1966, slightly more than 15 per cent of the incoming student body was Portuguese. By the mid-1970s, fully a quarter of incoming Clinton students were of Portuguese descent. In fact, by this point there were as many students of Portuguese as there were of Italian background at the school. As Carlos Teixeira and Robert Murdie have noted, most of the Portuguese immigrants who settled in downtown Toronto "came with little money, no English, and limited education."[8] The lack of English is especially important for understanding the second decade of European Clinton, as it explains why the school's pedagogical priorities remained largely as they had been since ESL classes were first introduced in the early 1950s. However differently configured, Clinton continued to serve a disproportionate number of students for whom English was not their first language and for whom life in Canada was still fresh and different. Indeed, the over-all proportion of first-generation students at Clinton – that is, those born outside of Canada – actually increased over the course of the new school's first decade. By 1975, close to 60 per cent of Clinton students were first generation, and the vast majority of them (like the Portuguese students) arrived with little or no English. The upshot is that the school remained committed to mounting a range of programs designed to integrate New Canadians into the mainstream. Indeed, it gave those programs a sort of second wind. As we saw in chapter 4, Clinton in the 1950s offered ESL classes largely thanks to the enterprising spirit of one teacher, Edward Parsons. Though Parsons himself bowed out of ESL teaching in the early 1960s, ESL programs remained a cornerstone of Clinton's program. By 1966–7 there were two dedicated ESL teachers at Clinton; by the early 1970s there were four. At its peak in 1974–6, Clinton had five full-time ESL teachers.[9]

The growth of ESL teaching at Clinton reflected the particular demographic patterns of Toronto's west end. It also reflected a more serious commitment on the part of the TBE to serve the needs of immigrant students. Speaking at the official opening of the new Clinton Street School in the fall of 1966, Kenneth Carson, the local school trustee, painted a "before" and "after" picture of the school board's commitment to ESL. "The object of a special board program," he explained, "is to help New Canadian students to improve their skills in speaking and writing English and in becoming successfully integrated in our society. Ninety-one teachers in the public schools are now assigned full-time to this program, more than twice as many as last year."[10] Trustee Carson emphasized the meteoric rise of ESL capacity to demonstrate the TBE's robust commitment to integrating New Canadian students. But what is equally (and inadvertently) striking about his statement is just how thin the board's commitment had been until that point. According to board data, in 1965 there were only twenty-eight teachers in the whole TBE who specialized in delivering ESL programs to New Canadian students in the board's "regular" elementary schools, even though schools like Clinton brimmed with such students.[11] It seems that as long as most of the "gateway" schools were concentrated in the downtown core, the board could easily ignore them. Once the immigrant population began to grow and disperse beyond the inner city, the school board snapped to attention.[12]

Still, once the TBE became engaged, the variety of programs it developed and its commitment of resources to ESL were impressive. Most schools adopted the Clinton practice of withdrawing students from their regular classes for a certain number of hours per week so that they could study English intensively, though few schools provided as many hours of ESL instruction per child as Clinton did.[13] Some schools offered a flexible "transitional" program that began with full-day ESL, tapered to part-time "withdrawal" classes, then concluded with periodic one-on-one tutorials as the student's command of English grew. For students over the age of twelve, the board created a "reception" school in the east end of Toronto, the Main Street School, which provided English immersion for a "segregated" population of newly arrived immigrant students. And exploiting the potential of otherwise empty schools, the board created a popular summer school in English as a second language. The program began as a pilot project at two schools in the summer of 1963. By 1970, the summer school program embraced twenty-one schools (including Clinton) and served almost 3,000 students.[14] Loren Lind estimates that, taken together, these various New Canadian programs reached a total of 6,000 children (and another 3,000 adults in evening classes) and absorbed about 5 per cent of the TBE's operating budget.[15]

As the TBE developed greater interest in immigrant education, it also seized control of the larger debate about what integration should entail. In this respect, the opening of the new Clinton coincided with a significant change in the dynamics of the integration debate in Toronto schools. In the 1950s and early 1960s, European Clinton acted largely on its own, working out an approach to educating immigrant students as it went along – equally blessed and cursed by the general indifference of the board and province under whose authority it acted. Once the Toronto Board of Education and the province of Ontario woke up to the importance of immigrant education, however, the debate shifted ground. Where "European Clinton I" had relative autonomy to make trail, "Clinton II" largely reacted to policy developments made at the board and provincial level. This is why, to understand Clinton in the late 1960s and early 1970s, we need first to appreciate the larger debate about diversity and citizenship in Toronto, Ontario, and indeed Canada.

In 1928, one of Toronto's school inspectors, George W. McGill, reported on the TBE's efforts "to make real Canadians out of those who are more or less unacquainted with our customs and ideals."[16] Language instruction was an important part of this process, but it wasn't only language with which teachers were concerned. "The teachers … are teaching English," McGill continued, "but they are also not losing sight of the broader aim, the Canadianizing of our foreign population."[17] Now fast forward some forty years. In 1970, the TBE produced a fact sheet describing its various ESL programs. The document defined students eligible for these programs as follows:

> A New Canadian child is any child who is unable to function success-
> fully in a regular school programme because his ethnic background
> reflects a culture other than our own. The school's responsibility is to
> help the immigrant child to function with ease and security in his new
> environment. The Toronto Board of Education understands and accepts
> this responsibility and uses its understanding as a basis for providing the
> immigrant student with every possible opportunity to involve himself
> with and commit himself to our culture.[18]

One might reasonably conclude from these book-ended statements, as some have, that the goals of ESL education in Toronto scarcely changed over the years – that they were rooted in "a rather crude version of cultural assimilation,"[19] which viewed cultural and linguistic differences as a "handicap" that needed to be overcome rather than an asset to be preserved and developed.[20] In fact, however, this apparent historical continuity is somewhat misleading, for by the mid-1960s the consensus surrounding the goals of ESL had begun to collapse. Even (or perhaps especially) within the TBE an alternative understanding of the purposes of ESL and the meaning of citizenship began to emerge.

The "turning point"[21] in this regard was the 1965 publication of a report produced by the TBE's research department entitled "Immigrants and Their Education."[22] The school board had asked the director of education to produce an audit of ESL services provided by the board, including the number of students taking ESL courses, where they came from, who taught ESL and how, what library resources were available, and so on. The research department ran with the assignment. It studied and synthesized old data, commissioned new surveys (both quantitative and qualitative), and produced a working paper it hoped would serve as a foundation for ESL in Toronto schools. The goals were ambitious and the language used to express them new and unfamiliar. The authors hoped their report would be the first step in the "development of an ongoing philosophy appropriate to providing an education for a *multi-culture* student population."[23]

The authors of "Immigrants and Their Education" wasted no time in announcing their disagreement with traditional approaches to immigrant education. The report began with a shot across the bow:

> There has been more and more discussion of "the New Canadian problem." Students who come from other cultures are faced with a different set of values and mores and often a new language. To refer to them as a problem is to do them an injustice. To recognize the numerous diverse problems that they face especially in the schools is essential. To assist these students to solve their problems, gain an education, and understand (though not necessarily believe) Canadian values and mores, all in the English language, is a complex task.[24]

The researchers wanted to flip the logic of assimilation on its head. The basic and longstanding goal of ESL education in Toronto schools was to assimilate immigrant children in a way that placed the onus squarely on the immigrant students and their families themselves. "Our school system and most of the schools," the report noted, "have tended to maintain themselves in a 'splendid isolation' waiting for the children from other lands to adjust to our city, our ways and our classrooms."[25] This approach was flawed. Rather than fixate on what immigrant students had to do to adjust to Canadian life, the report wanted to shift the discussion to what the *school system* should do to "improve its response"[26] to New Canadian students.

The improvement the researchers had in mind entailed a total rethink of the TBE's New Canadian programs. Most ESL programs, they noted, measured student success through some combination of proficiency in English and commitment to Canadian values. Implicitly or explicitly, conventional ESL programs expected "all new arrivals to 'learn our way'"[27] – even (or perhaps especially) if this meant checking distinctive ethnic and cultural identities at the Anglo-Canadian door. There was a clearly defined and fixed standard – the Canadian way – that immigrants were meant to aim for, and their status as citizens depended on how closely they came to reaching that goal. Those who achieved it became full citizens; those who fell short, like non-Christians, were considered citizens-minus. But what if the goal were not to *assimilate* immigrants but rather to *integrate* them into the polity? Imagine if citizenship were measured less by whether immigrants reached the Canadian standard and more by whether Canadians and immigrants could move towards each other in a way that created a healthy and dynamic mixture of cultures. Surely it would be far better, the report authors argued, to recognize that "the cultures of the new arrivals are valuable"[28] and to revamp New Canadian programs in a way that would "help the students understand, appreciate and learn about *each other and themselves.*"[29] The difference, in slightly caricatured form, came down to this: *Assimilation* is essentially uni-directional. It is a one-way educational path that gives immigrants the tools they need to become Canadian and an opportunity to shed incompatible cultural baggage along the way. *Integration*, on the other hand, is a "two-way street"[30] of mutual accommodation, of give and take, in which both established Canadians and immigrants have the ability – and the responsibility – to adjust their civic lenses.

This distinction between assimilation and integration is now a standard part of the social psychologist's lexicon.[31] In 1965, however, it was provocative, fresh, challenging, and in need of elaboration. For the TBE researchers, integration has at least two important advantages. The first, in their view, is that integration is superior to assimilation because it is less likely to produce the sort of ghettoization that undermines social harmony. Faced with a choice between adapting to Canadian values and maintaining what is familiar and dear, "immigrants have in many cases retreated to the solace and support of ethnic communities and organizations."[32] Who could blame them? The demand to assimilate "generates and maintains strong ethnic groups who isolate themselves in an attempt to preserve valuable elements of their heritage." The authors conceded that Toronto had largely escaped this sort of residential segregation, but this was largely a matter of luck. "Only the tremendous variety of immigrants, their mobility, and the continuing influx have prevented sharply defined ghettos from developing." If the city and its school system wanted to forestall this sort of ghettoization from occurring in the future, then immigrant students needed to feel that they could wear their cultural heritage on their sleeve wherever they lived. ESL programs that "draw on the resources and experiences of all students from all countries" – programs that integrate rather than assimilate – are therefore more likely to produce social harmony.

There is a real irony here. One of the most popular current criticisms of multicultural programs in Canada and elsewhere is that they encourage cultural and ethnic enclaves.[33] Multiculturalism, according to this critique, undermines social harmony because it allows, indeed encourages, immigrant communities to sustain their ethnic and cultural identities – even if some of these cultural practices conflict with prevailing norms in their new home. It is not that the TBE researchers weren't worried about the creation of culturally defined residential enclaves; they were. The difference – and here's the irony – is that these early multiculturalists thought the best way to prevent cultural conflict was to celebrate rather than constrain cultural diversity. Put in slightly different words, the TBE researchers believed school-centred cultural accommodation would pre-empt ghettoization, not cause it; for them, integration was a way to reduce cultural conflict rather than create it.

The second advantage of educational integration is that it encourages a degree of moral flexibility and openness at moments of significant change. Historical context is crucial here. Assimilation may have made sense when "Canadian values" were the tried-and-true gold standard and when many immigrants were fleeing religious and/or political oppression. But 1965 was not 1945, much less 1915. As the researchers were fond of pointing out, many of the families who immigrated to Canada in the 1960s did so in order to escape "the economic pressures of the home land."[34] They sought economic opportunity, not a cultural makeover. It is simply a "fallacy," they said, to believe that these students would have an epiphany "that things in Canada are better or more pleasant than in their native lands. Students, newly arrived in our schools, sometimes have different ideas as to what is better or more pleasant."[35] And why not? "It must not be forgotten that these new arrivals in our city have had a great deal that our Toronto-born pupils will never have." There was, indeed, much for rather parochial Toronto students to "envy." Why not integrate this diversity into the school program rather than place it in quarantine?

Besides, by the mid-1960s it was no longer clear what these immigrant students were supposed to assimilate *to*. Public intellectuals like George Grant lamented the disappearance of the old Canada beneath the juggernaut of American culture.[36] The Quiet Revolution in Quebec threatened to reconfigure, potentially massively, the political geography of the country as a whole. The preliminary report of the Royal Commission on Bilingualism and Biculturalism, published in 1965, began indeed from the premise that Canada was "passing through the greatest crisis in its history," which could lead either "to its break-up, or to a new set of conditions for its future existence."[37] And Toronto itself was in full metamorphosis, led by a Jewish mayor (Nathan Phillips), celebrating the construction of a new, high modernist City Hall,[38] but not quite willing to renounce its identity as Toronto the Good entirely.[39] Moments of acute vulnerability can sometimes become moments of openness to change. For the TBE researchers, this was one of those moments.

I have lingered on "Immigrants and Their Education" because it is such a striking – and early – example of the change in intellectual tone that gave rise to the idea of multicultural education in Toronto, indeed to the idea of multiculturalism more generally. I don't want to overstate the distinction between what went before (assimilation) and what came after (integration). Social change isn't like turning on a lamp, where light replaces darkness with the flick of a switch. In this regard it is important to understand that while the TBE researchers disagreed strongly with the way New Canadian programs were conceived and delivered, they did not mean to throw out the (ESL) baby with the (assimilationist) bath water. They urged the school board to think differently about ESL programs and to mount programs that would permit immigrant students to integrate themselves more easily and more comfortably into Canadian society. To that important extent, the researchers certainly wanted to relax the definition of what it meant to be "Canadian." But they never doubted that integration entailed some sort of transition from "them" to "us," and they had no qualms about requiring immigrant kids to make that journey. Had their version of integration not entailed a commitment to some form of "Canadianization," they would have dismissed the legitimacy and importance of ESL itself. They didn't.

In sum, the authors of "Immigrants and Their Education" were progressive, but hardly radical, reformers. It turns out they had lots of company. This brand of progressive reform caught on with parents deeply critical of school programs that disadvantaged poor and immigrant children, parents who wanted entry into mainstream Canadian life, not out of it. The reform agenda found an institutional home at the TBE where, by1969, a group of reform-minded trustees held a majority of seats.[40] And educational administrators, many of them influenced by activists like Paul Goodman, Jonathan Kozol, and A.S. Neill, worked from within the TBE to gather empirical evidence needed to mount and evaluate the reform agenda.

At the national level, the conversation about civic membership in those years was dominated by the Royal Commission on Bilingualism and Biculturalism (B and B Commission). One might be excused for thinking that a commission framed in terms of "biculturalism," and in which the questions that concerned the TBE researchers were consigned to a report on "other ethnic groups," might not be the most fertile ground for new approaches to socio-cultural diversity. In fact, however, the B and B Commission worked its way through precisely the same distinction between assimilation and integration that the TBE researchers had – and came to the same conclusion.

And since the commission took as part of its remit an analysis of the state of constitutionally mandated minority language education, the final report had lots to say about the connections between language, culture, and ESL as well.[41]

Still, no voice advocating educational reform spoke with as much authority, or to as large an audience, as the Hall-Dennis Commission, a blue-ribbon committee created by Ontario's minister of education in 1965. Like the Hope Commission (1950) before it, Hall-Dennis had a broad mandate to "set forth the aims of education"[42] for the entire public school system in Ontario. Unlike the Hope Commission, which was characterized by disabling internal dissent and thin external support, the Hall-Dennis committee spoke with one voice and built a case for wholesale educational change in a way that captured the public imagination. The commission's report, a glossy, coffee-table–style book entitled *Living and Learning*,[43] was a huge success when it was published in 1968. It sold 60,000 copies within months of its release and, as R.D. Gidney notes, "it attracted attention across the country and indeed the continent."[44] I can attest both to its appeal and its reach. I served as president of a federation of high school student councils in Winnipeg a couple of years after the publication of *Living and Learning*. At one point I was invited to address the local Rotary Club to explain, from a student's perspective, what the fuss associated with "the student movement" was all about. After trying unsuccessfully to find my own words to describe the need for wholesale reform in the schools, I let Hall-Dennis do the talking. In the end, my speech morphed into a warmed-over version of *Living and Learning* – with attribution but without the snazzy graphics.

What I found enormously appealing about the Hall-Dennis approach was the core idea that students should have the freedom – or as we liked to say, the right – to have a large say in what they learned and how they learned it.[45] The Hall-Dennis commissioners employed a biological metaphor to make the point. "Learning by its very nature is a personal matter," they argued:

> There is virtually a metabolism of learning which is as unique to the individual as the metabolism of digestion. Parents and teachers may provide

> stimulating experiences with learning in mind, but the actual learning
> experience is intimate and subjective, for each human being reaches out
> to the world in his own idiosyncratic way.[46]

This commitment to putting the individual student first was hardly new; what was different was the commission's purposeful commitment to root out practices that were inconsistent with the student-centred principle. If schools took "each child's learning experience as the basic nucleus of teaching," then it followed that "the child rather than the rules should be given primary consideration."[47] The problem with Ontario's schools in this light was that they were far too rule-bound, standardized, and austere – pickle factories, Lloyd Dennis called them.[48] The commission reported that during its extensive public consultations it "was told of inflexible programs, outdated curricula, unrealistic regulations, regimented organization and mistaken aims of education."[49] The obvious solution, as Hall-Dennis famously went on to propose, was simply to abolish many basic practices – like "lock-step systems of organizing pupils, such as grades, streams, programs, etc."[50] Everything at school, seemingly, was up for grabs, to be measured against the master principle that schools have a basic responsibility "to provide a child-centred learning continuum that invites learning by individual discovery and inquiry."[51]

R.D. Gidney has suggested that "over the decades that followed its publication, and especially in recent years, as memory of the sixties grows dimmer, the Hall-Dennis Report has attained almost mythic status, praised or blamed for changing the face of public education in Ontario."[52] The myth is more powerful than it is accurate. For one thing, there was a yawning gap between rhetoric and practice, between recommendations and adoption. There were lots of experimental programs launched in the wake of Hall-Dennis, but at a school like Clinton, as at so many others, the actual day-to-day classroom experience didn't change that much for most students. In the course of interviewing students who attended the school in the late 1960s and early 1970s, I was struck by just how conventional their classroom experience was. Much of it, in fact, flew directly in the face of Hall-Dennis. The kindergarten-to-grade-6 system of lock-step progress through grades, far from being abolished, remained (and remains) intact. Students who couldn't master the material in one grade were held back from the next, despite Hall-Dennis's dictum that "a child who is learning cannot fail."[53] For the most part students were still arranged by desks in rows, and Clinton was not one of the schools in which walls were removed to allow for open-concept instruction. Teachers continued to give lessons and assign homework. And those who questioned authority, even mildly, were still condemned to writing lines. True, there were changes at the margins. Several students remembered one teacher, variously described as "hippie-like" or "bohemian," who emphasized individual creativity by having her grade 3 students write poetry, and the number of field trips probably increased. But, by and large, the style of teaching and learning was not so different from the "flexible formalism" that had characterized Clinton in the late 1950s.

It is also easy to overstate or mythologize what some perceived as the "permissive and libertarian thrust of *Living and Learning*."[54] Read in isolation, the chapter in Hall-Dennis devoted to "the learning experience" could leave the impression that the commission basically thought of students as educational free agents who should be left to their own devices to choose the path best suited to "individual discovery and inquiry."[55] (That is certainly what I, campaigning for student rights in Winnipeg, thought – and hoped – the report meant.) But this reading misses Hall-Dennis's larger point. The commissioners understood very well that individual students were not, and could not be, educational free agents who could pick and choose how and what they wanted to learn in some sort of social and cultural vacuum. On the one hand, "the nature of society and its cultural values ... inevitably impinge upon the world of the child."[56] On the other, many individual students have complicated and unique "special needs" that have to be met in order for them to reach their potential. Hall-Dennis's goal was not naively libertarian, its aim not simply to deregulate schooling in a way that would expand individual choice in a market of individual discovery. Rather, the challenge, according to Hall-Dennis, was to find a way to situate individual students and nurture their learning in light of the many constraints that shape and affect individual students differently. Ontario's educational system was in dire need of reform because it had failed to put schooling in a context that was tailored to individual needs. It had neither kept pace with "big picture" cultural changes that affected every student nor demonstrated a firm enough commitment to "special learning programs" for those students with special needs. "One size fits all" may have worked in an earlier era. By 1968, according to Hall-Dennis, it was hopelessly outmoded.

This is where the themes of immigration and education re-enter the story, for the changing composition of Ontario's population was a perfect example of the sort of larger cultural change that schools needed to take into account. "Central to the Canadian fact," Hall-Dennis argued:

> are the roles of the English and French peoples in the founding of the nation; and their position in the bicultural social complex of Canada cannot be challenged. But a new issue arises, namely the role of the immigrant in Canadian society. This issue has significant implications.[57]

What were these significant implications? The commissioners were quick to connect the dots between this demographic trend and the country's cultural identity: "If the increase of the 'other Europeans' and the 'non-European' categories in the population is not accidental but a marked sociological trend, one wonders if now is the time to think not of Canadian biculturalism but of Canadian multiculturalism."[58] Never ones to play it close to the vest, the commissioners added this clear endorsement: "Ontario needs to be on its guard lest it miss this chance of developing a society that is truly multicultural."[59]

Hall-Dennis viewed the programmatic implications of this incipient multiculturalism through the lens of what it called "special learning experiences."[60] All children, the report maintained, "have the same basic needs. But the children of newly arrived immigrants may have exceptional needs, especially in language."[61] Hall-Dennis observed that those jurisdictions (like Toronto) that had mounted programs for New Canadians typically emphasized "linguistics and the acquisition of school language."[62] Echoing the TBE research-ers, Hall-Dennis pointed out that it was impossible to disentangle language from culture. And again like the TBE researchers, Hall-Dennis understood that, once cultural diversity was in play, schools had to take a stand on the meaning of citizenship:

> Furthermore, as far as education is concerned, the problem arises of whether the school, functioning according to the norm as a middle-class institution – predominantly British in heritage – should ignore the cul-tural values which the students' homes reflect or capitalize on them by adapting and incorporating them for their program.[63]

Given a choice between assimilation and integration, Hall-Dennis came down solidly in favour of integration. The commissioners wanted New Canadians "to feel like full-fledged Canadians as quickly as possible" and "active participants who know their rights and enjoy them."[64] But they insisted both that the Canadian idea of citizenship had room to accommodate ethno-cultural diversity and that this new diversity could enrich Canadian society:

> In a society which draws its students from various cultural and ethnic groups, a special and exciting challenge can be found in the interacting of the youngsters. Their interaction is educative. Furthermore, not only the student body but the whole school system should profit from such multiculturalism.[65]

Hall-Dennis occasionally fell back into the patois of paternalism when describing the needs of New Canadians. Still, the commis-sioners saw multicultural education as the leading edge of change, and they clearly wanted to signal its importance.

What had been new and unfamiliar conceptual territory for the TBE researchers in 1965 was, by the time Hall-Dennis reported in 1968, quite well mapped. Political and administrative support for multicultural education continued to grow thereafter, and, impor-tantly, a whole new cohort of committed and well-trained teachers appeared to deliver these integrative programs. When the TBE issued the final report on its large summer session for New Canadians in

1970, the authors noted that they had had no difficulty recruiting teaching staff to teach the 3,000 students because many had already taken "pervasive" in-service training offered by the TBE. "We already had at our disposal," the report observed, "a group of self-taught functionaries who had developed a sophisticated, mature and creative approach to the problem of cultural immersion and its relation to the development of language competence."[66] By the mid-1970s, in short, multicultural education had already established a root system, conceptually and institutionally, in Ontario's schools. In the words of one provincial curriculum guide, "multiculturalism is not a fad that will pass away. Even if immigration were to cease tomorrow, the nature of Canadian society will continue to change as children of culturally diverse parents continue to be born into this society."[67]

What did multicultural education mean on the ground? And how did it play out at a school like Clinton, which served as a gateway for so many immigrant students and their families? Unfortunately, the answers to these questions are not entirely straightforward. Begin with the central term "multicultural." Many people use the term, perfectly appropriately, to describe an ethnically diverse population. When Toronto is described as one of the most multicultural cities in the world, readers understand that this conveys a rough measure of the city's diversity. But to say that the Toronto Board of Education or the Hall-Dennis Commission or the government of Ontario came increasingly to support multicultural education is a bit different. Then the statement is not simply descriptive, it is prescriptive. It conveys an ethic, based on a moral judgment, that it is a good thing to develop practices that recognize, celebrate, and accommodate ethno-cultural diversity in public schools. Multiculturalism in this sense is no longer simply sociological or demographic; it becomes political.

This distinction between multiculturalism as description and prescription is important because the two senses of the term do not always align. It is perfectly possible, for instance, to imagine that a government might choose to pursue a policy of cultural uniformity to govern a demographically diverse, multicultural community.

Indeed, support for assimilation sometimes feeds off the fear that too much ethnic diversity may create instability unless it is counterbalanced by a singular cultural vision; this is how the Quebec Charter of Values was sometimes framed and defended. Whatever the merits of these views, the point is that it is important not to elide these two senses of the term "multicultural." We cannot really assess whether a school like Clinton developed an ethos of multiculturalism simply by showing that the school's student body became increasingly diverse over the years, though it did. Clinton's diversity provided the crucial background to school life over the period this book covers; it did not in itself dictate whether and how the school worked with that diversity.

If multiculturalism involves more than a description of diversity, it also entails something more than a commitment to cultural tolerance. Harold Troper, one of Canada's foremost scholars of ethnicity, argues that the introduction of federal multiculturalism policy in 1971 entailed a "radical reconstruction" of Canada's cultural vision. It dispatched the idea that there had to be an "overriding or primary national cultural tradition" and replaced it with the alternative view that "espoused respect for diversity and acceptance of pluralism as the true and only basis of an inclusive national identity." Thanks in part to this reconstructive cultural surgery, he says, "ethno-cultural groups are now assured that their cultural heritage has value, and they are free to retain as much of it as they can and desire."[68] Troper sums up the consensus that has formed around this approach like this: "For many Canadians in the early 1970s, multiculturalism simply translated as 'live and let live.'"[69]

The problem with Troper's historical summary is that it conflates two forms of multiculturalism that are actually quite different – what I call "old" and "new" multiculturalism. The adage "live and let live" encapsulates two important liberal ideas that sustained the "old" multiculturalism. The first is that individuals should be able to make their own decisions about the gods they worship, the people they associate with, the family traditions they honour, and other core decisions about the way they want to lead their lives. You can fancy it up in all sorts of ways, but the liberal promise comes down to creating a private space where personal choices flourish in all their heterogeneous variety. The second norm, which follows the first, is that governments have a corresponding duty to be "neutral" with respect to these core private decisions because when governments play favourites they stack the deck in ways that help some and hurt others. Choices aren't really freely made when they come either with benefits granted or burdens imposed by the state; that's why the liberal ideal is often described metaphorically in terms of a "level playing field." The Drew Regulations, discussed in chapter 3, are a textbook example of what happens when governments forget or disregard these liberal principles. And Rabbi Feinberg's powerful critique of the regulations provides a classic statement of the old multiculturalism. Recall his argument: religious freedom is central to liberal democracy. This means that governments mustn't endorse one religion over another because that sort of religious favouritism, exemplified by the Drew Regulations, "cannot fail to fan the embers of intolerance wherever a minority exists."[70] And in the post-Second World War mind, intolerance rhymed with totalitarianism, not liberalism.

Yet while multiculturalism as we now know it certainly depends on the sort of tolerance that Rabbi Feinberg emphasized, it can't just be about tolerating, or even celebrating, diversity. If it were we would "all be multiculturalists now"[71] because over the years – and thanks in part to the efforts of people like Rabbi Feinberg – "respect for cultural pluralism [has become] a basic norm of public discourse"[72] in most liberal democracies. No, the "new" multiculturalism is a bit different. It is more ambitious, more demanding, and more controversial, as its goal is not simply to celebrate diversity, but to take further steps to recognize, protect, and accommodate difference. The distinction between "old" and "new" is important because governments that are committed to multiculturalism in this more extended sense cannot afford to be completely neutral observers; they have to become more actively engaged, and sometimes entangled, in political and cultural controversies around accommodation. And this creates a set of complications that the "old" multiculturalism cannot, need not, and did not confront.

Compare these examples. The Drew Regulations withered on the vine in the late 1960s and 1970s because fewer and fewer public school boards in Ontario, especially in its larger cities, were willing to act in a way that so clearly and patently made schools the mouthpiece of Protestantism. Still, the regulations remained in force and were actively followed in some, especially rural, parts of the province. When they were ultimately challenged and struck down, in 1990, as a violation of the Charter of Rights, the Ontario Court of Appeal argued that public sponsorship of religion amounts to a form of indoctrination that cannot be squared with the idea of religious freedom.[73] In other words, the Drew Regulations were measured against the standard of the "old" multiculturalism – liberal neutrality that protects individual rights – and found wanting. In effect, the Court of Appeal declared as a matter of law what Clinton Street School had understood as a matter of fact from the very moment the Drew Regulations were promulgated.

Now consider the case of a school or school board that is asked to permit Sikh students to wear a small knife, a kirpan, strapped to their legs while they are on school property because this practice is required by their religious belief.[74] In a case like this, the authorities who preside over a multicultural school system have to decide whether they should step outside the principle of neutrality. They have to consider whether they should make an exception, for Sikh students, from a general or neutral rule banning weapons on school property – a general rule, that is, that remains in force for everyone else. This is the sort of accommodation request that the "new" multiculturalism, as an ethos and a policy, invites. This does not mean that the reason for the rule (in this case, schoolyard safety) is unimportant and can be set aside in the interests of religious freedom. It *does* mean that schools have to find ways both to achieve their policy goals and to respect religious belief. Whether you agree or disagree with the final disposition – the Supreme Court of Canada upheld the request by the Sikh students but imposed a set of conditions – the point is that the "new" multiculturalism involves much more than protecting the private space in which religious minorities, ethnic food, colourful parades, and "live and let live" thrive.

So how, then, are these "new" multicultural practices different? If they aren't guided by the principle of neutrality and the practice of "live and let live," what do they entail? And to what extent did they gain traction at a school like Clinton? Bernard Yack has help-fully described two of the functions of the new multiculturalism in terms of *border guarding* and *border crossing*. Border guarding is "the use of political authority to empower or protect distinct cultural communities."[75] When courts protect the rights of Sikh students to carry the kirpan; when school boards establish Afrocentric schools; when schools sponsor "heritage trips" to Asia for families who have adopted children from China; when schools offer heritage language programs for students whose linguistic and cultural roots are nei-ther English nor French – they are guarding borders in the sense that they are protecting or empowering cultural communities in a way that provides a counterbalance to the otherwise overwhelming gravitational force of a dominant culture.

It has to be said that, in the early years of what I have dubbed the new multiculturalism, this sort of border guarding was neither Clinton's priority nor its strong suit. I did hear some accounts of the ways in which the school went out of its way to tend the garden of cultural diversity; but, tellingly, these stories usually came from former teachers rather than from former students. One example that stands out is the school's support for after-school classes in Catho-lic education. The classes were the invention of Clara Tomasella, a longtime resident of the area, the parent of two Clinton students, and, from 1972 on, an educational assistant assigned to the kinder-garten classes. Mrs Tomasella had noticed that some of her young charges in kindergarten subsequently transferred to the Catholic school across the street. One of the incentives that led many parents to defect from Clinton was that the Catholic schools provided prepa-ration for first communion and confirmation within the school day. This spared parents and children alike the need to set aside their Saturday mornings to attend catechism class at the local church. Mrs Tomasella was both a devout Catholic and a strong supporter of public schools, so she hatched the idea of running after-school cat-echism classes at Clinton in the hopes of weakening the incentives to defect from the public system. First mounted in 1974, after-school catechism classes were organized by Mrs Tomasella at Clinton for nearly twenty years – with the school's blessing, if not always the bishop's.

Yet almost none of the students I interviewed spoke at any length about how the school encouraged them to take substantial pride in their cultural tradition. To be sure, there were folkloric presentations of Calabrian folk dancing at the Spring Thing (the school's annual talent extravaganza), but I heard many more accounts that replayed the theme of *The Sandwich* (see chapter 4), in which the school did little to help Vincenzo overcome the feeling that he didn't quite "fit in" because he ate a provolone and mortadella sandwich on crusty bread. One particularly reflective former student who attended the school in the late 1960s and early 1970s put it this way: "I think that Clinton [i.e, the teachers] did play a role ... in integrating (or assimilating) the students into the broader Canadian society in that they taught us values regarding education ... which may not have been instilled by parents at home. At the time this role was probably more assimilative than integrative, as the cultural diversity of the student body was really not reflected in the school curriculum (at least not to my recollection). So, throughout my years at Clinton (and beyond) I felt there was a 'gap' or discontinuity between home and school."[76]

Moreover, there was a darker side to border guarding in the schools. Guarding cultural borders can aim to protect and empower cultural minorities, but it can also be used to stigmatize and pigeonhole them. This is precisely what the controversy about "streaming" immigrant students into non-academic programs – which attracted considerable attention in Toronto in the 1970s – was all about. I heard about streaming on numerous occasions from former students, but one graduate in particular had an especially powerful way of describing how students were sorted into secondary schools. "It was pretty clear," she said. "The boys went to Central Tech, the girls went to Central Commerce, the smart ones went to Harbord (Collegiate) and the slow ones went to Bickford (Vocational)." It hardly needs adding that most of those who went to the technical, commercial, and vocational schools were the sons and daughters of immigrant parents, especially from Italy, Portugal, and the Caribbean. Most of the streaming occurred in the higher grades after students had left Clinton, but even at Clinton the ripple effect of streaming could be felt. One student recalled how an otherwise much-admired teacher gave her this career advice: "You're Portuguese," he observed. "You'll make a good secretary."

For the small number of black students, the challenge was less to overcome the low expectations of teachers than to combat name-calling and racial epithets in the schoolyard. As one put it, "I have only positive memories of my classrooms. It was in those public spaces like recess and going home for lunch … and after school. Those were the times I was confronted with racism … It was hard. There was … a lot of name-calling in the schoolyard." Nor was this sort of racism restricted to Caribbean-Canadian students. One former student, whose family like many others in the neighbourhood hailed from Calabria, remembers vividly being taunted by other students of Italian extraction because her somewhat swarthy complexion made her look "black."

If Clinton was slow to take up the multicultural task of *guarding* the borders of cultural diversity, it was considerably better attuned to some of the ways it could facilitate *crossing* those borders. As I argued in chapter 4, the Home and School Association was crucial in managing the interface between parents and teachers. Thanks to the well-attended monthly meetings, parents caught a glimpse of what their children's lives were like on the other side of the home-school border. But to cross the border – to have the school use its authority to bring cultural communities into contact with one another and to blur cultural boundaries – was more challenging. Clinton responded to the challenge in several ways. Staffing was one. Mrs Tomasella recalled how, in the fall of 1972, the school's principal, Edwin Kerr, approached her as she was delivering her children to school one day and asked if she would be interested in working as an assistant in one of the kindergarten rooms. She spoke English and Italian, came from the neighbourhood, knew everyone, and loved kids. She agreed and within a week began what turned out to be a thirty-year career at the school.

What Mrs Tomasella may not have known at the time is that her appointment was part of a deliberate TBE strategy to hire neighbourhood-based kindergarten assistants at schools like Clinton. The idea was to find staff who could serve as cultural translators – both to the school and to immigrant parents – in a way that would be mutually beneficial. Every spring she went door to door in the neighbourhood to recruit new kindergarten students and to explain to parents unfamiliar with the Canadian system what public school entailed and what they might expect. Once children were enrolled, Clara kept a watchful eye on students, teachers, and parents, alternately bringing them together and running interference between them as the situation required.

Staff like Clara Tomasella helped blur the boundaries between home and school. An increasingly diverse teaching staff helped expose students to different cultural registers. Here, too, the experience of border crossing was central to Clinton's new persona. An alphabetical listing of Clinton's teaching staff who presided over the last cohort of students in the old building (1964–5) begins like this: McArthur (principal), Cratchley (vice-principal), Allen, Campbell, Copeland, Countryman, Crate, Darrell, Dwyer, Flanagan, Garner, Golas, Hall, Howard, Jamieson … and ends with Wishart. To be fair, a few non-Anglo-Saxon names appeared along the way, but these were very much the exception to the (Anglo-Canadian) rule. Gradually but inexorably this changed, so that by the early 1970s the staff was far more heterogeneous. There were still plenty of names like Kerr, Eccles, and Knox, but beside them appear Chung, Goldstein, and Muto – and Angelo, Izumi, Mazza, and Nishi.

The effect of this staff diversity on students was often profound. Two examples stand out. One centres on Muriel Nishihama, the popular Japanese-Canadian teacher who arrived to teach grade 4 at Clinton when the doors opened in 1966 and was a mainstay of the teaching staff for many years thereafter. Students praised Ms Nishihama for her ability to instil a love of learning, especially reading, in her students. (A number, in fact, thought that she was essentially running a "gifted" program before such programs had been institutionalized.) But beyond this, what they remember is the way in which she expanded their cultural horizons. Among other things, she organized special lunches with and for her students around cultural themes, and at the end of the year she invited a few of the top students in the class to a special lunch. In one such case, she took her high achievers back to her home and introduced them to the rituals of a Japanese tea ceremony. As one former student recalled, this was the first time in her life she had ever used chopsticks.

The other notable pedagogical border-crosser was Edmund Gough. Described by his former students as tall, elegant, and a stickler for manners, Mr Gough arrived at Clinton in 1967 and remained there until his retirement thirty-plus years later. Mr Gough was black and originally from Trinidad, so he brought considerable potential for border crossing to the table. Though he says he did not cultivate this role, Mr Gough became a model (and sometimes a mentor) for a number of the black students at the school who came to him for advice about how to respond to racist bullying on the playground. He became a model as well for white students, simply by normalizing race. As one said to me, Mr Gough was the first black man she had ever really known outside Hollywood films and American television, and certainly the first in a position of authority. But Mr Gough also crossed borders by quite regularly accepting lunch or dinner invitations to his students' homes – and by encouraging other teachers to do the same. In this respect he was the leading edge of what became, by the mid-1970s, a concerted effort to bring the school to its community. This effort began with the way in which the school communicated with parents. In the late 1950s, as we saw in chapter 4, the Home and School Association offered to publicize its meetings in Italian as a way of communicating with parents who might otherwise not have known about the monthly home and school meetings, or might have been intimidated by them. By the mid-1970s this effort had expanded both quantitatively (by expanding the range of languages in a way that reflected the diversity of Clinton's population) and qualitatively. Now it was not just the Home and School Association but the school itself that communicated – from routine notices to report cards – in multiple languages.

When it comes to border crossing, however, no one was as proficient as the students themselves, and no subject elicited more enthusiasm from my interviewees than accounts of their friendships. Mary and Carolyn, the cross-cultural friends who watched Disney together every Sunday night; Anabel, the Portuguese woman who has maintained close ties with the Ukrainian and Jewish friends she made at school; Angela, whose best friends were her Caribbean and Greek classmates and the Chinese girl next door; Andrew and Peter, whose families were rooted in different eastern European worlds – just about everyone I interviewed had a story about friend-ships that crossed ethnic, cultural, or racial borders. To be sure, life on the playground was not always fun-filled. One graduate from the first decade of European Clinton described the school play-ground as a "hardscrabble" exercise in which ethnicity frequently enough was used as a pretext to administer rough justice. And even at their best, friendships were often tested by misunderstand-ing. One Anglo parent's plans for her child's birthday party were derailed because the Italian and Portuguese families to whom she sent invitations were mystified by the idea of a birthday celebration that did not centre on family. And another Anglo student told me that his non-Anglo friends were completely bewildered by a fam-ily vacation that consisted of long road trips to visit museums in distant cities. Still, virtually all of the former students I interviewed insisted that what made their experience at Clinton distinctive was the school's diversity and the opportunities for friendship that this diversity presented.

Of course, these border-crossing friendships did not simply self-generate. Looking back as adults, many students could see how their parents had attempted to steer their friendships in one way or another. In some cases this entailed creative ways of draw-ing boundaries. One graduate told me about her friend's mother who permitted her daughter to have trans-ethnic friends – but only as long as they played on the porch and did not actually enter the house. More often than not, though, parents seem to have encour-aged, or at least tolerated, their children's choices in friends; this was crucially important. One of my most memorable interviews was with two men who had been close friends at Clinton, had drifted apart over the years, but had re-established a close friend-ship more recently. They came from families whose approach to life in Canada was starkly different. One family's identity remained very much connected to Catholicism and the Hungary the parents had left behind. The other came from a family that wanted little to do with the eastern Europe of their past and embraced Canadian life with assimilative gusto. What was extraordinary about the inter-view was not that these boys became the best of friends at Clinton but that until they began talking about their childhood they had not realized just how different their family cultures had been. However different their families were, the boundaries that might have separated them were invisible to the children and ignored by the adults in a way that allowed this friendship to flourish.

Beyond parental guidance, the "take away" message from school offered subtle, yet powerful, reinforcement of these choices as well. In 1974, the Ontario Ministry of Education published a master statement on the aims of education to replace the Grey Book that had steered provincial curriculum policy since the 1930s. Entitled *The Formative Years*, the guide picked up where Hall-Dennis left off, declaring that Ontario's school curriculum grew out of "the philosophical commitment of our society to the worth of the individual."[77] From this basic principle followed the need to design curriculum that would allow students to "begin to develop a personal set of values by identifying value alternatives and their consequences, selecting personal values from the alternatives, internalizing the values selected, and acting in accordance with the values selected."[78] Even punishment reflected this core individualism. One student remembered how her grade 6 teacher had her stay after school to write lines after she protested about the amount of homework he had assigned. The sentence she was compelled to transcribe five hundred times might well have been the tag line advertising Ontario's educational philosophy: "I must take responsibility."

And what were these value-choosing, personal-identity-developing, responsibility-taking individuals to do with their heterogeneous cultural backgrounds? The answer from the Ministry of Education was clear: deploy these various cultural backgrounds in a way that will give individuals more to work with as they define their distinctive identities. The Canadian philosopher Will Kymlicka has famously argued that "the autonomy of individuals – their ability to make good choices amongst good lives – is intimately tied up with access to their culture, with the prosperity and flourishing of their culture, and with the respect accorded their culture by others."[79] He calls this "the 'liberal culturalist' position."[80] Yet well before this "liberal culturalism" became an object of philosophic discourse and debate in Canada and elsewhere, curriculum planners in Ontario had already seized on it as the cornerstone of what they called

"Multiculturalism in Action." As the phrase suggests, the ministry understood that schools would need assistance in developing ways to embed "liberal culturalism" in the day-to-day curriculum The challenge, they said, was "to provide a program that will give each child an opportunity to … develop and retain a personal identity by becoming acquainted with the historical roots of the community and culture of his or her origin, and by developing a sense of continuity with the past."[81]

This formulation is striking. It blends individual choice (children are given "an opportunity to develop a personal identity") with cultural connection ("the community and culture of his or her origin") in a way that provides a final insight into the real world of multiculturalism at Clinton – that is, the world as the students who were there perceived it. Following Yack, I have argued that multicultural education at Clinton engaged the school in various initiatives – from staffing to curriculum design to community outreach – that both guarded cultural borders and crossed them. Yet to fully understand the Clinton community in those days we need to add a third border activity – what I call *border choosing*. The school's actions were crucial in empowering and protecting cultural communities on the one hand (border guarding) and creating an environment that brought cultural communities into contact with each other on the other (border crossing). But those two functions could, and sometimes did, conflict with each other, so the success of these multicultural initiatives turned on how and where to draw these boundaries and how to police them. What made life on the cultural border work well at Clinton was the (relative) freedom students believed they had as individuals to decide, on their own terms, when to guard and when to cross; that they had the opportunity, within broad limits, to decide where and how to draw the boundary between "them" and "us" because this is what it meant, in the formulation favoured by Ontario's policy makers, "to develop a personal identity."

This boundary drawing captures an essential element of "multiculturalism in action," and I heard about it, in one form or another, time and time again: the graduate who was happy to embrace the World of Disney but who was still annoyed by the pressure to anglicize Italian names; the brother and sister who spoke cheerfully about their different trajectories – he remained "more Italian" while she became "more Canadian"; even the graduate who commented on the disconnect she felt between home and school, and who chose a profession that permitted her to reach out to ethno-cultural and other minorities so that their experience would be different from hers. All of these stories centred on the social and psychological space these students believed they had (or maybe seized) to draw boundaries in a way that made those boundaries easier to negotiate.

To be sure, these "ethnic options" (as the sociologist Mary Waters calls them) may be largely symbolic; they do not "determine where you live, who your friends will be, what jobs you will have, or whether you will be subject to discrimination."[82] But choosing cultural borders is far from the trivial exercise – akin to deciding between Coke and Pepsi – to which Waters compares it.[83] On the contrary, for many students of European Clinton the process of constructing a multicultural identity was an essential part of becoming Canadian, and they took it seriously. The seriousness and importance of this sort of civic project hit home when I spoke with Sergio. Brazilian by birth, Portuguese by extraction, Canadian by migration, Sergio has thought a lot about his identity. He explained that he has Italian and Portuguese friends whose "Portuguese or Italian heritage is very much at the forefront. It's really at the surface, and I don't think for me it is. I mean with the exception of my name, which kind of gives it away, other people wouldn't know, right, I could be Bob Smith and they wouldn't know there's this other world over here." Yet he did not consider himself completely assimilated. "I think I've been able to create a bit of a duality there in my life in that I think at one level I've stayed true to my culture and my background. I read and write Portuguese, I speak it fluently, I've maintained all that." Indeed, when it came down to it, he was able to appreciate many things that, as he pointed out, his interviewer simply did not have access to. "I've got the mungie cake thing going," he said, "and I've got the Portuguese, I've got the Brazilian, right, and you don't know what that's like. You don't know what it is to hear and understand Brazilian music and the poetry within it." And, he concluded, "It may go back to this, that this duality exists within me and they live happily together and I feel very, very, very fortunate that it exists."[84]

By the mid-1970s, the idea of multicultural education at Clinton was in full flower – give or take a rose petal on Pierre Trudeau's lapel. And then it changed again. On the one hand, the school's population became still more demographically multicultural. The core of European Clinton – Italian and Portuguese families – remained, but a significant number of Latin American and East Asian families moved into the neighbourhood, and the first wave of well-established Canadian families attracted by the proximity to major hospitals, universities, and the urban "buzz" joined them. What had been European Clinton for two decades became Global Clinton. On the other hand, while Clinton deepened its embrace of multicultural programs, it also discovered that the community's commitment to multicultural education had limits. Nowhere did these limits appear more clearly than in the debate, in the 1980s, over heritage language programs, and nowhere were the ideas of multiculturalism more vigorously debated. It is to this decade and this debate that we turn in chapter 6.

6

Global Clinton, 1975–1990:
"We Have Children from Lots of Countries"

Bidding farewell to Clinton in the mid-1980s, one newly minted graduate distilled her experience this way: "The things I will remember most about Clinton are the welcomings new children get from teachers and students and we have children from lots of countries."[1] The comment was perceptive. There were indeed children "from lots of countries." The school's demographic base, still solidly Italian and Portuguese, had recently broadened to include significant numbers of newly arrived immigrants from Latin America and East Asia. At the same time, firmly rooted Canadian families, many of them professionals lured by inexpensive housing and proximity to the downtown core, began to move into the area. This produced a level of socio-cultural diversity at Clinton that was unprecedented. As Jewish Clinton gave way to European Clinton in the 1950s, so European Clinton morphed, from the mid-1970s, into a school community that was different again. I call it Global Clinton.

And yet beneath the warm "welcomings" that greeted these new students, there was a serious, sometimes divisive, debate about how comfortably the terms "multicultural" and "citizenship" fitted together. The locus for that debate at Clinton was a proposal in the early 1980s to integrate "heritage language" and other multicultural programming – developed to connect students to their original languages and cultures – into the regular school day. The heritage language debate at Clinton became a signature issue, indeed a flashpoint, that tested the limits of the multicultural approach to education and citizenship. Just as critics of the Drew Regulations in the 1940s challenged the assumption that full citizenship required religious uniformity, and just as the wave of Italian immigrants into Toronto in the 1950s prompted progressive educators to distinguish between integration and assimilation as the basis of citizenship, so the debate over multicultural programming in the late 1970s and 1980s forced the Clinton community to revisit and rethink the terms of civic membership. In the end, the community not only discovered an approach to heritage languages that it could live with, it mapped out a form of moderate multiculturalism that endures to this day. The next two chapters tell the story of Global Clinton. Chapter 6 explains how the school adapted to several important demographic and pedagogical changes. Chapter 7 tells the story of the heritage language debate as it played out at the Toronto Board of Education, at Clinton, and in the collision between them.

The transition from Jewish Clinton to European Clinton in the 1950s had been swift, abrupt, and seismic. The transition from European to Global Clinton in the 1970s was slower and more incremental, but in the end equally decisive. Three broad changes characterize Global Clinton: the hyper-diversity of the student body; the school's steep decline in enrolment; and the impressive expansion of programs offered by the school, especially those nestled under the rubric of "special education."

Diversity goes to the heart of the Clinton experience, and the school's diversity is one of the things that its graduates across the generations recall with clarity and pride. The content and structure of education changed profoundly over the seventy years covered by this study, but references to Clinton's ethno-demographic diversity remained a constant throughout. Diversity is in the school's DNA, passed on from one generation to the next.

In fact, however, when Clinton graduates speak about the school's diversity, they clearly refer to two different, though related, phenomena. On the one hand, some point to the ways in which Clinton's student body was different from those of other public schools throughout the city. Toronto was famously (or infamously) dominated by Anglo-Protestants for the first five decades of the twentieth century, yet the same Anglo-Protestants were in the minority at Clinton. The *goyim* and mungie cakes might rule Toronto, but on the Clinton playground they were a clear minority. In this sense, to say that Clinton was diverse was to say that it was different from most other schools and from the rest of Toronto. At Clinton the minority was the majority, and several graduates who had attended other schools told me that this sociological fact made a real difference. At Clinton they were surrounded by students who were like themselves; it was a place, perhaps a singular place, in which they were not outsiders. Diversity in this sense describes Jewish Clinton and European Clinton particularly well.

On the other hand, a significant number of former students (sometimes the same ones, in fact) also spoke of Clinton's diversity as a way of describing the composition of the school itself rather than the school's relationship to the outside. Clinton was diverse not just because it was different from other schools or from the "Canadians" who dominated Toronto public life, but because the school was itself composed of children whose families came from different places, spoke different languages, and drew on different cultural traditions, yet who found themselves side by side in Clinton's classrooms. It is this second sense of internal diversity that made Global Clinton particularly noteworthy and special.

How diverse was Clinton in the late 1970s and 1980s? Social scientists have developed a statistical technique – called an ethno-fractionalization index – that estimates the probability that any two randomly selected individuals will come from the same group to calculate diversity of the sort I'm writing about. Imagine a population that is homogeneous in the sense that every individual shares a given characteristic – say, where their parents were born – with every other member of the population. Now imagine another population that is heterogeneous in the sense that no two individuals have parents born in the same country. Think of these alternatives as end points on a spectrum where 0 represents a perfectly homogeneous population and 1 represents a completely heterogeneous population. Working with the data that describe the population under study, one can then measure the extent or degree of diversity along the spectrum between homogeneity and heterogeneity. The higher the score, the more diverse the population.

Figure 6.1 Ethno-fractionalization, 1915–1985

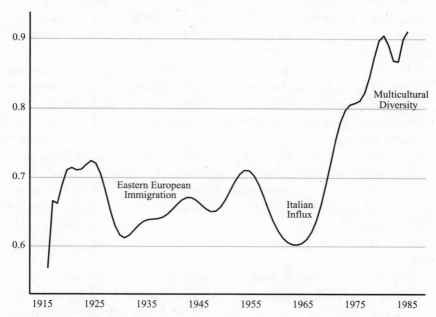

Source: Clinton data set

Figure 6.1 is an ethno-fractionalization index for Clinton that shows the dynamics of the school's diversity from 1915 to 1985. It measures the probability that any two randomly selected students will have fathers born in the same country.[2] Two things are striking: the first is that Clinton has always been a diverse school, never measuring below 0.6 on the ethno-fractionalization index; the second is that Clinton's diversity has varied considerably over the years. Note the lowest point, the most prominent "valley" in the graph that describes the mid-1960s. At this point, almost 60 per cent of Clinton students had a father born in Italy; most of the remaining 40 per cent had fathers born in Canada. As we saw in chapter 4, Clinton's demographic portrait at the time was significantly different from that of most other schools, and it faced challenges in integrating first-generation immigrant students in a way that most other Toronto schools simply did not. As a result, Clinton became a pioneer in developing ESL classes for first-generation immigrant students. But the school itself was not eye-catchingly diverse in the sense that most parents were born in one of two places – Italy or Canada.

Now look at the years that trace the lifespan of Global Clinton, roughly the mid-1970s to 1990. The ethno-fractionalization line rises steeply through the 1970s, as the school becomes increasingly heterogeneous, and peaks just before 1980 at over 0.9. This is extraordinary. It means that, by 1980, there was more than a 90 per cent chance that any two incoming Clinton students would have parents born in different countries, evidence that fits the school's self-understanding. Using languages spoken at home as their measure, the school's parent council conducted a survey in the early 1980s to understand just how diverse the school had become: astonishingly, well over forty languages were spoken in Clinton homes, including Inuktituk.

Figure 6.2 portrays this socio-demographic diversity from a slightly different perspective by describing Clinton's paternal origins in terms of five national and regional clusters – Canada, Italy, Portugal, East Asia, and Latin America. Look, in particular, at Clinton's composition in the early to mid-1980s. At that point, the moment when the debate over heritage languages was most intense, each of these five clusters accounted for at least 10 per cent of Clinton's population. In other words, there was no single, overwhelmingly dominant group that defined the school's identity, but rather an eclectic mix of socio-ethnic groupings all of which could claim a critical mass.

This heightened socio-ethnic diversity suggests that the neighbourhood surrounding Clinton was in flux. Nowadays, real-estate agents routinely try to entice potential buyers to the area with the tag line "steps to trendy Little Italy." This used to be more than a sales pitch. At its high-water mark in the early 1960s, fully 60 per cent of Clinton students were first- or second-generation Italian, and these students maintained a significant presence at the school through most of the 1970s. The irony, however, is that as Little Italy's reputation as an oasis of cosmopolitanism grew, the number of

Figure 6.2 Ethnicity by Father's Birthplace, 1970–1990

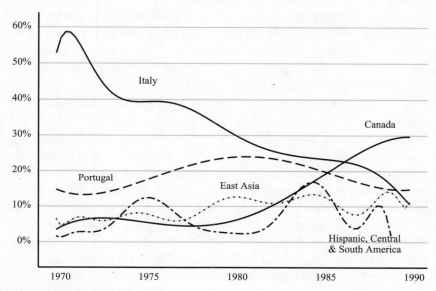

Source: Clinton data set

Italian families in the area actually declined. By 1975 only 40 per cent of the school's students were first- or second-generation Italian. By 1980 the figure was less than 30 per cent, and by 1985 just over 20 per cent. For many Italian families in the area, Clinton was a gateway rather than a destination, and as their prosperity grew so did their desire to move to bigger homes on larger lots in the suburbs. As one veteran teacher told me, "When I arrived at Clinton this was Little Italy. Now it's little Italian restaurants."

Where the Italian population waned at Clinton, the Portuguese population waxed. As I noted in chapter 5, the largest wave of Portuguese immigration occurred about a decade after the Italian, and in many ways the Portuguese pattern echoes the Italian. As more Portuguese immigrants arrived in Canada, more gravitated to Toronto's west end, and more Portuguese students attended Clinton. In fact, as Figure 6.2 shows, the Portuguese rise almost meets the Italian decline in the early 1980s, when both groups accounted for just under 25 per cent of Clinton's student body. But as Portuguese families became more firmly rooted and prosperous, like the Italian immigrants before them, they began to leave the downtown core. As a tradesperson who grew up in the heart of Portuguese Toronto put it to me, "I've now owned three different houses in [suburban] Mississauga. You can't argue with success." And with that success, the Portuguese presence at Clinton began to recede, albeit gradually.

In a 1978 article on special programs at Clinton, the *Globe and Mail* noted that the neighbourhood that feeds the school is "an Italian-Portuguese-Spanish speaking community where parents are very interested in their children's education."[3] The inclusion of Spanish in this description may surprise some readers, but in fact the journalist got it exactly right. Pushed from their homes by stagnant economies and political turmoil and pulled to Canada by more liberal immigration policies, Latin Americans became a new source of Canadian immigration through the 1970s. The numbers were comparatively small. Even at its zenith, in 1975, only 10,000 Latin Americans made their way to Canada.[4] Still, a disproportionate number of these Latin American immigrants settled in Toronto and Montreal, and of those who settled in Toronto, a disproportionate number settled near the intersection of Bathurst and College Streets – just around the corner from Clinton. Most of those who settled on the streets surrounding the school came from Ecuador and Colombia. A smaller number came from El Salvador, and, following the fall of President Allende in 1973, a handful arrived from Chile as well. Like the Italians and Portuguese before them, most of the Latin American immigrants were young, and soon enough had school-age children of their own. The result is that by the mid-1980s children of Latin American immigrants accounted for close to 15 per cent of the school's population.

The arrival of families from a variety of East Asian countries – especially China and Vietnam – broadened the Clinton community still further. In general, there were two sorts of Asian immigration stories at Clinton. The first centred on families who came from southern China or Hong Kong in the late 1960s or early 1970s, spoke Cantonese, were admitted to Canada because they were sponsored by family members, gravitated to the Clinton area because it was close to the original Chinatown on Spadina Avenue, and tended to work in factories or in poor-paying service jobs. The second immigration story typically was about families who came from Vietnam, Taiwan, and Hong Kong in the late 1970s and early 1980s, spoke a language other than Cantonese, had fewer family connections to Canada, were admitted either because they were refugees or because they had entrepreneurial aspirations, yet who, like those in the first story, were initially consigned to low-paying, labour-intensive jobs.[5] The confluence of these two immigrant streams meant that there was a critical mass of East Asian students at Clinton – at least 10 per cent of the student population – from the late 1970s on. However different the stories, the arrival of East Asian students added a dimension to the Clinton community that was fresh and unfamiliar.

And then there were the "white painters," the mildly pejorative term used to describe the young professionals who began to snap up houses in downtown areas like those surrounding Clinton. Thanks to the enormous expansion of postsecondary education in the 1960s, most came with university degrees and many with additional professional training. Architects, city planners, ad executives, teachers, clergy, writers, engineers, lawyers, professors – all of these and more bought and began to renovate (endlessly) houses in the Clinton catchment area. For most of them, the neighbourhood was not a gateway but a destination, the place where they expected to set down roots. Most settled happily into the community as it gentrified, and most thought the area's cosmopolitanism was one of its most attractive features. Soon enough they too were sending their children to Clinton. The take-up was impressive. What began as a trickle in the mid-1970s grew quickly in the 1980s, so that by the end of the decade fully 30 per cent of Clinton students came from families that basically fitted this description.

What did the white painters have in common? I have described the other tranches of Global Clinton in socio-ethnic terms – Italian, Portuguese, Latin American, and East Asian. While it would be tempting to think of the young professionals as the second coming of Anglo-Protestant Toronto, this description doesn't quite fit. In the first place, they weren't "Anglo" in any meaningful way, being both more varied and more cosmopolitan than the traditional rendering of the term Anglo usually allows. Nor did most of them self-identify

as Protestant. (One of the problems I had in gathering data on religious affiliation of Clinton parents in the 1980s, indeed, is that many
of them either did not answer the question or stated that they had
no religious affiliation.) A more helpful way to place the young professionals may be to consider immigration status, for here there is an
important contrast with other members of Global Clinton. Most of
the Portuguese, Latin American, and East Asian members of Global
Clinton were first-generation (or early second-generation) Canadians. As Figure 6.3 shows, more than half of all Clinton students
in the 1970s were born abroad. Apart from the 1950s (at the height
of Italian immigration to the area), no decade has recorded more
first-generation students than the 1970s. The young professionals,
on the other hand, were largely second- and third-generation Canadians, and as they became a larger part of the Clinton school community in the 1980s their presence altered the immigration balance
within the school significantly. Where in the 1970s roughly half of
Clinton students were first-generation, in the 1980s only about 30
per cent were first-generation, and this figure was falling.

This recalibration matters. As long as most Clinton students were
first- or early second-generation immigrant students, the basic need
to help them make the transition to Canadian society largely defined
how the school saw itself and shaped how it performed. As we have
seen in previous chapters, there were important debates about what
the ideal citizen should look like, but as long as Clinton thought of
itself first and foremost as a gateway school one could connect the
historical dots in a way that told a neat and tidy story that began
with assimilation, moved through integration, and ended with multiculturalism. The arrival of the young professionals complicated the
school's mission, and with it the school's story. It is not that the white
painters were hostile to multicultural approaches – far from it – but
they did have other priorities that they considered at least as important. In the end, as we will see in chapter 7, the task of reconciling these
various, often competing, goals created conflict within the school and,
more importantly, between the school and the Board of Education.

Global Clinton was more socio-ethnically diverse than anything
that had preceded it. It was also considerably smaller. Whatever
the story of Clinton may be, one thing it demonstrates clearly is the

Figure 6.3 Immigration Status by Decade

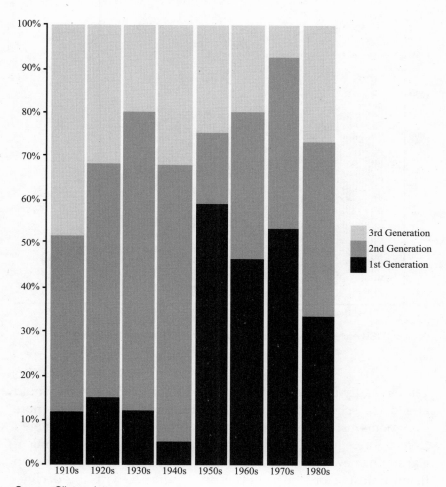

Source: Clinton data set

notorious difficulty of accurate, long-range enrolment planning. In the mid-1950s, the Toronto Board of Education was taken by surprise when immigrant families flooded into the area; the board spent much of the next decade scrambling to find places for their children. In the mid-1960s the planners who designed the "new"

Figure 6.4 Enrolment Trends, 1935–1988

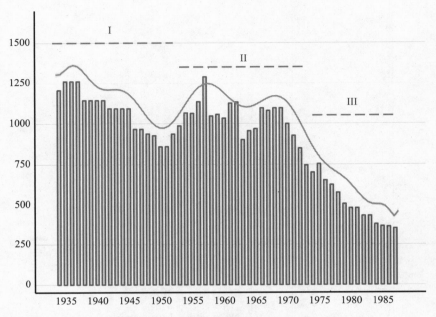

Source: TDSB Archives (1935–67); Ontario Ministry of Education (1966–88)

Clinton badly underestimated the number of students who would attend the school; the school's architects ultimately added more classrooms just as the shovels broke ground. Global Clinton suffered from a different sort of planning problem. Following the building of a gleaming new school for a thousand-plus pupils, enrolment began to fall almost before the paint was dry. Figure 6.4 charts this decline. When the new school opened for the 1966–7 academic year, there were almost 1,100 students enrolled. By the mid-1970s, as European Clinton morphed into Global Clinton, enrolment had dropped to about 750 students (a decrease of 31 per cent from the school's opening attendance a decade earlier). By the late 1980s, enrolment was essentially in a free fall, eventually bottoming out at a mere 350 students – a decline of another 53 per cent.[6] No one had expected such a steep and rapid decline in enrolment.

Clearly, Clinton's precipitous decline in enrolment did not occur in a vacuum. If the enrolment of a neighbourhood school declines, it is a safe bet that this trend reflects a larger population decline in the community that feeds it. This is certainly what happened to Clinton: between 1961 and 1991, the Clinton catchment area lost 42 per cent of its population.[7] What is even more striking – and more directly related to school enrolments – is that, during the same time period, the neighbourhood's population of children under the age of fourteen shrank by 77 per cent. Narrow the temporal boundaries slightly and the same pattern emerges. Between 1976 and 1991, the start and finish of what I call Global Clinton, the total population in the area declined by 20 per cent. The population of children under fourteen fell by three times that amount – 62 per cent. In other words, the decline in Clinton's enrolment simply reflected the larger demographic fact that fewer people, especially fewer school-age children, were living in the area. This connection seems intuitively obvious, and it is confirmed when one looks at enrolment patterns in other public schools in the area, notably Montrose and Grace, where a similar decline occurred.[8] Nor were these demographic trends limited to public schools. The introduction of full funding for Catholic schools notwithstanding, enrolment in the two major neighbourhood Catholic schools, St Francis and St Lucy's, also declined, though the fall was neither as early nor as steep as at the public schools.[9]

Long-term declines in enrolment invariably produce fraught discussions at school boards about whether to shut down underpopulated schools. The extended Clinton community, to its credit, looked at its enrolment decline somewhat differently – not as a crisis to be managed but as an opportunity to provide programs that would address a variety of unmet needs. The most ambitious example of this strategy was the creation of Centro Clinton Daycare in 1974, an inspiration that came more from outside the school than from within. The proposal was spearheaded by a community association called the Centro Organizzativo Italiano (or COI), from which the daycare took its name. The story of COI is an almost textbook example of the way in which the needs of immigrant associations fitted hand in glove with the federal government's strategy to "promote citizenship" in immigrant communities.[10] Based in Toronto's west end, it began as a loosely organized voluntary association of recent Italian immigrants, obtained sponsorship from the West End YMCA, then secured funding from the federal government – first through a Local Initiatives Program grant, then directly from the Citizenship Branch of the Secretary of State and the United Way. Boasting a membership of some 400 people, COI described its mission as "to provide for the interpretation of material and to render information to immigrants and to educate immigrants in the awareness of the Canadian community and to help and stimulate self-help for immigrant groups."[11] As one well-connected supporter put it, their work in solving everyday problems for ordinary people was "almost miraculous."[12]

The need for a daycare facility in the community reflected the basic fact that "there are many working mothers; mothers who would like to work but had no suitable place to leave their children; and mothers who had to work evenings when their husbands were home to look after the children but who would much prefer to work during the day."[13] From the outset, it was clear that Centro Clinton Daycare would serve the local community and would be run by the local community. "As there are no factories, hospitals or other employers of large groups of people in the area, the centre would probably remain a fairly local one of help primarily to mothers who would leave their children on the way to work."[14] The COI was right. One of the attractive features of the daycare was that, unlike many others, it opened at 7 a.m. and closed at 6 p.m. – long enough for working mothers to drop their children, get to work, work a full shift, and return for pickup. And, sure enough, once the daycare opened, the children came. What began in 1974 as a facility that cared for about fifteen three- to six-year-olds in one room on the main floor of Clinton quickly expanded to serve more children, across a greater age range, and in more rooms. Indeed, already by 1978, Centro Clinton Daycare had essentially taken over most of the first floor of the school, offering full-day care for toddlers, half-day care for children in kindergarten, and an after-school spin-off program for children up to age nine. As the *Globe and Mail* put it, "Clinton Street Public School is one city elementary school that is doing something positive about its empty rooms."[15]

But the idea of a daycare at Clinton was not just about solving a space problem or providing a safe and secure place where working parents could park their pre-school children during the day. Rather, the COI's goal was to have the daycare help prepare immigrant children for Canadian schooling. "The area to be served," noted the proposal, "has many Italian and Portuguese people, as well as a few Chinese and other ethnic groups. One aim is to encourage the children to learn to speak English, in a relaxed atmosphere, especially those from non-English speaking homes so that they will be at less of a disadvantage, and able to communicate better with the teachers when they enter the regular school system."[16] This was not a one-way street, however, for "at the same time an effort will be made to make the children feel at home in the centre by having Portuguese and Italian speaking teachers. The children will also be encouraged to feel proud of their own cultural heritage."[17] In other words, Centro's mission was both to cross borders and to guard them. These were complementary, not contradictory, educational – and citizenship – strategies.

The experience on the ground was encouraging. Maria Azevedo, now the daycare's director, began at Centro as a part-time teacher in 1975 and vividly remembers switching back and forth between Portuguese and English with both parents and children.[18] With parents who had difficulty communicating in English, her job was to convey important information to them in Portuguese. Not infrequently, she was called on to serve as a translator for teacher-parent interviews, for daycare board meetings, and for other official school events. With the children, she found herself using Portuguese to help them get their linguistic bearings, explain how things worked, and soothe the feelings of anxious newcomers. She was not alone. Indeed, according to a 1989 article in the *Globe and Mail*, five of eleven staff at Centro Clinton at the time were fluent in a language other than English. "In the room reserved for kindergarten-age children, a map of the world shows that the children's parents and grandparents hail from Bolivia, Chile, Vietnam, Colombia, Italy, Poland, the United States and Canada. In every respect, the staff speak their language."[19]

One of the other distinctive features of Centro Clinton Daycare is that it provided integrated space and care for children with developmental disabilities, either to help prepare them for the school's special programs or, for those already of school age, to provide care after the school day had finished. The inclusion of special needs children in the daycare was a direct result of the expansion and refinement of special education programs, not just at Clinton but in Toronto, and indeed in North America more generally, in the 1970s. To be sure, these programs did not appear out of thin air. As Jason Ellis and Paul Axelrod point out, the Toronto Board of Education had a long tradition of mounting special education programs, and already by 1945 "the TBE had an established special education system, with a wide range of classes and programs addressing the needs of some 2,900 children and adolescents identified as having disabilities and learning difficulties."[20] The largest program – so-called "auxiliary classes" – was established for "mentally defective" and "backward" children at the height of the eugenics movement, roughly at the time of the First World War. Renamed "opportunity classes" in 1937, this program typically catered to students who had scored between 50 and 75 on standard IQ tests. Most schools in Toronto, including Clinton, had such opportunity classes by mid-century. In the 1950s and 1960s, somewhere between twenty and thirty-five students (or about 1 to 3 per cent of the student body) were consigned to the two opportunity classes at Clinton – one for younger, the other for older students.

Beyond this, the TBE had created a series of specialized disability programs over the years. Most were centred in one school (or a few schools, depending on demand) that served as magnets for the students enrolled in them. (As we saw in chapter 3, Clinton served as the hub for deaf education from 1924 to1953.) The TBE sponsored open-air classes that catered to students who were vulnerable to diseases such as tuberculosis (for which sunlight and fresh air were thought to be the best antidotes),[21] sight-saving classes for children with reduced vision, and orthopaedic classes for children with physical disabilities. The crowning achievement of this era, however, was the opening, in 1953, of the Sunny View School, a facility dedicated to students "with physical disabilities and [in a separate wing] deaf children."[22] The result was that, "by 1956, there were some 3,500 Toronto students – out of a total enrolment of 83,000 – receiving one form or another of special education"[23] – sufficient in innovation and scale to permit school officials to yield to the all-too-familiar temptation among Toronto boosters to think that their way of doing things should serve as a model for other North American cities.[24]

This mid-century consensus on special education in Toronto's schools, however, came under attack in the early to mid-1970s – just as European Clinton was becoming Global Clinton. Calls for reform to the prevailing system of special education came from all sides. One especially trenchant critique was launched by a group of women, the Treffan Court mothers, who maintained that the board's special education programs in effect streamed poor and immigrant children into dead-end vocational programs. (As someone close to the system once quipped, participation in vocational programs meant "going nowhere at your own pace.") This critique seized the attention of a number of social scientists (who demonstrated that the intuition of the Trefann Court mothers about streaming was, in fact, spot on), and it captured the imagination of the progressive members of the school board, the Hall-Dennis Commission, and policy entrepeneurs as well – among them the minister of education, Bette Stephenson. Health professionals pointed out that mid-century notions of special education had not kept pace with medical research on learning disabilities and urged policy makers to develop more differentiated programs to help those with cognitive disabilities, including those previously labelled "uneducable." From an altogether different side of the spectrum came pressure to invest more resources in the "best and brightest" by developing a stronger and better organized infrastructure of programs for "gifted" students.

Unlike Centro Clinton Daycare, which began and remained a bottom-up, parent inspired, and community-driven initiative, the reforms to special education in the mid-1970s were largely top down; that is, once they began, it was governments at various levels that shaped the policy and programmatic contours. Whichever direction the causal arrows point, the effects of this new emphasis on special education on the life of the school were enormous. Consider three snapshots of special education at Clinton taken a decade apart. In 1966–7, Clinton's first full year of operation in its new building, special education consisted of two Opportunity Classes (which enrolled twenty-six students) and one "special program" in English as a second language. A decade later, in 1976–7, the commitment to special education had expanded somewhat; it comprised one full-time and two part-time ESL teachers, two "special program" teachers who taught students at various ages and with varying forms and degrees of learning disabilities, and one teacher assigned to a "behavioural" class for students who had difficulty coping with the regular classroom environment. By 1986–7, another decade on, the expansion of special education was unmistakable. By this point there were two full-time teachers for "learning disabled" students, a teacher who ran a behavioural class, a teacher assigned to the gifted program, and another special education teacher who both served as the school's guidance counsellor and ran what was called the learning centre. Add to this a group of educational assistants assigned to help the special education teachers in their classrooms, then fold in another set of teachers (and assistants) who were supplied and paid by the Metropolitan School Board[25] to run programs for children with more severe developmental delays, especially Down's syndrome and autism. Even this underestimates the presence of special education programs in the school because, beyond the staff based at Clinton, the TBE furnished a range of other experts (speech therapists, social workers, and psychologists, for example) who spent time at Clinton as part of a regular rotation among a "family" of similarly situated schools.[26]

The expansion of special education at Clinton, like the establishment of the daycare, took advantage of the concurrent decline in the school's enrolment. In a word, there was lots of space to house these new classes and programs, and with the space came the flexibility necessary to determine, program by program, whether an "integrated" or "segregated" model of special education worked best. Like many other schools in Toronto, Clinton ultimately organized its special education program around a model that was known, in the argot of the time, as "continuum of care," in which the amount of integration varied with the severity of the disability.[27] Those with more severe developmental delays were assigned to largely self-contained classes, those with less severe disabilities worked in regular classrooms but spent scheduled time in the learning centre receiving one-on-one or small-group instruction, and those in between (like the "learning disabled") lived a sort of hybrid existence, though one that tilted towards self-containment.[28]

Marlene Danicki, who taught special education at Clinton for thirty-five years, noted that when she began teaching learning-disabled classes in the late 1970s the idea was that students would spend two years in her class before re-integrating into regular classrooms. In fact, however, this rarely happened. Her original group of eight students stayed with her and, as younger students arrived, the class simply grew.[29] The school certainly understood the advantages of integration. As a Clinton brochure from 1986 put it, "interaction between handicapped and non-handicapped students facilitates positive attitudes and awareness towards handicapped people in general and also serves the handicapped child with appropriate role models." And yet, as the same brochure admitted, this contact (especially with the developmentally delayed students) tended to be informal and usually occurred outside the classroom. "The opportunities for interaction amongst the students occur for the most part during recess, lunchtime, special school events, field trips, and the inclusion of small groups or individuals in special program areas such as physical education, music, library, and kindergarten classes."[30]

And what of school life for students in the regular stream? More often than not, when I asked graduates of Global Clinton about their years at the school, the most vivid memories centred on extra-curricular activities and special events. There was a computer club that introduced students in grades 1 to 3 to elementary programming with Commodore 40s, and there were many other clubs besides: "two art clubs, weaving and sewing clubs, three choirs, chess and French clubs, square dancing and disco dance clubs and a jogging club."[31] There was the ever-popular Mr West, who took clusters of students to Dufferin Mall, gave them each $20, and invited them to spend it any way they wished – all in the interests of applying the math they were learning in class to the real world. There were sports teams, of course, and field trips, and the sleepover camp-cum-science centre that is the Island School. There were opportunities for students to support "worthy causes," among them the Terry Fox Run, the Stop 103 Food Bank, and the World Wildlife Fund. The annual

Fall Fair (an enduring and profitable institution) began in the late 1970s, and musicians, artists, and troubadours visited the school on a regular basis. And just about everyone remembered the hot lunch program (especially the cabbage rolls!) that operated through most of the era.

For Principal Ed Kerr these sorts of activities were "the icing on the cake" that did "so much to enrich our boys' and girls' education."[32] But the heart of Clinton, he insisted, was the academic program. In most respects, Clinton was a thoroughly conventional, mainstream school. It was not, and had no aspiration to be, like the alternative schools that had begun to spring up across the city that sported names like SEED, Alpha, and Contact. Nor was it one of the inner-city schools chosen to pilot "new methods of instruction in an effort to raise academic achievement"[33] There were standard-issue classrooms with walls, rows of desks, a good library, desk work and homework, and report cards. Like most schools, there were many competent teachers and a few memorable ones. When I asked former students to assemble an informal hit parade of their best teachers, names like Ed Gough, Muriel Nishihama, Gary West, and Janet Hoosen turned up again and again. To be sure, there were one or two outliers among the teaching staff. One interviewee recalled her grade 6 teacher who believed in self-directed learning: "We had a couch in our classroom. I don't really remember having any formal lessons about anything ... All I did that year was read a lot of Stephen King books because I felt like it." But this was the exception rather than the rule. In most respects, Clinton was a quite typical school, not so different from countless others in cities across North America.

Still, "conventional" does not necessarily mean unreflective or hidebound. The school's official mantra was that Clinton provided "a developmental approach to learning to accommodate the diverse needs of our children which are the result of the diversity of their learning abilities, ethnic origins, environmental backgrounds, and learning styles. This approach acknowledges that there is no one way to learn and that children may vary in their chronological age."[34] The emphasis on diversity spoke both to the school's commitment to individualism and to its basic egalitarianism. *Each* child was different; *every* child deserved an education best suited to her particular strengths and needs. The problem was that, as enrolment declined and the staff complement shrank correspondingly, the school's leadership had fewer means to mount the sort of "balanced" program students deserved and the ministry and board required. "Securing such a 'balance,'" Principal Kerr observed in 1978, "is not easy in a Junior School."[35] Clinton was well known, he said, for its "special emphasis" on the teaching of reading; this remained non-negotiable. A new curricular module dedicated to environmental studies had recently been introduced and had been piloted by Clinton teachers in 1977–8; the module was mandated by the ministry, and the school had little flexibility even if it had wanted it. Yet despite these various curricular and personnel constraints, Clinton found a way to rebalance its curriculum and to direct resources to two other priorities – music and physical education.

The story of how music was mainstreamed is particularly revealing. Clinton had long prided itself on its music program and over the years had nurtured more than its share of musical talent – Louis Applebaum (composer), Esther Gartner (cellist with the Toronto Symphony), Victor Feldbrill (conductor), Jerry Gray (folk singer), and Zal Yanofsky (drummer with the Lovin' Spoonful) among them. In the 1970s and 1980s, Lorraine Pace was the driving force behind Clinton's extra-curricular music program. Kindergarten teacher, talented pianist, lover of Broadway musicals, and impresario, and known for her big hats, blonde hair, and dramatic gestures, Mrs Pace cut an impressively flamboyant figure. One graduate said that she and her friends used to think of Mrs Pace as Marilyn Monroe's twin. Every year she organized the Spring Thing – the extraordinarily popular school-wide variety show. No less memorable were the Friday afternoon sing-alongs in the gymnasium in which Mrs Pace introduced students to Broadway show tunes and vaudeville standards. Perched at the piano at the front of the gymnasium, she deployed her infectious enthusiasm to teach senior students tunes that they could sing as fillers between acts of the Spring Thing.

The other musical force at the school was Nancy MacDonald, whose teaching assignment placed her in the primary grades but whose advanced training as a vocal coach put her in charge of the Clinton choirs. For school choirs of the time, the annual Kiwanis music festival was the gold standard. In 1977–8, for instance, Clinton entered no fewer than twelve choirs in the competition, a remarkable showing by any measure.[36] Professional musician Richard Reed Parry (Clinton, 1986–9) describes this experience as "life-changing":

> I feel blessed to have had the music teachers I did at Clinton. Nancy Mac-Donald was a beautiful, beautiful choir teacher. She had music, choral music, deeply ingrained in her, and was so marvellously good at sharing that music and teaching it to young people, and challenging us all to dig in and sing. She would routinely pick a student at random to sing alone and sing in front of each other, as well as shaping us into fine form year after year to go compete in the Kiwanis Music Festival, all of which remains one of the most exciting musical moments of my upbringing.[37]

Still, music was an extra-curricular activity, and as a result musical education reached only those students who chose to become involved. Understanding both the importance of music and the unique gifts of Ms MacDonald, the staff in 1978 "agreed to take on an extra two students in their classrooms so that Miss Nancy Mac-Donald could teach music to all classes."[38] And what happened for music occurred as well for physical education, which was upgraded at the same time from a purely extra-curricular subject to a core teaching area with a dedicated staff member assigned to it.

It is clear, in other words, that despite the decline in enrolment, Global Clinton still had enough administrative flexibility to rebalance its teaching program in a way that brought subjects like music and physical education into the pedagogical mainstream. What, then, of the array of programs that fell under the general rubric of multicultural programming? Given the socio-demographic diversity of the Clinton community, did it not make sense to expand and mainstream ESL, heritage language programs, third-language courses, and other multicultural curricular initiatives? Among his own extra-curricular activities, Principal Kerr sat on a working group struck by the Toronto Board of Education that answered this question with a resounding "yes." As we will see in chapter 7, his own school was not so sure.

7

Global Clinton and Heritage Languages

The extraordinary diversity that characterized schools like Clinton provoked a heated and divisive debate about multicultural programming that embroiled the Toronto Board of Education and its schools for fully a decade – essentially from 1975 to 1985. The decisions about music and physical education emerged more or less organically from Clinton itself. The provenance of the multicultural initiatives is more complex, but, however it is described, it is clear that the TBE played a major role. Led by a group of left-leaning, progressive trustees and supported by a like-minded and rapidly growing professional staff, the board had both the commitment and the resources to ensure that the multicultural question remained near the top of the policy agenda throughout the period. The board's ongoing commitment and the basic consistency of its analysis were impressive. An issue paper on multiculturalism entitled "The Bias of Culture"[1] begat two reports from a working group on multicultural programming,[2] which led to two reports from the sub-committee on race relations,[3] which produced two more reports on language policy.[4] Never before (or since, really) had questions of culture, race, and language received such thematic treatment from the TBE.

Why did the board approach multicultural programming with such a combination of urgency and persistence? Why did it mobilize when it did? And what did its proposals entail? The board's reasons for taking multicultural programming seriously, and the reasons for its particular timing, were many and various. Some of the triggers were external. The federal government had announced its official support for the principle of multiculturalism in 1971; the Toronto board was now poised, and believed it had a duty, to transform principle into policy. Lest anyone miss the connection, the board's 1975 working group on multicultural programs used Prime Minister Trudeau's statement to the House of Commons on multiculturalism as an epigraph with which to adorn the title page of its report.[5] The board was also aware that Toronto's Catholic school board had already taken steps, aided by the government of Italy, to provide Italian language and culture classes in schools with large Italian-Canadian populations. Some observers have suggested that the public board was anxious not to be left behind, especially since public schools (among them Clinton) were already losing students to their Catholic neighbours.[6] A third, more abstract, impetus for multicultural programming came from educational researchers who advanced an early version of the now-ubiquitous argument linking education and globalization. As the board saw it, linguistic versatility is bound to be an enormous asset in "the global village."[7] The upshot was that Toronto schools needed to be far more ambitious in providing instruction in languages and cultures beyond English and French so as to prepare their students for the world in which they would live and work. "In today's complex world, any country which aspires to play a significant role in international diplomacy, economy, science or art must have specialists in these fields who are proficient in the languages of the world."[8] And there were other educational benefits besides. It was "practically self-evident" that "language is so vitally related to thought, knowledge and social activity that it is not an overstatement to say that it is language which makes us human ... Proficiency in two or more languages expands, refines and strengthens the student's cognitive capacity" and so is key to "achieving academic success."[9]

It seems clear, though, that most of the pressure to upgrade and expand multicultural programming in Toronto schools was locally sourced and grown. It reflected the board's own sober judgment that it needed to "face" the profound changes entailed both by "the reality and the goal" of education in a multicultural society.[10] Anyone who had taken the trouble to visit a school like Clinton would have seen at first hand just how profoundly the socio-demographic composition of Toronto schools had changed over the years. As I've suggested in earlier chapters, it took the school board far longer than it should have to appreciate this seismic change. When it finally did open its eyes, however, the effect was electric. Stung by criticisms that poor and immigrant students were ill-served by the school system, the TBE, in 1970, commissioned a systematic benchmark survey of its students. Dubbed the Every Student Survey (ESS), the audit revealed just how fundamentally the cultural base of Toronto's school population had changed and how closely immigrant status and academic performance were related.

The Every Student Survey quickly became the empirical standard against which the board measured its programs. When the first working group on multicultural programs reported in 1975, it began its analysis by pointing out that "within the City of Toronto's public school system, the vast majority of children come from extra Anglo-Canadian cultures and for more than half of these children, English is not their first language."[11] Where the education system that Egerton Ryerson had built was Anglo-Canadian from top to bottom, the TBE now had to own up to "the shocking recognition ... that within the space of a decade its CULTURAL BASE HAS BECOME INCOMPATIBLE with the cultural base of the society which supports its endeavour."[12] Or, to put it another way (and the working group had a special talent for making the same point in several different ways): "Multiculturalism is an organic reality which forms the basis for the ordering of all human affairs in the Toronto community at large. Multiculturalism is *not* an organic working reality which forms the basis for the ordering of the Toronto school system's operation."[13]

The deep and serious mismatch between the school system's dominant culture and the heterogeneous multicultural backgrounds of its students produced toxic results:

It is generally known that school transmits A DOMINANT MESSAGE to the young personality for whom the cultural heritage which that institution represents is alien. In its simplest terms, the message is that the cultural heritage in which his personality anchors itself is invalid. Silent, certainly, non-verbal, persistent and unmistakable, the message bombards his consciousness from all sides of the new cultural enclave manifest in the classroom, the hallways and the offices of the school, to say nothing of the blunt expectations, directions and instructions of the staff which control it.[14]

The tensions created between the school's dominant culture and the student's original culture were debilitating. "Unable to participate in any meaningful way in the new culture and discouraged with the lack of meaning and value of the old, the student's perception of himself becomes that of a non-person" or a "marginal non-entity."[15]

This account of what happens when an Anglo school system collides with an extra-Anglo student body was meant to describe the reality of Toronto schooling in the mid-1970s. What were the possible remedies? From the outset, the working group rejected piecemeal reforms that might "ameliorate the conditions" but would not "eliminate the causes"[16] of this cultural tension. To understand the causes, one needed a clear-headed set of principles based on a coherent "philosophy" – the working group's preferred term for its task. And to develop a coherent philosophy one needed a basic normative and moral lens through which to see the subject clearly. For the working group, the idea of equality provided the lens that put the issue of multiculturalism into sharp focus.

The focus on equality (or equity) ran like a red skein through much of the board's work in the 1970s and 1980s. As Gaskell and Levin have pointed out, the progressive reformers who accounted for a majority of the board's members "wanted more attention on the experience of students growing up in poverty, more involvement of local communities in decision making, the teaching of languages other than English, and a system-wide critique of racism, sexism, homophobia, and class bias."[17] The multiculturalism question was particularly fertile soil for this equity-focused direction because it allowed the reformers to nurture two branches of equality from the same stalk. On the one hand, the various working groups built the case for multicultural programming around the idea of equality as equal status. "Although languages may differ in their usefulness in various contexts such as the scientific, educational, or political, they are equal in their humanizing and socializing capacity. Hence, from a strictly educational viewpoint all languages are equal."[18] To give preference to English and French was, in effect, to establish a hierarchy of languages in school that was no more justifiable in principle than establishing a hierarchy of races in society. To the extent that schools privileged English and French and "outlawed" others,[19] they created a linguistic hierarchy that turned schools into sites of dominance and inequality. And just to make the point clear, the working groups went out of their way to identify the struggle for real multiculturalism with campaigns against racism whenever they could. "Elitism and racism" worked together to obscure "the true face of our multicultural Canada."[20]

The working groups seem to have been well aware that framing Anglo cultural dominance this way would be hard for many in their audience to swallow, so they offered a second frame that made essentially the same point but did so in the more congenial language of individual rights and personal development. By this account, "every child has an equal right to preserve a vital link with his/her heritage; hence to recover or maintain the language of his/her ancestors is a legitimate expectation."[21] The 1975 draft report produced by the first working group emphasized the ways in which the prevailing approach to cultural integration in the schools relegated the New Canadian student "to an amorphously marginal half-life in the dim corridor somewhere between the two worlds which the mutually discrete cultures represent."[22] The final report, produced a year later, adopted a more upbeat tone. "In order for these children to develop a positive self-image and feel good about participating, both as members of a family unit and members of a classroom unit, the schools should provide them with a means of recognizing their own cultural and linguistic heritage as a matter of routine school experience."[23] Either way, the goal should be "to provide equal educational opportunities to all children, and secondly, to do so without the loss of the child's personal identity and cultural integrity."[24] Or to put the argument in a way that combined the two egalitarian rationales: Helping students to maintain their original language and culture "would function to dispel the negative impact of the dominant culture on the personal development of these children."[25]

What went for culture went for language as well. The 1982 working group concentrated its attention on the linguistic implications of this egalitarian approach. In its view – widely shared by scholars of language and education – it was impossible to engage non-Anglo cultures seriously without providing instruction in languages other than English. "Language," the working group argued, "is so intimately linked with culture that a profound understanding of a culture is impossible without knowing its language. The educational system must play a significant role in the cultivation of these languages."[26] Both the provincial and federal governments paired their commitment to *multi*culturalism with a commitment to *bi*lingualism. Given the intimate connection between language and culture, this policy choice made no sense to the TBE working groups. "It is paradoxical," the report observed, "that in a country which boasts a policy of multiculturalism children should be discouraged from using the languages which they have inherited."[27] Clearly, "the Canadian government's policy of multiculturalism needs to be rounded off with a policy of multilingualism."[28]

This broadly egalitarian approach produced a suite of four program proposals to raise the profile of multiculturalism, broadly conceived, in Toronto schools. The first, and least controversial, was a recommendation to "immediately improve and increase the resources for English language instruction,"[29] both by sharply increasing the number of ESL teachers to meet growing demand and to require higher threshold standards for teachers moving into the area to ensure that ESL and high-quality teaching went hand in hand. At least in principle, it was hard for anyone to oppose the expansion of ESL programs. Who, after all, would object on philosophical grounds to making the transition to "Canadian life" quicker and easier? Nor was it difficult to support the working group's second major initiative, the expansion of academic "booster" programs. School age immigrant children often arrived in Toronto with "uneven educational background(s)" which left them "deficient" in subjects such as mathematics, reading, and writing.[30] Rather than attribute these deficiencies to irremediable intellectual deficits, it made much more sense to give these students special, intensive tutoring that would allow them to join their grade level as soon as possible. This was the rationale for "booster" programs, and the same logic supported the use of languages other than English to help young students make the transition to English-based instruction. The TBE's experimental program at General Mercer School, which drew heavily from Italian-speaking families, was the model for this approach. The Grande program (named after its principal advocate) had "proven to be a practical method at the kindergarten level for the smooth transition from the third language to English."[31]

The third (linguistic) and fourth (cultural) sets of programmatic proposals were more ambitious and pushed the working groups into more controversial territory. On the linguistic side, the working groups argued vigorously that the TBE should broaden its commitment to third-language instruction so as to give extra-Anglo students the tools to preserve and maintain their cultural roots. Heritage language programs, taught in the schools but by instructors from the cultural communities themselves, were an obvious place to start. There was, as it turns out, a weak and a strong version of the heritage language programs. The weak version would have schools sponsor such programs as an extra-curricular, after-school activity. The stronger version, which the working groups supported on both pedagogical and philosophical grounds, would have heritage languages integrated into the regular school day. Beyond heritage programs, both working groups (1975–6 and 1982) went out of their way to advocate third-language training. The first working group was intrigued by the experiments in bilingual English-Chinese education that had been staged at two downtown Toronto schools, Ogden and Orde Street.[32] The second working group (1982) was established in part to respond to requests from the Armenian and Ukrainian communities to establish bilingual schools in which their languages would have equal status with English. This working group was broadly sympathetic. It was particularly telling, it argued, that other provinces (notably Alberta, Manitoba, Saskatchewan, and Quebec) were far ahead of Ontario in developing bilingual schools where as much as half the instruction was conducted in "third" languages like Ukrainian. The introduction of bilingual and trilingual programs at all levels of the school system would be a "bold departure in [the board's] language policy."[33] But such boldness was necessary if the TBE hoped to redeem the promise of its multicultural approach.

As to culture, here, too, the working groups stressed the need to act decisively. This was particularly true of the 1975–6 committee. As we saw in chapter 5, by the mid-1970s the subject of multicultural curriculum and pedagogy was beginning to receive sustained attention from royal commissions, ministry policy makers, educators, and school communities. The working group was unimpressed, for what it saw around it was not a budding movement of cultural openness but a world in which the story of Canada was told entirely in terms of English and French immigrants and their encounter (as the group put it) with "Native People." In that account other immigrants, settlers, and builders were "invisible."[34] This was a serious pedagogical issue because marginalization of this sort – akin to racism[35] – cut students off from their cultural heritage, undermined their personal identity, and damaged their potential to succeed in their studies. What was needed was root-and-branch change: "It is obvious to the Work Group that inclusion of appropriate and accurate multicultural content in the curriculum spells out the need for a thorough and complete review of *all* curricula and a massive infusion process for the purpose of redesigning *all* forms of aids to learning from textbooks through to library holdings."[36] Only then could the school "prevent the growth of ethnocentrism and racism which have prevailed in the past."[37]

The working groups had plenty of moxie. They also faced plenty of obstacles. The first was legal. Ontario's Education Act sets out the broad legislative framework, the legal architecture, within which schools in the province must operate. Among other things, the act essentially stipulates that instruction in public schools must be carried out in either English or French, an obvious problem for the advocates of bi- or multilingual schools. The first working group exhorted the provincial government to change the act to permit multilingual teaching, as other provinces like Alberta had done. When it became clear that the government had no intention of acceding to the request, the TBE played administrative cat and mouse – exploiting loopholes here and finding ways to experiment there. The linguistic activists did chalk up one victory. In 1977, the provincial government agreed to sponsor and fund heritage language programs – which in the Toronto board meant classes either after school or on weekends. Whatever the constraints, these extra-curricular heritage language programs quickly became popular fixtures in many schools. This included Clinton where, in the first year (1977–8) alone, the school had seven heritage language classes – three Italian, two Spanish, one Portuguese, and one Greek.[38]

The second working group (1982) was able to nudge heritage language programs slightly farther along the track. The provincial government continued to rebuff the most ambitious proposals to create full-bore bilingual and trilingual schools, but it did announce plans, in 1982, to extend the regular school day by half an hour a day or 150 minutes per week. The board's language committee pounced on the possibility that these extra minutes could be used for heritage language classes, effectively upgrading the status of the program from extra-curricular to integrated. Even then, though, there were significant qualifications. Eligibility for integrated heritage language programs applied to only about a dozen downtown schools, Clinton among them. And even in these schools, the programs would not be established unless and until a referendum had been held at the school to confirm that the community wanted language programs held during regular school hours.[39]

The second obstacle was political. Over the course of their lives, both of the working groups (1975–6 and 1982) held extensive public consultations – hearings, public meetings, formal presentations, informal soundings, scholarly briefings, and study tours to other jurisdictions. They quickly discovered that the public was deeply divided over the multicultural proposals. The debates were, as Cummins and Danesi put it, "divisive and bitter,"[40] characterized by long, acrimonious public meetings that kept the rhetorical pot boiling throughout the period. By and large, "the extra-Anglo ethnic population"[41] was solidly behind the working groups. Indeed, "in most cases, community presentations requested much more than the Draft Report (of 1975) actually proposed."[42] But a large number of individuals and groups emerged out of the woodwork to oppose even fairly modest initiatives in multilingualism.[43] The provincial government's program, established in 1977, to fund (largely) after-school heritage language programs produced a "vehemently hostile" reaction from opponents; "in the words of a Ministry official, the phone rang constantly for three weeks with people voicing their disapproval."[44] The issue escalated from there. The Toronto Teachers' Federation was dead set against the integration of heritage language programs into the school day and, in the wake of the second working group's initiative, organized a work-to-rule protocol to advertise their concerns. The nadir, though, was reached in March 1984 when one of the members of the second working group was accused of assaulting a person opposed to the language proposals outside a meeting hall.[45] Clearly, as the first working group put it with uncharacteristic understatement, "there is a fundamental disagreement about the relationship between language, culture and education."[46]

I've already outlined the working groups' equity-based argument for broad and deep multicultural programming. How did they understand the opponents' ideas? To be sure, there were many practical objections and worries about implementation that led some who were otherwise sympathetic to the thrust of multicultural programming to withdraw their support or at least equivocate. If heritage language teachers were not fully certified and accredited, would they be competent in the classroom? What sort of alternative programming would be developed for the students who chose not to enrol in heritage language classes? Would attention to heritage languages make it more difficult for immigrant students to master English? Were these initiatives too expensive? And so on. Still, it is hard to see how these practical reservations could produce the deep bitterness that characterized the multiculturalism debate. Differences about how programs will be rolled out can spark disagreement, but they don't usually lead to shouting matches, personal attacks, and scars that, even after thirty-five years, have not entirely healed. So what, as a matter of principle, led a significant number of trustees and vocal constituents to oppose the recommendations of the working groups?

For their part, the working groups thought that the dispute over language training in the schools was so rancorous because it exposed two starkly different ways of thinking about what "real" multiculturalism entails. I say "real" because, as the working groups conceded, their opponents both on and off the board did not for the most part repudiate multiculturalism altogether. But, from the perspective of the working groups, their opponents' version of multiculturalism was thin, limited, and ultimately hypocritical. As the working groups saw it, their opponents (especially those, like teachers and principals, who belonged to the school system itself) believed that "it is the inherent right of the extra Anglo-Canadian population to maintain and cherish their original cultural heritage and their language in Canada." Yet at the same time, they rejected the idea "that the school system has any responsibility to become actively involved in the culture and language maintenance process itself. The grounds are that the business of the school is education and not the maintenance of cultures and languages other than French or English!"[47] Rosario Marchese, who was a school trustee at the time of the second working group, recalled with evident frustration the attitude of some members of his constituency: "We're here and we should leave it to the parents to teach their children the language and it shouldn't be done at school."[48]

For the critics of the working groups' initiatives, multiculturalism was a lot like religion; it should be confined to the private sphere. As with religious freedom, individuals have broad discretion or choice to preserve their original language (or not) and associate with others dedicated to preserving that culture (or not). This is what it means to have a "natural right" – the working groups' term[49] – to maintain one's linguistic and cultural heritage. But like the right to religious freedom, this heritage right also means that there should be a clear boundary between the cultural freedom individuals enjoy in private and the cultural rules they must obey in public. Again, to appropriate the summary articulated by the first working group, by this view, "culture and language development is the responsibility of the home. The school's responsibility is education."[50]

But as the working groups were quick to point out, this sort of bright-line separation between a private sphere (where linguistic, religious, and cultural diversity flourish) and a public space (where education rules) is naive because education is also a crucial vehicle for the transmission of language and culture. It's all very well to say that extra-Anglo communities have the right to maintain their original languages and cultures in private, but the rules are different for English and French. Unlike all other languages (and cultures) in Canada, they alone have a private *and* a public status that shapes and feeds the definition of what it means to be a citizen, an equal member of a particular political community. Think again about religion, especially in the context of the controversy surrounding the Drew Regulations in the 1940s. As we saw in chapter 3, the issue for the Jewish community was not simply whether the Drew Regulations violated a student's individual right to religion. If that alone had been the issue, the religious exemption provided for non-Christians might well have settled the matter. Rather, the Canadian Jewish Congress argued vigorously that the real problem with the Drew Regulations was that they conveyed the unmistakable message that non-Christian students could not be full and equal members of the community because Ontario was a Christian province. In their view – a view shared by many liberal thinkers – the state must be neutral when it comes to fundamental rights. It can't load the dice in favour of one religion without compromising the idea of equal citizenship for others.

The working groups criticized their English-first opponents on basically the same grounds. One can tell extra-Anglo communities that they have complete freedom to maintain their original languages and cultures, but when their children attend school it is only English and French that really count. To the working groups, the schools' overall goals were perfectly transparent. For all of the talk about multiculturalism, the mission remained to assimilate immigrant children to "a single dominant cultural base"[51] in a way that was less direct but no less clear than the Drew government's vain attempts to create a school system based on Christian religious instruction. Jim Cummins and Marcel Danesi, two scholars who have written and consulted on these questions for forty years, put the point like this: "The vehemence of the negative reaction to heritage language instruction in the public school system can be understood in the context of the persistence of Anglo-conformity ... in the hearts and minds of many Canadians. Thus, while 'multiculturalism' contributes a surface veneer to Canadian identity, at a deeper level, in English Canada, identity is still largely rooted in Anglo-conformity."[52] And, truth be told, there were many interventions in the debate that lived up (or down) to this portrayal. Predictions of balkanization and ghettoization were rife. Speaking to the proposal to create a Ukrainian language school, the *Toronto Star*'s warning was typical. In an editorial entitled "Don't Balkanize Schools," the newspaper drew out the consequences of culturally distinct schooling: "Toronto could, at worst, end up with something of a segregated school system: a white Anglo-Saxon Protestant core of schools, surrounded by a smaller network of ethnic schools. The danger of fragmentation is all too real, as fully half the children in our schools speak English as a second language."[53]

The differences between those who favoured integrated heritage programs and those who opposed them were deep and pervasive. Yet in one crucial way the two positions were oddly, but powerfully, similar: both sides in the debate framed the issues surrounding heritage language and culture in terms of a binary, either-or choice. However the positions were formulated – public versus private, thick versus thin, genuine multiculturalism versus assimilation, unity versus balkanization – both sides portrayed them as if they posed a stark choice between mutually exclusive alternatives. In one version, opposition to extended heritage language and culture programs reflected elitism and racism; in the other, support for them launched schools down a slippery slope towards segregation and ghettoization. There was little room left, and certainly no principled room, in the middle to bridge these alternatives in either version, which is one of the reasons the debate was so rancorous, polarizing, and resistant to compromise.

This consensus on the binary nature of the issues shaped the debate in Toronto schools in the late 1970s and 1980s, and it continues to shape much of the multiculturalism debate to this day.[54] But it is badly overdrawn – on both sides – and needs to be questioned. It is, I believe, a false dichotomy that actually obscures more than it clarifies.

This is where Clinton re-enters the story. One reason to be suspicious of the heritage language dichotomy is that it really does not describe, and I believe cannot explain, the way the heritage language debate played out at Clinton Street School – and other schools like it. Clinton was one of the dozen or so schools in downtown Toronto identified as prime candidates for integrated heritage language programming that followed from the 1982 working group's study. As I noted above, integrated language programs were subject to a local option. Once a school had been identified as a candidate, a highly structured process of consultation and debate within the local school community followed. This consultation then led to a school-wide referendum among parents who were asked to accept or reject integrated heritage language programming in their school. The parents' choice ruled.

The task of leading the school community through this process fell in the first instance to the school's parent council. In Clinton's case, the old Home and School Association, which used to draw 150 or 200 parents to monthly meetings (see chapter 4), had atrophied badly over the years. Putting the best face on it, Principal Kerr reported in 1978 that while parental involvement in general was "disappointing" there was at least "a small core of enthusiastic, hard working Mothers and Fathers."[55] As the Clinton community changed, though, it began to attract more professional parents who enjoyed working at the interface between local communities and large bureaucratic organizations like school boards. The number of parents who regularly attended meetings was still modest; then, as now, meetings attracted at best a couple of dozen parents. But those who were involved, as co-chair Sally-Beth MacLean recalls, were upbeat and committed. They worked under a new name (the Clinton Educational Community Association or CECA), reorganized themselves so as to appeal to more parents, and cut their organizational teeth successfully on one of the most intractable of all parent council issues: how to improve the school playground. Still, navigating the heritage language question posed a challenge of another order altogether.

The proposal for integrated heritage language classes at Clinton dominated the CECA's agenda for the better part of two academic years, 1983–4 and 1984–5. During the first year, the deliberations were largely internal. Sensibly enough, the sub-committee struck to study the question went on two field trips to visit nearby schools where integrated heritage language programming was already up and running. Neither impressed the Clinton group. School "A," which was largely Portuguese, had seized the opportunity to regularize integrated language teaching that was already operating under the radar. The results were mixed according to the Clinton observers. The heritage teacher praised the new format and reported that students responded better to her instruction and that, as a teacher, she felt better integrated into the school. But the Clinton group also noted that the extension of the school day had meant that extra-curricular activities (like sports and music) had withered because parents didn't want their children to stay yet longer at school. This was especially troubling for the Clinton parents because, at Clinton, it was through such extra-curricular activities that cultural mixing and integration occurred most successfully. They worried, too, that the quality of the "concurrent" program offered to those students not in heritage language was "inadequate"; and that enrolment in heritage language classes had actually decreased rather than increased under the integrated model.[56] Besides, a school that had such an overwhelmingly large representation of one heritage population was not really a good model for Clinton, which was so much more heterogeneous and in which, therefore, the logistics of mounting many heritage classes simultaneously were different and more complicated.

School "B" was, in this respect, more similar to Clinton. It offered a total of six heritage classes, including Greek, Spanish, and, importantly, one on Black Culture. Moreover, the school's principal had scheduled heritage classes for the first period after lunch three times a week so that the classes did not appear as if they were some sort of lesser value add-on to the regular school day. The Clinton group remained unconvinced. Most of the heritage classes included children from kindergarten all the way to grade 6 (which made the teacher's job somewhere between challenging and impossible), the quality of the concurrent program was suspect, extra-curricular activities had essentially "dissolved," and the debate that led to the program's creation had left "wounds [that] had obviously not healed." As the Clinton group concluded, "The study group unanimously hopes that we can avoid similar problems at Clinton, whichever way the decision goes."[57] The heritage language sub-committee duly reported back to the CECA steering committee and to the school as a whole. While it was clear to anyone who had followed the study tour what the sub-committee thought, the committee itself was "very careful to examine all sides of any issue brought before it. It takes this responsibility for fairness very seriously."[58]

If in the first year of the heritage consultation the CECA largely pulled its punches, in the second year it came out fighting. There were two major differences between Year One and Year Two. The first is that what had been a debate that was largely run by, and confined to, Clinton parents and teachers became a larger and more contentious discussion led by officials from the school board. The Planning Committee established by the TBE was chaired by the area superintendent and included the two local school board trustees, professional staff whose function it was to serve as intermediaries between ethnic communities and schools, representatives from umbrella ethnic organizations, and several other board employees who served as consultants. The school, for its part, was represented by two members of the CECA and two representatives from the existing after-school heritage language program. The Clinton parents felt outnumbered and under siege. So configured, the consultation was almost perfectly designed to deteriorate into a pitched battle in which the two blocs on the committee dug in their heels in ways that did not exactly promote bridge-building. The Clinton representatives complained bitterly that the board representatives were not the least bit interested in hearing from the school community but took every opportunity to "sell" integrated heritage language programs, to muzzle those who disagreed, and to engage in dirty tricks to influence the outcome. The board members, for their part, found the Clinton representatives obstructionist and "destructive" in their opposition to integrated heritage language programs.[59] How else to describe the filibustering list they compiled of more than forty questions – from process and design through content and implementation – all of which were meant to sow doubts about the legitimacy and usefulness of the program.[60] All of this contributed to the adversarial tone – us versus them – of the debate.

Photo 1. A kindergarten class seated in a circle. Note the five stained-glass panels at the back. Three surviving panels are on display in the current school library. No date, presumed 1930s. Clinton Street School Archives.

Photo 2. A class photo with cadets in front, 1920. The cadet corps had an important presence at Clinton in the interwar period. Cadets had access to the rifle range in the school's basement. Clinton Street School Archives.

Photo 3. The original Clinton Street School (1888), the annex (1923) behind it, and the main building (1913) behind it, viewed from Clinton Street. The school dominated the neighbourhood landscape. TDSB Museum and Archives Department, Historical Photo Collection.

Photo 4. Clinton Street School (1913–1965), viewed from Manning Avenue. The arched doorway is the girls' entrance. The separate boys' entrance was on the other (north) side of the building. TDSB Museum and Archives Department, Historical Photo Collection.

Photo 5. A class photo, 1929. The playground was constructed of wooden planks before it was replaced with pavement in the 1930s. Clinton Street School Archives.

Photo 6. A class photo, 1937. Note the ornate desks riveted to the floor, the chalk-drawn maps of Canada and North America, and the boy (centre-left) wearing a Toronto Maple Leafs sweater. TDSB Museum and Archives Department, Historical Photo Collection.

Photo 7. A household science class, 1920s. Note the array of food, including root vegetables, herbs, preserves, and the Bunsen burner cooktops. Clinton Street School Archives.

Photo 8. A manual training class, 1920s. Note the fully equipped workbenches complete with wooden tools. Clinton Street School Archives.

TORONTO PUBLIC SCHOOLS

REPORT CARD

19...3.8   19...39.

Pupil...*Helen Devon*...

Grade...*11*......   Teacher...*F. Mc*...

Principal...*W. A. Scholfield*...   School...CLINTON ST.

Message from the Superintendent of Schools:

This report card makes provision for a record of progress in school subjects and for a record of progress in some of the qualities of a good citizen. It is expected that parents, teachers and pupils will all recognize that excellence in the development of the personal qualities mentioned is as important as a good standing in the subjects of study. To that end the best possible co-operation between the home and the school is absolutely necessary.

C. C. GOLDRING.

Photo 9. A Student Report Card, cover, 1938–9. This template was used in Toronto schools in the 1930s and 1940s and bears the imprimatur of C.C. Golding, the director of education. The report card recorded both academic achievement and "progress in some of the qualities of a good citizen." Clinton Street School Archives.

CITIZENSHIP

Improvement is Desirable in the Items Marked—X

	Sept.	Oct.	Nov.	Dec.	Jan.	Feb.	Mar.	Apr.	May	June
HEALTH HABITS: Sitting, standing and walking correctly										
Keeping clothing, hands, face and teeth clean										
Coming to school well rested										
Observing rules of safety										
RELIABILITY: Respecting public and private property										
Being trustworthy										
SELF-CONTROL Making effort to control temper										
Refraining from quarrelling and complaining										
CO-OPERATION: Respecting the rights of others										
Showing good sportsmanship										
COURTESY: Being polite in speech and actions										
INDUSTRY: Making good use of time										

Photo 10. A Student Report Card, citizenship grades, 1938–9. The "qualities of a good citizen" comprised both individual traits (e.g., self-control) and social virtues (e.g., cooperation). Clinton Street School Archives.

TORONTO DAILY STAR

TORONTO, MONDAY, NOVEMBER 14, 1938

OCTOBER CIRCULAT

DEAF CHILDREN WILL "FEEL" VOICES AS THEY NOW "FEEL" MUSIC

NEW "PHONOTACTOR" MACHINE WILL BE GIVEN TO CLINTON SCHOOL BY THE STAR

To help fight the isolation of deafness which rests upon a number of Toronto children, The Star has ordered a "phonotactor" from | Prof. Robert H. Gault of Northwestern university, who will have it built especially in his college laboratory at Evanston, Ill. Children | who learn to take advantage of various deaf aids at Clinton Street school already are taught to place their finger-tips on the top of a | piano (TOP) in order to "feel" the music which they cannot hear. Much after the same fashion, Dr. Gault's machine picks up a speaker's voice through a microphone and | transmits it to a device corresponding to a loudspeaker. Sensitive fingers placed on the "phonotactor" will help the children "hear" by means of vibration.

Photo 11. Deaf students standing beside a piano, "feeling" music. Between 1924 and 1953, Clinton served as Toronto's only school for deaf students. The Clinton program was known for its controversial use of the "oralist" approach. Source: *Toronto Star*, 14 November 1938.

Photo 12. A class photo on the school steps with a student holding Union Jacks, 1941. Patriotic wartime activities were an important part of the Clinton experience during the Second World War. Clinton Street School Archives.

Photo 13. A staff photo, 1939. At the time there were 28 classes serving approximately 1,150 students. This included graded classes from kindergarten through grade eight, as well as specialized classes for household science, manual training, "auxiliary," and deaf education. Clinton Street Public School Archives.

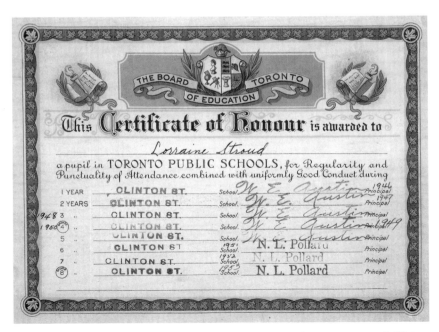

Photo 14. A Student Honour Certificate. Approximately 9 per cent of Clinton students earned these certificates, which were used widely in Toronto schools in the 1930s and 1940s. Clinton Street Public School Archives.

Photo 15. A classroom photo, 1959–60. Note the mural depicting Amsterdam, back left. Clinton Street School Archives.

Photo 16. A classroom photo, 1961–2, with Principal McArthur at top left. Compare the number of students here (fewer than 30) with the number in 1937 (more than 40). Clinton Street School Archives.

Photo 17. Clinton Street School, opened in 1966. In its first year of operation, about 1,100 students attended the school – nearly three times the current population. Photo courtesy of Vincenzo Pietropaolo, 2016.

Photo 18. Centennial Mural, 1967. Note the self-consciously diverse portrayal of Canada's population. Clinton Street School Archives.

Photo 19. Clara Tomasella, parent, kindergarten assistant, and extra-curricular program organizer welcoming students in three heritage languages – Italian, Spanish, and Portuguese. Clinton Street School Archives.

Photo 20. Clinton students at the Toronto Island Science Camp, 1980s. The science camp, located just beyond the Toronto harbour on Lake Ontario, has been a fixture of the student experience in Toronto since the 1960s. For many Clinton students it was the first experience of overnight "camping" away from home. Clinton Street School Archives.

Photo 21. Ed Gough, teacher, 1978. Mr Gough was a revered teacher, role model, and track coach for more than 30 years. TDSB Museum and Archives Department, Historical Photos Collection.

Photo 22. Students at their desks in a typical classroom, 1978. In an era of pedagogical experimentation, Clinton remained committed to "flexible formalism." TDSB Museum and Archives Department, Historical Photos Collection.

Photo 23. A staff meeting, 1978. Principal Ed Kerr (middle) leads the discussion. TDSB Museum and Archives Department, Historical Photos Collection.

Photo 24. The Clinton School choir singing at Massey Hall, 1977. Clinton's school choir was a fixture at the annual Kiwanis Music Festival, especially in the 1970s and 1980s. Clinton Street School Archives.

Photo 25. The Clinton School choir was chosen to sing for Pope John Paul II during his visit to Toronto in 1984. Clinton Street School Archives.

Photo 26. Lorraine Pace at the piano leading a sing-a-long, n.d. Mrs Pace, a much beloved kindergarten teacher, organized the annual variety show, the Spring Thing. Clinton Street School Archives.

Photo 27. The Clinton choir, directed by Nancy MacDonald, n.d. Originally hired as a primary grades teacher, Ms MacDonald's talents as a music teacher led the school to reorganize its staffing so that she could teach music full-time. Clinton Street School Archives.

Photo 28. Kindergarten teacher Lorraine Pace helping a student to form letters, 1978. TDSB Museum and Archives Department, Historical Photos Collection.

Photo 29. Clinton athletes assembled for a track meet, 1980s. Clinton Street School Archives.

Photo 30. Clinton Street School Fall Fair, late 1970s. Note the portrait of former Prime Minister Pierre Trudeau in the background. Clinton Street School Archives.

Photo 31. Cohen's Fish Market, Clinton Street at College Street. This was one of many businesses that served families of Jewish Clinton. Photo (1970) courtesy of Vincenzo Pietropaolo.

Photo 32. Little Italy, World Cup Celebrations, 1970. Photo (1970) courtesy of Vincenzo Pietropaolo.

The second difference between Year One and Year Two is that the stakes were higher: this broader consultation was meant to provide parents in the school community with the background information they needed to vote in a school-wide referendum on the subject. Here again, charges and counter-charges abounded about misinformation conveyed, scare tactics deployed, and secret ballots compromised. In the end, the Clinton community voted against integrated heritage language programs by a comfortable though not overwhelming margin.[61] And soon enough things at Clinton returned to the status quo ante. Still, the heritage language debate left its mark. As one member of the parent council said to me, "My blood still boils – and I was on the winning side."

How does the Clinton experience fit into the multicultural binary, the "either-or" formulation, I described earlier? It would be convenient to say that the Clinton episode proved what the working groups and their supporters had been saying all along – namely, that opposition to integrated heritage language programs reflected the continuing domination of Anglo-centrism in Toronto schools. But this interpretation doesn't quite work. In the first place, the opposition to integrated heritage language programs at Clinton was not simply an Anglo issue. Opponents were drawn, in various ways and for various reasons, from all of the major sub-communities at the school. Indeed, one of the most passionate and effective interventions at the large public meeting held to discuss the proposal was by a multilingual, non-Anglo woman who opposed the program because she thought this form of classroom teaching amounted to language training "lite."

More importantly, these Anglo parents didn't really fit the assimilationist mould. They didn't lecture ethnic communities about the need to learn Canadian ways, didn't prophesy the fragmentation of the Canadian polity if the school mounted integrated heritage language courses, and didn't identify with the "rednecks" (their term) who thought that immigrants should just "suck it up" and make the transition to Canadian society. Jim Clarke, who had been a member of the sub-committee that visited the two schools where integrated heritage language was in operation, recalled that there had been a lot of scepticism about the quality of heritage language teaching. "But there was no one who said, you know, they should just forget it and learn English." He continued: "I don't remember anyone ever talking about whether it was a good idea from the point of view of ethnic parents for their children to have their backgrounds reinforced."[62] Quite the opposite. From the perspective of the self-consciously cosmopolitan, largely Anglo newcomers to the neighbourhood, "the rich multiple cultural mix" was one of the attractive things about the Clinton area.[63] As one woman, then a "newbie" now a long-time resident of the community, put it, the cultural mix was one of the "special" things that Clinton had going for it and one of the reasons families like hers chose to settle in the community.

Nor did the CECA or the school consign heritage languages or cultures to the private sidelines. Those who were opposed to integrated heritage language programs did not insist that Clinton should have nothing to do with multicultural programs. Far from it. To build on the distinction I introduced in chapter 5, Clinton continued to promote both border guarding and border crossing – with the support of the CECA, parents, and the school's leadership. The school continued to sponsor four after-school heritage language programs, despite their imperfections. It still organized catechism classes, sang for the Pope, furnished report cards in several different languages, hired multilingual staff (especially in the main office), supported Centro Clinton Daycare, and provided multicultural services "to maintain communication with ethnic groups and agencies which provide support services."[64]

Beyond this, the school did its best to attract diversity-themed special exhibits and performances from outside the school itself. One early and striking example was a visit from the authors of *The Sandwich,* shortly after the book's publication in 1975. As co-author Ian Wallace recalls, Clinton students were particularly excited because the book was set at their school. But what impressed him both at Clinton and at other schools across the country was that "many students shared highly personal accounts of incidents in their lives when they had been laughed at, taunted, or experienced discrimination of some kind, and we embarked on a moving and thoughtful discussion that sometimes shocked other students ... and made teachers aware of situations that they had previously been unaware of." Indeed, he remembers that "many teachers commented that they read the book at the beginning of each school year to establish respect for everyone in their classrooms."[65]

The Sandwich had such a powerful effect because when it was published it was one of the few resources available to teachers, parents, and elementary-aged students that dealt explicitly and probingly with issues of diversity. That changed – quickly. The Inner City Angels, one of whose earliest and most significant supporters was a Clinton graduate,[66] brought a wide range of performances, many of them diversity-themed, to inner city schools (including Clinton). The Board of Education, through its Race Relations Department, developed its own travelling shows, like "The Invisible Kid" – a short play aimed to raise awareness of racism.[67] Another regular visitor in the mid-1980s was the story-teller Caroline Parry, a Clinton parent and author of *Let's Celebrate! Canada's Special Days* – a spectacularly successful children's book.[68] Conceived in 1984 and published in 1987, *Let's Celebrate* was an exercise in both border guarding and border crossing. It provided children with a description of, and a guide to, important cultural festivals around the world, brilliantly arranged by season so that the various holidays and celebrations appeared simultaneously familiar and different. With total sales of over 80,000 copies, *Let's Celebrate* became a staple not just at Clinton but in many, many other schools in Canada and beyond.[69] These sorts of initiatives may not have met the high bar set by some members of the school board, but they certainly demonstrated that Clinton did not accept the idea that students should check their cultures at the schoolhouse door.

And yet, clearly, there was still a wide gulf between the supporters and the opponents of integrated heritage language classes at Clinton. Part of the disagreement turned on whether the program suited the particular conditions of the school, and much of the debate centred on nitty-gritty questions of design, fit, and workability. But there was more to it, I think. As the parents on the CECA saw it, public schools had to balance the need for immigrant students to learn English with the legitimate desire to maintain their original language and culture. As Sally-Beth MacLean put it, "I think it's important for the children of [immigrants] to have pride in their origins, pride in their country that they have roots to. And I believe that it's very important for them to become as articulate and well educated as possible in the dominant language, whether it's English or French, but it's equally important for them to be proud of their roots."[70] The members of the two working groups probably would have agreed with the basic thrust of this statement. The big difference is that the Clinton parents believed that after-school or weekend heritage language classes were a "perfectly okay"[71] way to honour and achieve this double purpose. In their view, a decision not to integrate heritage language classes into the regular school day was not a demeaning denial of full citizenship; it was a perfectly acceptable way to balance two important educational goals.

The point is that these Clinton parents defied the either-or, black-and-white binary way of thinking about citizenship in Canada. They didn't subscribe to a "thick" theory of multicultural citizenship, which would have imposed a duty to integrate minority languages into the school day. But neither was their attachment to multicultural citizenship so "thin" that it could only support the most superficial forms of diversity. The Clinton parents, instead, landed right in the middle. They supported a moderate multiculturalism that ventured into territory that assimilationists considered dangerous but stopped short of what the TBE believed equity demanded.[72]

This moderate multicultural approach carried the day at Clinton; it continues to serve as a useful, and I believe defensible, way of thinking about multicultural citizenship in Canada and other diverse societies. To understand the distinctiveness of Clinton's approach to multiculturalism we need, briefly, to switch lens settings to zoom out in a way that will reveal the broader intellectual topography of the Clinton debate. As Will Kymlicka (among others) has shown in detail, the idea of multicultural citizenship became popular in the West as a response to, or a reaction against, the idea of "the unitary, homogeneous nation-state ... In this model, the state was implicitly (and sometimes explicitly) seen as the possession of a dominant national group, which used the state to privilege its identity, language, history, culture, literature, myths, religion, and so on, and which defined the state as the expression of its nationhood."[73]

The upshot of this fusion of nationalism and political power was that those who did not belong to the dominant (usually majority) group had either to shed their original culture and assimilate or face exclusion from the full benefits of citizenship – or both. The vicious possibilities of such a fusion were on display in Nazi Germany, but in truth "virtually every Western democracy has pursued this ideal of national homogeneity at one point or another, as have virtually all post-communist and post-colonial states."[74] This includes some countries, like Canada, which portray themselves as open, immigrant states but which nevertheless "at some point or other had the goal of inculcating a common national language and culture."[75] Nor is this just a history lesson. The "new nationalism," as Michael Ignatieff called it in *Blood and Belonging*,[76] roiled politics in the 1990s in places as different as the former Yugoslavia, Northern Ireland, Kurdistan, and Quebec. And the growing electoral presence of anti-immigrant parties in many countries (notably in Europe) means that the argument remains a hot political issue to this day.

Multiculturalism was, and is, an explicit response to this sort of ethno-centric nationalism. While it has taken many different forms, the basic idea of multiculturalism "involves the repudiation of the older idea that the state is a possession of a single national group. Instead, the state must be seen as belonging equally to all citizens." What this means, telegraphically, is that "a multicultural state repudiates any nation-building policies that assimilate or exclude members of minority or non-dominant groups."[77] Pierre Trudeau famously captured the spirit of these ideas, and the contrast with ethno-centric nationalism, when, in 1971, he proclaimed multi-culturalism as the Government of Canada's official policy. "There cannot be one cultural policy for Canadians of English and French origin, another for the original peoples and yet a third for all others. For although there are two official languages, *there is no official culture*, nor does any ethnic group take precedence over any other. No citizen or group of citizens is other than Canadian, and all *should* be treated fairly."[78]

If there is no official culture, then what is the basis of Canada's national identity and a citizen's allegiance? For Trudeau and others, the short answer to this question is that a powerful set of "shared values" connect Canadians – citizen to citizen, group to group, and region to region. In Trudeau's vision, the Charter of Rights provided a distilled statement of those values, but there are other versions and sources as well. One of the many government reports published in the midst of the Canadian constitutional crisis of the 1990s put it this way: "Canada is a country that believes in freedom, dignity and respect, equality and fair treatment, and opportunity to participate. It is a country that cares for the disadvantaged at home and elsewhere, a country that prefers peaceful solutions to disputes. Canada is a country that, for all its diversity, has shared values."[79] By the time it reported in 1975, the first TBE working group thought it unnecessary to spill any ink whatsoever to explain why multicultural programming deserved thematic treatment, because multiculturalism itself had already become part of the Canadian creed. It was "a desirable social goal" that was recognized and shared "by [the] Canadian people."[80] The basic contrast is this: where citizenship in an ethno-centric state depends on one's pedigree and connection to a privileged ethnic group, citizenship in a "civic" state depends on one's acceptance of certain core values. It is not descent, but consent that matters.[81]

The idea that shared values are the foundation of a benign form of nationalism that is civic rather than ethnic in nature is obviously attractive – especially to those of us whose professional life is dedicated to the proposition that ideas are important. There are, however, several significant, and related, problems with this notion of civic nationalism. The first is that it exaggerates the extent to which civic (or even constitutional) values are the foundation of national sentiment. After all, there are many countries in the world that identify themselves as being committed to liberal democratic principles and the institutions that go along with them – individual rights, the rule of law, regular elections contested by multiple parties, a basic distinction between public and private, and so on. But that hardly makes their citizens or their ideas of citizenship interchangeable. Every Anglo-American country (to name only those most similar to each other) would claim that it, like Canada, believes in "freedom, dignity and respect, equality and fair treatment, and an opportunity to participate." But this doesn't mean that Americans, Australians, the British, Canadians, and New Zealanders are interchangeable and would fit easily in each other's shoes. Or to make the same point more bluntly: the longstanding rivalry between the United States and Canada in Olympic hockey invariably produces vivid demonstrations of national pride on both sides, but you cannot explain the intensity of these national moments by parsing the subtle differences between the First Amendment on the one side and Section 1 of the Charter of Rights on the other. National differences run much deeper than that.

If the theory of civic nationalism exaggerates the importance of values in constituting national identity, it also underestimates, or even misunderstands, the importance of culture and cultural legacies in constituting national identities. The fact is, *pace* Trudeau, all countries produce an official culture; they create stories about themselves that weave together an authoritative national culture and identity from many and various strands of social experience. Since modern states can't replicate the relative intimacy of the Athenian *polis,* they are left to create what Benedict Anderson famously called "imagined communities"[82] that link citizens across time and space. Nations in this sense are intergenerational communities. They derive their strength from the fact that their members "share something that connects them back in time to a particular point of origin and forward into an indefinite future. As such, they share predecessors and successors who are regularly invoked to deepen the ties that bind the living and extend their sense of obligation to past and future generations."[83] Citizens may share political ideas and values, but these aren't enough on their own to create and sustain national identity. What you need are cultural artefacts like language, symbols, stories of origins, memories of traumatic or heroic experiences, and so on, "that link the members of nations to past and future generations." When people affirm "particular lines of cultural heritage as a source of mutual concern and loyalty [they establish] the kind of intergenerational community characteristic of nations."[84]

In this sense, culture is crucially different from religion. Liberal states can and should distance themselves from establishing or inculcating particular religious doctrines. But they can't distance themselves in the same way from culture "if only because they must use cultural tools and symbols to organize, exercise and communicate political authority. States cannot therefore provide us with culture-free sites for the construction of political identity. Political identities ... are bound, to a certain extent, to take on the form of inherited cultural artifacts."[85]

In the project to construct national identities schools play a crucial role because that is where the potential citizens we call children are introduced to key elements of a country's identity – its language (or languages), history, institutions, symbols, and other cultural artefacts. That the Canadian story has usually been told in English and French; that the account of its early history usually centres on the interplay among French, English, and Indigenous peoples; and that the story of Canada is presented as a progressive march "from colony to nation" – all of this reflects an attempt to expose students to a set of core cultural memories that will generate "the desire to live together" here and now in what Ernst Renan famously called "a daily plebiscite."[86] Does this story and its cultural legacy expose a cultural "bias," as the TBE working groups complained? Of course it does. But no country can fully escape "the bias of culture"[87] because for better or worse no country is willing to say that its national identity is simply a blank slate that is up for grabs.

So what use is multiculturalism then? One part of the answer, viewed from a highly specific vantage point, is that the sort of moderate multiculturalism that emerged at Clinton is important to ensure that cultural diversity has an important place in the story of nation-building itself, that it becomes part of the country's cultural heritage that connects past, present, and future. Because culture is constructed or invented,[88] it is inherently dynamic. Unlike nationalisms that are based on membership in a certain ethnic group or that determine eligibility for citizenship by tracing blood lines, standards that are largely fixed, the cultural stories that countries tell about themselves are more malleable. There is a significant opportunity, therefore, to make diversity an essential part of a country's story, to supplement and constrain the master narrative and, indeed, to own up to frankly distasteful parts of that legacy. Introducing students to that legacy in a way that makes them identify with it as their own is hugely important. And one way to accomplish that is to have them see people like themselves in it.

Multicultural citizenship is a question of more or less, not either-or. Like most policies of moderation, it has to defend itself from critics on both sides. From one side, the criticism is that moderate multiculturalism doesn't go far enough, that it is really a policy of "assimilation by stealth"[89] or, worse, a policy that both conceals and legitimizes racism and colonialism.[90] From the other, the criticism is that it goes too far, that in their hurry to embrace multiculturalism Canadian schools (like other Canadian institutions) have abandoned our British or French cultural heritage and hollowed out what it means to be Canadian. That, I take it, is part of what is at stake in the recent niqab debate and former Prime Minister Harper's reference to "old stock" Canadians.

With the Clinton experience at my back, I clearly interpret things differently. The traditionalist's concerns seem vastly overstated. It is hardly as if the traditional Canadian story has been completely displaced. There is still a site in Toronto (Fort York) where students learn how British North Americans repulsed the American invaders in the War of 1812. English and French (in several different forms) remain the core languages in the city's schools. And all the major school holidays that are observed and celebrated (whether formally or informally) – Thanksgiving, Hallowe'en, Remembrance Day, and Christmas in the fall term, Easter and Victoria Day in the spring – have been around for a long time and remain solidly in place.

Yet by the same token, it is important to acknowledge and credit just how significantly and meaningfully the "cultural story" told in schools has changed. When I attended elementary school on the Prairies in the 1960s, nothing was said about the treatment of Chinese-Canadians or the wartime internment of Japanese-Canadians or the cultural genocide of Indigenous peoples. I had never heard of the Underground Railroad, the small number of Jewish students in my class disappeared for religious holidays that our teachers made no attempt to explain, and I had no clue what the few Catholics in my neighbourhood believed or what they found meaningful in their religious experience. It's not just that the schools I attended were less diverse than Toronto schools then or almost any urban school now, although that is certainly true. Rather, it is that the account of Canada's cultural heritage we received was much, much narrower than what is offered today. Comparing the heritage curriculum then and now is like night and day.

This change didn't occur by accident. It happened because teachers and principals and parents and school boards thought it was important to "imagine" the country's history differently, in a way that gave a far more prominent place to themes that, as the working groups pointed out, were largely invisible in the standard account. When faced with the choice, Clinton rejected integrated heritage language classes where other schools embraced them. But they did not reject the idea of multicultural citizenship. This remains *their* cultural legacy.

8

Conclusion:
Remembering the Answers

"Everything's different now." Whether referring to the school's physical structure, what was learned and how, or the rhythms of neighbourhood life, "change" was a theme to which the former students I interviewed returned again and again. Take, for starters, the social and economic structure of the neighbourhood around Clinton School. The sort of gentrification that began during Global Clinton has continued apace. There are still enough Italian and Portuguese "old timers" to make a difference, but the socio-economic centre of gravity within the community has clearly moved. Here's a telling example: 414 Markham Street is a three-storey, red-brick Victorian at the corner of Markham and Ulster, five minutes by foot from Clinton. In 1931, Might's City Directory listed the occupants as "Foreigners," subsequently identified as the Labour League Mutual Benefits Association, part of a cluster of left-wing Jewish organizations in the neighbourhood that embraced collectivist values, promoted Yiddish culture, and nurtured a spirit of internationalism.[1] From that it morphed into the Hebrew Free High School, and from that 414 Markham became a small synagogue. And now? The building has been converted into an upscale bed and breakfast called Posh Digs. That, in a nutshell, is how the community has changed.

Not surprisingly, Clinton School has changed in ways that mirror the demographic changes around it. In a 2012 parent census, more than half of Clinton families reported an annual household income of over $100,000 – twice the level of that in the Toronto District

School Board as a whole and significantly higher than the level in other schools in the area's "family" of schools.[2] As with wealth, so with diversity. To be sure, the school continues to embrace teaching about diversity and in other ways to provide a platform for diversity-enhancing activities. Its teachers are able to draw on extensive resources surrounding multicultural pedagogy, and the larger curricular framework developed by the provincial ministry of education gives diversity pride of place. But Clinton is no longer the "gateway" school for immigrant children that it used to be; nor is it as diverse as the rest of the Toronto public school system is now. A demographic snapshot or two makes the point: In the 1950s, close to 60 per cent of Clinton students were first-generation immigrants. In the 1980s, more than 30 per cent were first generation.[3] Now only about 10 per cent of Clinton students were born outside Canada – the lowest level since the 1940s and roughly half the level in the Toronto public school system currently.[4] Put the other way round, more than 70 per cent of current Clinton students have at least one parent who was born in Canada – twice the level of Toronto school parents as a whole.[5] Not since the 1940s has Clinton had such a large proportion of firmly rooted second- and third-generation Canadian families.

Yet despite these recent trends, the larger Clinton story speaks more powerfully than ever to the themes of citizenship and diversity because it reminds us just how easy it is to drift off course in the face of heavy weather. One marker of this drift is the striking resurgence of controversy over the recognition of minority (especially non-Christian) religious practices and institutions in Canada.[6] I referred briefly in the context of the Drew Regulations to the controversy over the Quebec Charter of Values, which, had it been implemented, would have banned public servants from wearing conspicuous religious symbols while discharging public functions. But Quebec is hardly alone in its willingness to rethink and restrict religious accommodation. One of the defining issues of the 2015 Canadian federal election concerned the Harper government's intervention to prevent a Muslim woman from wearing a niqab at the ceremony conferring her Canadian citizenship. Although the Harper government was defeated, it is striking that more than 70 per cent of Canadians agreed with its position that a woman should not be allowed to wear a niqab at a citizenship ceremony; almost two-thirds believe that a federal public servant should not be allowed to conceal her face when dealing with the public.[7]

So despite (or perhaps because of) the apparently relentless secularization of North American society, the treatment of religious minorities has returned as a significant political issue. From a liberal perspective, the niqab controversy may be fraught, but in principle it shouldn't be a hard case.[8] An individual's right to conscience and belief (Canada) and the free exercise of religion (United States) are not merely fundamental, they are the *first* rights listed in both the Canadian Charter and the U.S. Bill of Rights. To use the formulation made famous by John Stuart Mill, in a liberal democracy governments may only interfere with an individual's religious rights if their exercise inflicts some discernible harm on others. True, the definition of what constitutes "harm" is not entirely self-evident,[9] but in both Canada and the United States courts have developed techniques and tests to deal "reasonably" with the combination of ambiguity and passion that goes with the terrain. In the absence of some compelling justification (connected, for instance, to national security) and in the presence of some less intrusive alternative (like having a niqab-wearing woman expose her face privately to a female official to confirm her identity) there is no good reason to prohibit a Muslim woman from covering her face at a citizenship ceremony. Even if many non-Muslims and even Muslims find this practice offensive or degrading, at the end of the day it is her decision, not mine or yours. One may need to summon up every ounce of self-restraint to allow her to act as she will, but that is what the commitment to liberalism in general, and to freedom of religion in particular, requires. The central Canadian ideals are individualism and freedom of religion; they take precedence over other concerns.

This liberal argument is a powerful one, but, judging from the public opinion soundings noted above, most Canadians apparently don't see things this way. One reason may be that the Harper government chose to frame the niqab debate in terms of shared citizenship, not individual rights. This was a shrewd strategic move. Prime Minister Harper understood that his political appeal to citizenship would resonate with many who agreed that this sort of religious accommodation "is not the way we do things here."[10] As he put it to the House of Commons, "Why would Canadians, contrary to our own values, embrace a practice that is not transparent, that is not open and frankly is rooted in a culture that is anti-women ... That is unacceptable to Canadians."[11] That the issue arose in the context of a citizenship ceremony added a dollop of symbolism that was both unmistakable and powerful.

The history of Clinton School may be helpful in sorting out the relevant issues here. To be sure, the story I've told is about one school, in one city, at three different times in the past – limitations that, individually and collectively, suggest caution about generalizing from the experience. Yet in one respect the Clinton story is a particularly attractive basis for questioning and, perhaps, rejecting the ideas of citizenship articulated by Mr Harper (and apparently shared by many others). The reason is that, long before Mr Harper entered politics, Clinton also put citizenship first. The crucial difference is that, over the course of the twentieth century, what I have called the three Clintons – Jewish, European, and Global – arrived at judgments about citizenship that contrasted sharply with those of Mr Harper. Mr Harper's key questions were who belongs and under what terms. Clinton posed similar questions about citizenship, but it furnished answers that were more clearly consistent with the broad liberal tradition that Canada has always embraced – answers that have, over many decades, proven their practical worth for the quality of the lives lived in this community and beyond. My ambition in writing this book has been to remember and to restore these answers.

How do the three Clinton stories bear on our current citizenship dilemmas? Let me draw out their logics in turn. The story of Jewish Clinton and its reaction to the Drew Regulations is the most distant historically, but its subject is probably the closest to our current situation. Then as now, religious identification was clearly central to the story. Then as now, the religious minority was treated by many with suspicion if not outright hostility. And then as in the current debate, citizenship was defined in a way that made it impossible, by definition, for religious minorities – Jews then, devout Muslims now – to be considered full and equal citizens. Governments may encourage immigration (especially for economic reasons) and may confer civic legal status, but full and equal citizenship – a real sense of belonging, of having public standing, of being a somebody – isn't possible as long as citizenship is defined by standards that many religious minorities can't possibly meet without betraying their own religious identity. The Drew Regulations underscored the fact that Jews didn't fit squarely into Canadian society. For "citizens minus," like Jews under Drew, the civic calculus will always be governed by a subtraction sign.

The alternative, as Rabbi Feinberg articulated it and Clinton School practised it, is to convert the civic calculus from subtraction to addition by finding shared traits and cultivating practices that can build a bridge to full citizenship without erasing religious differences. In the case of Jewish Clinton, the school was galvanized by the shared desire for social mobility (tied to superior academic achievement). Quietly yet forcefully, what I've called the Axis of Good at Clinton resisted the provincial government's impulse to accentuate difference. It showed, instead, what could happen when Jewish parents and Anglo-Protestant teachers worked together in ways that acknowledged, then bridged, those differences. A similar strategy is needed in the current climate. Building, as Jewish Clinton did, on the shared insight that schools are crucial in helping immigrant communities "get ahead" might not be such a bad place to start.

The Harper government did not restrict its concern, however, to religious minorities or to practices that follow directly from religious belief. Shortly before the election was called in July 2015, Parliament passed the Zero Tolerance for Barbaric Cultural Practices Act,[12] and during the election campaign itself the government announced its intention to create a "tip line" that would enable "citizens and victims" to report "barbaric cultural practices" such as forced marriage, female genital mutilation, and polygamy to the authorities.[13] These legislative and administrative moves broadened considerably the scope of the government's interest. It is important to understand that the government's goal in enacting the legislation and creating the snitch line was not simply to proscribe these practices. That could have been accomplished – or already had been accomplished – by making them criminal acts or otherwise prohibiting them. The government's goal, rather, was to link these "barbaric cultural practices" to an understanding of citizenship. It is not just that the people who engage in these practices were deemed bad, it is that they were deemed un-Canadian; by rooting them out the government was acting "to ensure the integrity of our immigration and citizenship programs."[14]

But this is an odd way to think about citizenship, about what it means to belong, because it implies that citizenship is really defined by what it is not (viz. barbaric) and by the threat of contamination by outsiders. Such a conception pushes citizenship back on its heels. In this regard, too, Clinton's approach provides an emphatic counterpoint, for where the Harper government did its best to fortify the country's cultural borders, Clinton sought to relax them. The approach of European Clinton and the Toronto Board of Education to incorporating a large number of first- and early second-generation immigrant students speaks eloquently in this context. The TBE's strategy – developed, as we saw in chapter 5, in the mid-1960s – turned on the distinction between assimilation and integration, on the idea that cultural contact was a "two-way street," and on the simple, but powerful, observation that Toronto's students might well learn valuable things from their newly arrived classmates. In embracing diversity, schools like Clinton put hope before fear.

In truth, siding with integration over assimilation was something of a gamble. Who really knew whether integration would provide a smoother path to citizenship? Who could be sure that the invitation to integrate wouldn't lead to cultural ghettoization and fragmentation? Who really could predict whether multiculturalism would become so superficial and banal that the very "multi cultures" themselves would abandon it? Yet the empirical evidence strongly suggests that the gamble paid off. For the most part integration has made the path to Canadian citizenship easier.[15] For the most part multicultural citizenship has led neither to acute fragmentation nor to the creation of parallel societies.[16] And for the most part multiculturalism remains one of the self-evident truths of Canadian political discourse – unlike in some other countries.

What accounts for this (relative) success? There is no single answer – there never is – and I don't claim to have found the "right" causal explanation. What I can say is that, over time, schools like Clinton worked out what they needed to do to cultivate the sort of multicultural citizenship that their commitment to integration through diversity implied. In chapter 5, I suggested that, as the commitment to multicultural citizenship grew, such schools developed three broad strategies: border-crossing, border-guarding, and border-choosing. It is not that Clinton produced the only or the authoritative recipe for multicultural citizenship. Some initiatives worked there better than others, and some things that worked at Clinton might not have worked as well at other schools. But what stands out – and what I think does have more general applicability – is that Clinton deployed all three types of bordering – crossing, guarding, and choosing – in ways that created a dynamic combination. It is the mix, I believe, that is key. Having made a commitment to integration over assimilation, the school understood that it had to encourage its students to cross cultural borders – in both directions and in various ways. Clinton also understood, however, that it had a responsibility to use its authority to guard borders by protecting and empowering distinct cultural communities. It understood, in other words, the inner logic of multicultural citizenship because it realized that "without the existence of cultural borders, there are no borderlands for the border crossers to occupy."[17] Yet without permission for individuals to cross, blur, and even customize these cultural boundaries to some extent, the multicultural project would run the risk of seizing up, frozen in the place that the state decreed; that is why border-choosing is important as well. Precisely how these three components are configured will vary from school to school, conflict to conflict, time to time. But the take-away from the Clinton story is that any credible approach to multicultural citizenship requires that all three elements be present in ways that both complement and counterbalance each other. Multicultural citizenship is not a single, monolithic set of policies; nor is it an à la carte menu from which you can pick and choose as you like. It is a package deal.

Yet even if I've got the history right, some might argue that the past is no guide to our current situation because multicultural policies simply aren't equipped to respond effectively to the current challenges posed by increased global migration. This argument comes in two rather different forms. The first, more common in Europe, is that the current waves of tension, anti-immigrant sentiment, and religious extremism demonstrate that multicultural policies have "completely failed."[18] As one Canadian journalist has put it with characteristic bluntness, the "belief that the modern progressive state can socially engineer its way to harmony ... is a dangerous delusion."[19] The coincidence of the arrival of large numbers of Syrian refugees together with the escalation of jihadist violence will surely test the integrative capacities of many European countries. It remains far from clear how all this will play out.

The second argument, more common in North America, is different. It is that in some ways multiculturalism has been *too* successful – that it has become one of those sacrosanct, but empty, bromides that has little substance yet that no one dares question. The problem, by this argument, is that the multicultural emperor has no clothes. Either multiculturalism is really just a way of disguising the Anglo-conformism that has always constituted Canadian society, or its superficiality makes it dangerous. If the premise underlying official multiculturalism in Canada is that the country has "no official culture," then we have made ourselves vulnerable to those who believe strongly in the truth of their culturally illiberal and religiously orthodox convictions.[20] There is no "there" there, which may explain why, in a better-late-than-never response, the Harper government thought it important to patrol cultural boundaries more vigilantly, polish up our best Anglo-Canadian symbols, and put them back on display.

There is, in fact, an element of truth to these criticisms. The conventional wisdom is that the government of Pierre Trudeau seized on the strategic usefulness of multiculturalism as a way of negotiating the treacherous politics of Canada-Quebec relations. By this reading, "the formula that gradually emerged – multiculturalism within a bilingual framework – was essentially a bargain to ensure white ethnic support for the more urgent task of accommodating Quebec."[21] This stratagem meant downplaying, even denying, that there was any "official culture" in Canada because that would have threatened support for this national unity strategy outside of Quebec. But the consequence, whether intended or not, was to imply that Canada, at its core, doesn't really stand for much of anything at all. The best that could be said, in the searing metaphor of novelist Yann Martel, was that Canada was "the greatest hotel on earth."[22]

Seeing multiculturalism through the eyes of a school's history is a useful corrective to this interpretation. The fact of the matter is that Clinton Street School (especially in its incarnation as Global Clinton) didn't look at the issue of cultural diversity in terms of national unity. It didn't have to, and besides, it had more pressing issues to address – like dealing with a kaleidoscopic variety of daily challenges that flowed from the challenge of integrating immigrant students as smoothly as possible into Canadian life. Where the mega-constitutional politics of the time were played out against the backdrop of Canada-Quebec relations, the micro-politics of Clinton were not so constrained, and this freed the school in important ways to build multicultural citizenship from the ground up rather than apply it as a policy directive from the top down – to find its distinctive path in a way that defined integrated citizenship as a matter of "more or less" not "either-or." For a school like Clinton, the goal was not to abandon the notion of an "official culture." Rather, the challenge was to pay respect to the country's political and cultural legacy while also adapting that culture to the needs and aspirations of its new citizens.[23] Finding the right balance at Clinton between acculturation and adaptation was all part of the daily routine. It was also, as it turns out, the process through which it constructed multicultural citizenship.

Ernest Renan once described the "spirit" of the modern nation as consisting of two principles: "One lies in the past, the other in the present. One is the possession in common of a rich legacy of memories, the other is present-day consent, the desire to live together, the will to perpetuate the value of the heritage that one has received in an undivided form."[24] Renan's observation speaks to what Clinton did and what public schools continue to do; for, like the nations Renan described, schools are sites of "a daily plebiscite" – or perhaps better, a daily conversation – about civic identity. If nothing else, I hope this book has contributed to this conversation between past and present by recovering one school's legacy in a way that will help it (and others) affirm the present and navigate the future.

Notes

1. Introduction

1 C.C. Goldring, "Are We Hitting the Target in Our Educational Effort?" Address to the Ontario Urban and Rural School Trustees' Association, 21 June 1955, 12. Toronto District School Board Archives, Goldring Papers.
2 Ibid., 1.
3 Ibid., 7.
4 Ibid., 11.
5 Noel Pollard, "Message from the Principal," *Clinton Chronicle*, April 1960, 3 (emphasis added). Clinton Street Public School Archives, Folder Q.
6 The scholarly literature on the connection between schooling and citizenship in Canada is extensive. My goal in these notes is not to be comprehensive but to be helpful. To that extent I will use the notes to provide readers who want to explore the subject further with a few sources that, in my view, are especially good places to start. In that spirit, allow me to suggest several quite different works that deal directly with education and citizenship: Eamonn Callan, *Creating Citizens: Political Education and Liberal Democracy* (Oxford: Clarendon Press, 1997); Lorna McLean, "'There is no magic whereby such qualities will be acquired at the voting age': Teachers, Curriculum, Pedagogy and Citizenship," *Historical Studies in Education* (Fall 2010): 39–57; Ken Osborne, "Public Schooling and Citizenship Education in Canada," *Canadian Ethnic Studies*, 32, 1, (2000): 8–37; and Amy Von Heyking, *Creating Citizens: History and Identity in Alberta's Schools, 1905–1980* (Calgary: University of Calgary Press, 2006).

7   Take, for instance, the current mission statement of the Toronto District School Board: "To enable all students to reach high levels of achievement and to acquire the knowledge, skills, and values they need to become responsible members of a democratic society."
    See www.tdsb.on.ca, accessed 5 June 2016.
8   See J.M.S. Careless, *Toronto to 1918: An Illustrated History* (Toronto: Lorimer, 1984), Table V, 201.
9   See Mark Fram, "19th-century Suburbia, 21st-century Cool (or How to Build a City)," in Dennis De Klerck and Corrado Paina, eds, *College Street – Little Italy: Toronto's Renaissance Strip* (Toronto: Mansfield, 2006), 43–61.
10 *Clinton Public School, 1888-1988,* Clinton Street Public School Archives, 2.
11 Information about when houses were built, who owned them, and what occupants did for a living was compiled from *Might's Toronto City Directory*, various years.
12 Clinton Street was apparently named after Sir Henry Clinton (1811–1864) who served as the secretary of state for the colonies between 1859 and 1864 under the administration of Lord Palmerston. He seems to have visited Canada only once (in 1860), and because he left the post in April of 1864, his successor, Edward Cardwell, played a much larger role in the run-up to Canadian Confederation, the serious consideration of which only began in September 1864 in Charlottetown.
13 *Clinton School, 1888–1988,* 7.
14 Stratton Holland, "They Study for the Space Age – in an 1863 School," *Toronto Star*, 1 July1967.
15 Careless, *Toronto to 1918*, Table VI, 201.
16 This description is based on the Clinton School data set that I have compiled on the basis of a random sample of registration cards. The data set is discussed in greater detail later in this chapter.
17 On Empire Day and some of the other school holidays, see Matthew Hayday and Raymond B. Blake, eds., *Celebrating Canada, Volume I: National Holidays, Annual Celebrations and the Evolving Contours of Canadian Identities* (Toronto: University of Toronto Press, 2016).
18 The phrase was (and is) often capitalized, a usage that is followed in this book.
19 Frederick Crowe, *Christ and History: The Christology of Bernard Lonergan from 1935 to 1982* (Toronto: University of Toronto Press, 2015), 12.
20 Richard Alba and Mary C. Waters, "Dimensions of Second-Generation Incorporation," in Richard Alba and Mary C. Waters, eds., *The Next Generation: Immigrant Youth in a Comparative Perspective* (New York: New York University Press, 2011), 1.
21 United Nations, Department of Economic and Social Affairs, "International Migration Report, 2015," accessed at www.un.org/en/

development/desa/population/publications/migration/index.shtml.
For an insightful analysis of the ways in which this migration is changing
cities, see Doug Saunders, *Arrival City* (Toronto: Knopf, 2010).

22 Alba and Waters, *Next Generation*, 1.

23 See Marc Morjé Howard, *The Politics of Citizenship in Europe* (Cambridge: Cambridge University Press, 2009), especially chapter 1.

24 See also Triadafilos Triadafilopoulos, *Becoming Multicultural: Immigration and the Politics of Membership in Canada and Germany* (Vancouver: University of British Columbia Press, 2012), and Ruud Koopmans, Paul Statham, Marco Giugni, and Florence Passy, eds., *Contested Citizenship: Immigration and Cultural Diversity in Europe* (Minneapolis: University of Minnesota Press, 2005).

25 Leading North American scholars of this sociological approach include, among others, Richard Alba, Jeffrey Reitz, Mary Waters, and, from an earlier generation, Nathan Glazer and Raymond Breton. For the most recent, comprehensive analysis of integration in Europe and North America, see Richard Alba and Nancy Foner, *Strangers No More: Immigration and the Challenges of Integration in North America and Western Europe* (Princeton: Princeton University Press, 2015).

26 See, for instance, Antoine Bilodeau, ed., *Just Ordinary Citizens? Towards a Comparative Portrait of the Political Immigrant* (Toronto: University of Toronto Press, 2016).

27 Christopher Cochrane, "The Effects of Islam, Religiosity, and Socialization on Muslim-Canadian Opinions about Same-Sex Marriage," *Comparative Migration Studies*, 1, 1 (2013): 147–78.

28 Irene Bloemraad, *Becoming a Citizen: Incorporating Immigrants and Refugees in the United States and Canada* (Berkeley: University of California Press, 2006).

29 Ibid., 26–30.

30 Ibid., 9.

31 Ibid., 215–52.

32 See ibid., 29–30, figure 2 and figure 3.

33 See Leslie Pal, *Interests of State: The Politics of Language, Multiculturalism and Feminism in Canada* (Montreal: McGill-Queen's University Press, 1993).

34 Desmond King et al., *Democratization in America: A Comparative-Historical Analysis* (Baltimore, MD: Johns Hopkins University Press, 2009), 5.

35 *Clinton Public School, 1888–1988*, Clinton School Archives. Other anniversary-inspired publications from neighbouring schools include Central Tech Alumni Association, *CTS 1915–2015: 100 Years of Excellence*; *Orde Street Junior Public School Centenary Yearbook, 1915–2015*; and Harbord Alumni Association, *The Happy Ghosts of Harbord, 1892–1992*.

36 Gerald Grant, *The World We Created at Hamilton High* (Cambridge, MA: Harvard University Press, 1988); David F. Labaree, *The Making of an*

American High School: The Credentials Market and the Central High School of Philadelphia, 1838–1939 (New Haven: Yale University Press, 1988); Colleen Gray, *No Ordinary School: The Study, 1915–2015*, published for The Study by McGill-Queen's University Press (Montreal, 2015). The creation of charter schools in the United States has also produced a steady stream of institutional biographies, among them Seymour Fliegel, *Miracle in East Harlem: The Fight for Choice in Public Education* (New York: Crown, 1993), and Mary C. Bounds and Wyatt Tee Walker, *A Light Shines on Harlem: New York's First Charter School and the Movement It Led* (Chicago: Chicago Review Press, 2014).

37 The data set was constructed using a method of systematic random sampling. We made the decision early on to use families as a unit of analysis so that we could track family dynamics over the course of their Clinton careers. Accordingly, 1,709 families were sampled, yielding 3,711 unique individuals. The cards were sampled evenly across the entire range of cards, so that there was no oversampling. The data were stored in panel format, listing each grade and data for each student. This produced a total of approximately15,000 observations.

38 A. Alan Borovoy, *At the Barricades: A Memoir* (Toronto: Irwin Law, 2013).

39 I carried out most of the seventy-five interviews myself, though invaluable help was provided by a group of undergraduate students who undertook approximately a dozen of them on my behalf. Most interviewees were recruited through a modified snowball method (one graduate suggested another, and so on), but a significant number came unsolicited – either by providing contact information on the Alumni section of the Clinton Public School website or (as with one graduate whom I met by chance at a Toronto Raptors basketball game) by volunteering in unanticipated ways.

An obvious challenge facing anyone undertaking interviews of this sort arises from the fallibility of the subject's memory and the tendency for memories to be structured, reordered, and edited by subsequent events. Here I follow Neil Sutherland (*Growing Up: Childhood in English Canada from the Great War to the Age of Television* [Toronto: University of Toronto Press, 1997], at 7) in thinking that interviews are nevertheless useful inasmuch as they bring to light recurring patterns or "scripts"; the more often these scripts appear, the more reliable the recollection.

All of the interviews were conducted in a manner that complied with the ethics protocol developed at, and approved by, the University of Toronto. Most of the interviews have been transcribed. The Toronto District School Board also provided ethics clearance for the project.

40 The scholarly literature on the subject of citizenship and diversity in Canada is bountiful. The most important single voice is almost certainly

that of Will Kymlicka, who has produced a steady stream of books and articles on the subject. See, for instance, *Multicultural Citizenship* (Oxford: Clarendon Press, 1995) and *Multicultural Odysseys: Navigating the New International Politics of Diversity* (Oxford: Oxford University Press, 2007). Other important figures include Charles Taylor and his colleague Gérard Bouchard, who have developed, in the Quebec context, the idea of "interculturalism" as opposed to "multiculturalism." See Gérard Bouchard, *Interculturalism: A View from Quebec* (Toronto: University of Toronto Press, 2015), and Charles Taylor, "Interculturalism or Multiculturalism?" *Philosophy and Social Criticism* 38, 4–5 (May/June 2012): 413–23.

Kymlicka, in particular, has been sensitive to the need to track how theoretical commitments (like the commitment to multiculturalism) actually play out in practice as a function of policy. He and Keith Banting have produced remarkable work that speaks to the "real world" of multiculturalism, both in Canada and farther afield. See Keith Banting and Will Kymlicka, eds., *Multiculturalism and the Welfare State: Recognition and Redistribution in Contemporary Democracies* (Oxford: Oxford University Press, 2006). Banting provides an updated version of the central chapter in that volume in "Canada as Counternarrative: Multiculturalism, Recognition, and Redistribution," in Linda A. White, Richard Simeon, Robert Vipond, and Jennifer Wallner, eds., *The Comparative Turn in Canadian Political Science* (Vancouver: University of British Columbia Press, 2008), 59–76. In the field of education, I would be remiss if I did not mention the magisterial work of Ronald Manzer, who devoted a significant part of his scholarly career to understanding the democratic dynamics of education policy in Canada and other Anglo-American democracies. See Ronald Manzer, *Canadian Public Schools and Political Ideas: Canadian Education Policy in Historical Perspective* (Toronto: University of Toronto Press, 1994) and Ronald Manzer, *Educational Regimes and Anglo-American Democracy* (Toronto: University of Toronto Press, 2003).

2. Jewish Clinton, 1920–1952

1 James Lemon, *Toronto since 1918: An Illustrated History* (Toronto: Lorimer, 1985), 50.
2 *Toronto Star Weekly*, 8 December 1917.
3 Morley Safer, "Clinton Street School Remembered," 11 November 2012, Clinton Street Public School Archives.
4 Ontario, Department of Education, *Programme of Studies for Grades I to VI of the Public and Separate Schools* (Toronto: Department of Education, 1940), 5.

5 J.M.S. Careless, *Toronto to 1918: An Illustrated History* (Toronto: Lorimer, 1984), Table VIII, 202. See also Louis Rosenberg, *Canada's Jews: A Social and Economic Study of Jews in Canada in the 1930s*, ed. Morton Weinfeld (Montreal: McGill-Queen's University Press, 1993), 33.

6 Gerald Tulchinsky, *Canada's Jews: A People's Journey* (Toronto: University of Toronto Press, 2008), 144–5.

7 See Careless, *Toronto to 1918*, Table VIII, 202.

8 See Lemon, *Toronto since 1918*, Table VIII, 196.

9 For helpful but quite different accounts of The Ward, see John Lorinc, Michael McClelland, Ellen Scheinberg, and Tatum Taylor, eds., *The Ward: The Life and Loss of Toronto's Immigrant Neighbourhood* (Toronto: Coach House Books, 2015); Stephen A. Speisman, *The Jews of Toronto: A History to 1937* (Toronto: McClelland and Stewart, 1979), 81–95; and Ruth Frager, *Sweatshop Strife: Class, Ethnicity, and Gender in the Jewish Labour Movement of Toronto, 1900–1939* (Toronto: University of Toronto Press, 1992).

10 Daniel Hiebert, "The Geography of Jewish Immigrants and the Garment Industry in Toronto, 1901–1931: A Study of Ethnic and Class Relations" (PhD diss., University of Toronto, 1987), 277.

11 Ibid., 299. For the purposes of his study, Hiebert analysed Jewish residential patterns in nine different areas of Toronto's west end. Area 9, bounded by Bathurst on the east, Dovercourt on the west, College on the south and Bloor on the north corresponds almost perfectly to the Clinton catchment area. The only difference is that the Clinton boundary did not extend as far west as Dovercourt. This makes little difference for the analysis, however, since most of the Jewish residents in Area 9 lived east of Dovercourt.

12 Ibid., 289.

13 According to Hiebert (299), 53 per cent of residents in the Clinton area were connected to the garment industry in one way or another. At the Clinton School itself, the proportion of students who had parents in the garment industry seems to have been somewhat smaller. According to the occupational information provided by the registration cards, approximately one-quarter of Clinton students in the 1930s and 1940s had a parent working in the garment industry.

14 See Hiebert, especially chapters 7 and 8. See also Gerald Tulchinsky, *Joe Salsberg: A Life of Commitment* (Toronto: University of Toronto Press, 2013); and Frager, *Sweatshop Strife*.

15 Gerald Tulchinsky, "The Jewish Experience," in Roger Hall, William Westfall, and Laurel Sefton MacDowell, eds., *Patterns of the Past* (Toronto: Dundurn, 1988), 314.

16 Hiebert, 303. Hiebert (299) also notes that the Clinton catchment (Area 9 in his study) "was obviously a popular destination for upwardly mobile

Jewish families" as "over one-third of all Jewish factory owners lived in this area."

17 Ibid., 272–4.

18 Ibid., Table 8.18 (upper), 332.

19 Ibid., Table 8.18 (lower), 332. Not only did the Clinton area have a relatively high level of home ownership, the average value of homes was somewhat higher than in the rest of Jewish Toronto. According to Hiebert's figures, the average property value across Jewish Toronto was $3,217 in 1931. In the Clinton area, it was $4,495. In the course of my interviews, graduates would sometimes refer to the value of their childhood homes and to the relative "poshness" of various streets in the neighbourhood. This anecdotal evidence aligns well with Hiebert's analysis.

20 Ibid., Table 8.11, 328.

21 See Roberto Perin, *The Many Rooms of This House: Diversity in Toronto's Places of Worship since 1840* (Toronto: University of Toronto Press, forthcoming), especially chapter 4 for a detailed discussion of synagogues in the neighbourhood.

22 On Salsberg the best source is Gerald Tulchinsky's *Joe Salsberg*.

23 In the 1945 election, MacLeod won with 33.6 per cent of the vote, followed by Frank Williams (Conservative), who polled 29.6; Albert Russell (CCF), who received 20.5 per cent of the vote; and Arthur Farmer (Liberal), who took 16.3 per cent of the vote. Because polling stations were usually situated in private homes, it is possible to analyse the geographical distribution of the vote. Where MacLeod received just over a third of the total vote in the constituency as a whole, in the polling stations located in the Clinton catchment, he won 51.5 per cent of the vote – almost twenty points higher. Ontario, Lesiglative Assembly, Sessional Papers, vol. LXXVIII, Part IV, 319–22.

24 Salsberg won the 1945 election (against three opponents) with 52 per cent of the vote. He won Markham Street with a remarkable 63 per cent. Ontario, Legislative Assembly, Sessional Papers, vol. LXXVIII, Part IV, 353–6.

25 Cited in Frank N. Clarke, "'Keep Communism Out of our Schools': Cold War Anti-Communism at the Toronto Board of Education, 1948–51," *Labour/Le Travail* 49 (Spring 2002): 99.

26 Jack Quarter, interview by author. Toronto, 14 February 2014.

27 Clarke, "Keep Communism Out," 93–119.

28 Peter Campbell, *Rose Henderson: A Woman for the People* (Montreal: McGill-Queen's University Press, 2010), especially chapters 8 and 9.

29 "Mistake to Change Name of School," *Toronto Telegram*, 6 April 1937. See also Campbell, *Rose Henderson*, 274. The choice of Clinton presumably had

something to do with the fact that Henderson lived on Montrose Avenue, which was in the Clinton school catchment.

30 Safer, "Clinton Street School Remembered."

31 Rosenberg, *Canada's Jews*, 254–5. If one includes those Jews born in Britain, the figure rises to 97 per cent.

32 Howard Moscoe, Transcript of the Human Book Event, Clinton Street Public School, October 2012.

33 Hughes introduced kindergartens into the school system in 1883, which made Toronto the second city in North America after St Louis to have public school kindergartens.

34 See R.D. Gidney, *From Hope to Harris: The Reshaping of Ontario's Schools* (Toronto: University of Toronto Press, 1999), 14 and 289 (Figure I).

35 On the strategy of differentiation in American schools at the time, see the classic account in David Tyack, *The One Best System: A History of American Urban Education* (Cambridge MA: Harvard University Press, 1974), 177–98.

36 For a period during the First World War, Clinton took gender separation one step further and created all-boys' and all-girls' classes. A description and analysis of this (apparently short-lived) practice became the focus of W.A. Craik's article on Clinton. See *Toronto Star Weekly*, 8 December 1917.

37 *Clinton Street Public School, 1888–1988*, 22.

38 See Jason Ellis, "'Inequalities of Children in Original Endowment': How Intelligence Testing Transformed Early Special Education in a North American City School System," *Higher Education Quarterly* 53, 4 (November 2013): 401–29.

39 Cited in ibid., 411.

40 P.F. Munro, *An Experimental Investigation of the Mentality of the Jew in Ryerson Public School Toronto* (Toronto: University of Toronto Press, 1926), 6.

41 Cited in Ellis, "Inequalities," 413.

42 This is the basic argument of Jason Ellis in "'Backward and Brilliant Children': A Social and Policy History of Disability, Childhood, and Education in Toronto's Special Education Classes, 1910–1945" (PhD diss., York University, 2011).

43 See Ellis, "Inequalities," 414–23.

44 Ellis, "Backward and Brilliant Children," 105.

45 Figures were compiled by the author from annual reports, published by the Toronto Board of Education, which provide a school-by-school audit of teachers, their educational qualifications, years employed by the board, previous experience, salary, and the class to which they are assigned. A complete set of these annual lists is available in the Clinton Street School Archives.

46 The best account of Clinton's deaf education program and how it fitted into the national and international context is Jason A. Ellis, "'All

Methods – and Wedded to None': The Deaf Education Methods Debate and Progressive Educational Reform in Toronto, Canada, 1922–1945," *Paedagogica Historica: International Journal of the History of Education* 2013, 1–19.

47 Ibid., 10. The director of education who made the comment is C.C. Goldring, cited in chapter 1. As Ellis points out, the irony here is that Goldring made this progressive pitch "in a radio address, a medium inaccessible to deaf people."

48 Ibid., 13.

49 Ibid.

50 One graduate recalled that some of the deaf students played on an integrated volleyball team. Another recalled school-wide concerts at which the deaf students performed.

51 See, for instance, Doreen Kronick, *They Too Can Succeed: A Practical Guide for Parents of Learning Disabled Children* (San Rafael, CA: Therapy Publications, 1989); Doreen Kronick, *New Approaches to Learning Disabilities: Cognitive, Metacognitive, and Holistic* (Philadelphia: Grome and Stratton, 1988); and Doreen Kronick, ed., *Learning Disabilities: Its Implications to a Responsible Society* (Chicago: Developmental Learning Materials, 1969).

52 Doreen Kronick, interview by author, Toronto, 22 July 2013.

53 After making a presentation on this part of Clinton's history, a pediatrician and Clinton parent who specializes in treating students with an array of learning disabilities told me that the referrals he receives frequently employ the same cluster of words – annoying, nuisance, disruptive – to describe the students he has been asked to assess and treat. Personal communication, Dr Mark Feldman.

54 A. Alan Borovoy, *At the Barricades: A Memoir* (Toronto: Irwin Law, 2013), 7–8.

55 Neil Sutherland, *Growing Up: Childhood in English Canada from the Great War to the Age of Television* (Toronto: University of Toronto Press, 1997), 192.

56 Ibid.

57 R.D. Gidney and W.P.J. Millar, *How Schools Worked: Public Education in English Canada, 1900–1940* (Montreal: McGill-Queen's University Press), 209.

58 Toronto Board of Education, *Annual Report 1932*, 102 (Dr P.F. Munro, Inspector; italics in original).

59 Judith N. Shklar, "A Life of Learning," in Bernard Yack, ed., *Liberalism without Illusions: Essays on the Liberal Theory and Political Vision of Judith Shklar* (Chicago: University of Chicago Press, 1996), 264–5.

60 *Clinton Courier*, 1942. Clinton Street Public School Archives.

61 Sutherland, *Growing Up*, 208.

62 Safer, "Clinton Street School Remembered."

63 Paul Axelrod, "No Longer a 'Last Resort': The End of Corporal Punishment in the Schools of Toronto," *Canadian Historical Review* 91, 2 (June 2010): 261–85. See also Mona Gleason, "Disciplining the Student Body: Schooling and the Construction of Canadian Children's Bodies, 1930–1960," *History of Education Quarterly* 41, 2 (Summer 2001): 189–215.

64 The data discussed here come from hardcover registers, dating from 1932 to 1970, that provide a record of the administration of corporal punishment at the school. The information includes the student's name, the date, the infraction for which the student was punished, the number of "slaps" administered, the student's teacher, and the person administering the punishment (usually the principal or vice-principal). These registers are held in the Clinton Street School archives.

65 This does not mean that 236 separate students were strapped. Some students were recidivists who were "slapped" on more than one occasion.

66 The reduction in the number of strappings in the mid-1930s may well reflect the fact that, in 1934, C.C. Goldring, the director of education, felt "compelled … to send out a circular suggesting more caution in punishing pupils" when it was revealed that, in 1933, a total of 11,000 strappings had occurred in Toronto schools. Campbell, *Rose Henderson*, 192. Even then, as Campbell goes on to point out, there were still 2,465 strappings between March and June of 1934 system wide.

67 Axelrod, "No Longer a 'Last Resort,'" 266.

68 The offences listed in the paragraphs below all come from the corporal punishment registers for the years 1932–49.

69 Sutherland, *Growing Up*, 192.

70 *Clinton, 1888–1988*, 16.

71 Ibid., 20.

72 One example is Alan Borovoy, who reconnected with his grade 3 teacher, Miss Nicoll, as an adult and made a point of calling her every year on her birthday until her death. Human Book Event, October 2012, Clinton Street Public School.

73 *Clinton, 1888–1988*, 16.

74 Safer, "Clinton Street School Remembered."

75 Gidney and Millar, *How Schools Worked*, 352.

76 In their analysis of teaching experience across English Canada in the first decades of the twentieth century, Gidney and Millar note that "between 1929–30 and 1936–37 alone, for example, average experience in Ontario increased by about two full years, from 9.5 to 11.6 years" (Gidney and Millar, *How Schools Worked*, 136). The average teaching experience at Clinton was higher at both ends of the period sampled by Gidney and Millar. In 1929–30, teachers at Clinton had, on average, 14.3 years

of experience. In 1936–37, it was slightly less – 13 years – though still above the Ontario average. As Gidney and Millar go on to point out, rural teachers tended to have less experience than urban teachers, so the Ontario average is not particularly meaningful. As they say, "during the 1920s in Ontario the average experience of rural teachers was 4 or 5 years; in urban communities it was more like 12 or 13" (Gidney and Millar, 137). This would suggest that the experience of Clinton's teaching staff was not so different from other staffs in city schools. Clinton data compiled by author.

77 Safer, "Clinton Street School Remembered."

78 Paul Axelrod, "Beyond the Progressive Education Debate: A Profile of Toronto Schooling in the 1950s," *Historical Studies in Education* 17, 2 (October 2005): 241.

79 *Toronto Star Weekly*, 23 December 1916.

80 See Gidney, *From Hope to Harris*, 14 and 289 (Figure I).

81 *Clinton Courier*, 1942.

82 The evidence for exceptionally high academic achievement at Clinton is indisputable. In addition to everything else, the registration cards record the "Destination" of all students at Clinton, including those who transferred to another school or moved out of the city and those who graduated. Using the subset of those students who attended grade 8 at Clinton in the 1940s, one can compare the proportion of Clinton students who continued to secondary school (or at least qualified for more schooling) with the Ontario student population as a whole. As I noted in the text, even using the most generous measure, the proportion of Ontario students who continued schooling past grade 8 at the end of the 1940s was somewhere between 61 and 67 per cent. The contrast with Clinton is striking. At Clinton, 84 per cent of students who attended grade 8 pursued formal education after they left Clinton – about 20 points above the Ontario average. Moreover, most Clinton graduates (70 per cent) went into the academic stream (which for students in the neighbourhood meant Harbord Collegiate). Seventeen per cent entered the "commercial" stream (usually Central Commerce), and 13 per cent went to technical school (usually Central Technical School). Clinton figures calculated by the author from the Clinton data set.

83 See note 2 above.

3. At Clinton You're a Somebody

1 Paul Axelrod, "Beyond the Progressive Education Debate: A Profile of Toronto Schooling in the 1950s," *Historical Studies in Education* 17, 2 (2005): 241.

2 Ontario, Department of Education, *Programme of Studies for Grades 1 to 6 of the Public and Separate Schools* (Toronto: Department of Education, 1940), 7.

3 Jan Morris, *Farewell the Trumpets: An Imperial Retreat* (Harmondsworth, Middlesex: Penguin, 1978), 322.

4 Ibid., 323–4. See also William J. Smyth, *Toronto, the Belfast of Canada: The Orange Order and the Shaping of Municipal Culture* (Toronto: University of Toronto Press, 2015).

5 *Toronto Telegram*, 22 September 1924. Cited in Stephen A. Speisman, *The Jews of Toronto: A History to 1937* (Toronto: McClelland and Stewart, 1979), 321.

6 Irving Abella and Harold Troper, *None Is Too Many: Canada and the Jews of Europe, 1933–1948* (Toronto: University of Toronto Press, 2012).

7 See Gerald Tulchinsky, *Branching Out: The Transformation of the Canadian Jewish Community* (Toronto: Stoddart, 1998), chapter 7; Irving Abella, "Anti-Semitism in Canada in the Interwar Years," in Moses Rischin, ed., *The Jews of North America* (Detroit: Wayne State University Press, 1987), 235–46; and Speisman, *The Jews of Toronto*, 318–23. One particularly important form of explicit discrimination was the use of "restrictive covenants" – contracts that include conditions or restrictions, for instance, on the sale of property – to prevent Jews from buying property in selected neighbourhoods. The attempt to abolish restrictive covenants was one of the important projects undertaken by the Canadian Jewish Congress in the 1940s and 1950s. The memory of such restrictive covenants is said to have made Jewish landlords, for instance in the Kensington Market area, to be more open to renting property to Afro-Caribbean immigrants. One product of this landlord-tenant relationship was something called the Spee and Dee (Spadina and Dundas) society, which, for many years, brought these two communities together for an annual reunion in Kensington Market.

8 Tulchinsky, *Branching Out*, 198. See also Cyril Levitt and William Shaffir, *The Riot at Christie Pits* (Toronto: Lester and Orpen Dennys, 1987). As both Tulchinsky and Levitt note, one of the striking features of the Christie Pits Riot is that both Italian and Ukrainian youth came to the aid of the Jewish fighters. For an evocative portrait of Toronto's Jewish community during the period and its political, cultural, and social transformation over the middle decades of the twentieth century, see Rick Salutin, "The Conversion of the Jews," in his book of essays entitled *Marginal Notes* (Toronto: Lester and Orpen Dennys, 1984), 218–45.

9 See, for instance, Ted Schmidt, *Shabbes Goy: A Catholic Boyhood on a Jewish Street in a Protestant City* (Toronto: n.d.).

10 *Clinton Public School, 1888–1988*, 26.

11 Ralph Halbert, interview by author, Toronto, 21 January 2015.

12 The story of the Montreal strike is told by Roderick MacLeod and Mary Anne Poutanen, "Little Fists for Social Justice: Anti-Semitism, Community, and Montreal's Aberdeen School Strike, 1913," *Labour/Le Travail* 70 (Fall 2012), 61–99. There were also strikes in Toronto in 1918 and 1919, when a teacher at King Edward School (just to the east of Clinton) refused to raise a "Zion flag" among the flags representing Allied forces at the end of the First World War. The strike, which began at King Edward, apparently spread to several other nearby schools though not, it seems, to Clinton. See Shmuel Shamai, "The Jews and the Public Education System: The Students' Strike over the 'Flag Fight' in Toronto after the First World War," *Canadian Jewish Historical Society Journal* 10, 1 (1988): 46–53. According to Gerald Tulchinsky, Joe Salsberg was also involved in a student strike at nearby Lansdowne School to protest the singing of Christmas carols. See Gerald Tulchinsky, *Joe Salsberg: A Life of Commitment* (Toronto: University of Toronto Press, 2013), 14.

13 The story was told by Alan Borovoy at the Human Book Event, Clinton Street School, October 2012.

14 Joyce Timpson, e-mail message to author, 13 May 2015.

15 "Alumni Memories," Clinton Street Public School Archives.

16 The report card was standard issue in Toronto schools throughout the Jewish Clinton era. There are several examples in the Clinton Street Public School Archives.

17 Ontario, Department of Education, *Programme of Studies for Grades 1 to 6 of the Public and Separate Schools* (Toronto: Department of Education, 1937), 5–8.

18 "Alumni Memories," Clinton Street Public School Archives.

19 Ontario, Department of Education, "Regulations and Programme for Religious Education in the Public Schools" (Toronto: Department of Education, 1949), 5.

20 Ontario, Department of Education, "Regulations and Programme for Religious Education," 6.

21 Robert M. Stamp, *The Schools of Ontario, 1876–1976* (Toronto: University of Toronto Press, 1982), 177–8.

22 Ontario, Department of Education, "Regulations and Programme for Religious Education," 8.

23 Martin Sable, "George Drew and the Rabbis: Religious Education in Ontario's Public Schools," *Canadian Jewish Studies* 6 (1998): 30.

24 Martin Sable, "Keeping the Faith: The Jewish Response to Compulsory Religious Education in Ontario's Public Schools, 1944–1990" (PhD diss., University of Toronto, 1999), 11. An article-length version of the argument Sable makes in his dissertation can be found in Sable, "George Drew and the Rabbis," noted immediately above.

25 Cited in Stamp, *Schools of Ontario*, 178.

26 Cited in ibid., 177.

27 As Stamp notes, the Drew government was also concerned about shoring up (and building) its support with Ontario voters should its minority government fall for want of legislative confidence. The religious education plan, in other words, was crafted in part to highlight the differences, and to drive a wedge between, Drew's Conservatives and the opposition CCF. It was a strategy that "swung many middle-of-the-road voters over to the Conservative camp." Ibid., 179.

28 As Martin Sable shows in detail, the Jewish community itself was divided between those who, like Feinberg, thought it was important to protest the Drew Regulations and others who were more reticent to "rock the boat." See Sable, "Keeping the Faith."

29 Cited in ibid., 34–5.

30 See ibid., 35.

31 Heather Laing, "Religious Education in Ontario," in Nancy Christie and Michael Gauvreau, eds., *The Sixties and Beyond: Dechristianization in North America and Western Europe, 1945–2000* (Toronto: University of Toronto Press, 2013), 250.

32 Sable, "Keeping the Faith," 49.

33 Lilian E. Cox, Mary Entwistle, and Rotha M. Reed, *Stories of God and Jesus: Grade II* (Toronto: Ryerson, 1944), 4. Subsequent references will be provided in the text, with the grade (e.g., II) of the volume followed by the page (e.g., 4).

34 "Teachers' Guides, Grades One to Six," apparently prepared for the Canadian Jewish Congress, submission to the McKay Commission, 1966, 5–6. Ontario Jewish Archives, F.17, S.5-4-4, file 43.

35 Max Sherman to Canadian Jewish Congress, 2 April 1945. Ontario Jewish Archives, F. 17, S, 5–4-4, file 10.

36 See Sable, "Keeping the Faith," 98–9, n26. In 1962, Arthurs prepared a memorandum for the Canadian Jewish Congress on the legal basis for a challenge to the Drew Regulations. A key member of the Canadian Jewish Congress team at the time was Alan Borovoy, Clinton, class of 1945.

37 F.M. Catzman and B.G. Kayfetz, "Religious Education in Public School," 4 February 1955, Ontario Jewish Archives, F17, S. 5–4-4, file 10. There were enough such incidents over the years that, in January 1957, the Canadian Jewish Congress prepared a brief for Premier Leslie Frost that provided a list and summary of some of the more egregious examples. "Brief of the Canadian Jewish Congress ... on the matter of religious education in the public schools presented to the Prime Minister of Ontario, in January, 1957." Ontario Jewish Archives, MG6H, Sydney M. Harris, File 70.

38 "Survey of Jewish Education in Greater Toronto," produced by the Education Committee of the Canadian Jewish Congress and Division II of

the United Jewish Welfare Fund, 1944. Ontario Jewish Archives, Fonds 67, series 12-1, file 7. According to the survey, there were 53 Jewish students at Regal Road and 275 at Palmerston.

39 According to the same survey, there were 581 Jewish students at King Edward, 693 at Clinton, and the largest number, 778, at Lansdowne – all of which were in the corridor along College Street between Spadina and Grace. In the case of Clinton, the Jewish population accounted for approximately 55 per cent of the total school population.

40 Canadian Jewish Congress, "Interview with Mr. Phimister," March 1952. Ontario Jewish Archives, F.17, S. 5-4-4, file 6.

41 Ibid.

42 M.C. Cohen, "Report on Conversations with Jewish Teachers in the Toronto Public Schools," 30 April 1952. Ontario Jewish Archives, F.17, S.5-4-4, file 6.

43 The Springfield Plan, outlined in the Clinton Home and School Association Bulletin of April 1945, was developed as a program for "teaching democracy" in Springfield, Massachusetts. The program was inspired, the Clinton summary suggested, by the realization "that children had been taught that they lived in a perfect democracy, yet their experiences proved otherwise. Therefore, it was decided to point out the weaknesses and show how democracy could be strengthened." To this end, elementary school students engaged in "joint projects" that stressed "living and working together." The Springfield Plan became the subject of a documentary (or a "talking film") that "shows how the Springfield Plan, designed to promote racial understanding and tolerance, operates." The film was shown to a joint meeting of the Clinton, Palmerston, and Essex Home and School Associations in February 1946. What is especially interesting, in light of the Drew Regulations, is that the Springfield Plan was the creation of the National Conference of Christians and Jews in the United States. See Clinton, "Home and School Bulletin," April 1945 and February 1946, Clinton Archives, Folder G.

44 For a suggestive example of this phenomenon in the American setting, see Douglas S. Reed, *Building the Federal Schoolhouse: Localism and the American Education State* (New York: Oxford University Press, 2014), 254.

45 Christie and Gauvreau, eds., *The Sixties and Beyond*, 3–4.

46 For good introductions to this question, see Laing, "Religious Education in Ontario"; R.D. Gidney and W.P.J. Millar, "The Christian Recessional in Ontario's Public Schools," in Marguerite Van Die, ed., *Religion and Public Life in Canada: Historical and Comparative Perspectives* (Toronto: University of Toronto Press, 2001), 275–93; and Lois Sweet, *God in the Classroom: The Controversial Issue of Religion in Canada's Schools* (Toronto: McClelland and Stewart, 1997).

47 I take up the question of cultural heritage and diversity in chapter 7.

48 Laing, "Religious Education in Ontario," 262.
49 Gidney and Millar, "Christian Recessional," 275.
50 Ibid.
51 *The Corporation of the Canadian Civil Liberties Association* v. *The Minister of Education and the Elgin County Board of Education* (1990) 71 O.R. (2d) 341.
52 Laing, "Religious Education in Ontario," 254.
53 "The Bible and the Schools," *United Church Observer*, 15 February 1961. This is an unsigned editorial, but it is presumably the work of Al Forrest, who was the magazine's editor at the time and whose relationship with the Canadian Jewish community was particularly testy because of his views on the Middle East.
54 *Clinton Courier* (1942), 1–2. Clinton Archives, Folder G.
55 My formulation here is a play on the term used by Alan Cairns to discuss the place of Indigenous people in the Canadian constitutional structure. See Alan Cairns, *Citizens Plus: Aboriginal Peoples and the Canadian State* (Vancouver: University of British Columbia Press, 2001).
56 R.D. Gidney, *From Hope to Harris: The Reshaping of Ontario's Schools* (Toronto: University of Toronto Press, 1999), 23. As Gidney notes, the Hope Commission became politically disabled because its plan for reorganizing Ontario's schools would have severely affected the status of Catholic schools. In Gidney's words: "A lengthy minority report argued the injustice and illegality of all such proposals, and the entire report suffered as this particular part of it became a political hot potato: ... Weighed down by such hefty baggage, the Hope Report sank from sight, leaving hardly a ripple of memory behind it." Gidney, 24.
57 Canadian Jewish Congress (hereafter CJC), "Religious Education in Ontario Schools," Brief submitted to the Royal Commission on Education, 19 September 1945, 7.
58 Ibid., 12.
59 Ibid., 12.
60 Ibid., 2. Emphasis in original.
61 Ibid. Emphasis in original.
62 Ibid. Emphasis in original.
63 Ibid., 3.
64 Ibid.
65 Ibid.
66 Lynne Marks, "*Kale Meydelach* or *Shulamith* Girls: Cultural Change and Continuity among Jewish Parents and Daughters – A Case Study of Toronto's Harbord Collegiate Institute in the 1920s," *Canadian Women's Studies* 7, 3 (1986): 88; also available in Ruby Heap and Alison Prentice, eds., *Gender and Education in Ontario: An Historical Reader* (Toronto: Canadian Scholar's Press, 1991), 291–301, quotation at 297. Clinton was one of the schools that fed Harbord Collegiate.

67 Esther Tile, interview by author, 21 October 2013.
68 "Keep Yule Out of School: Feinberg," *Globe and Mail*, 2 December 1950, 1–2.
69 See Sable, "George Drew and the Rabbis."
70 CJC, "Religious Education in Ontario," 2.
71 *Charter Affirming the Values of State Secularism and Religious Neutrality and of Equality between Women and Men, and Providing a Framework for Accommodation Requests*. Bill 60. Quebec, National Assembly, 40th Legislature, First Session, 2013: 2.
72 CJC, "Religious Education in Ontario," 13.
73 Ibid.,12.
74 Bernard Yack, *Nationalism and the Moral Psychology of Community* (Chicago: University of Chicago Press, 2012), 48.
75 Ibid., 46.
76 Ibid.
77 Ibid., 170.
78 Ibid., 174.
79 Ibid., 49.
80 Morley Safer, "Clinton Street School Remembered," 11 November 2012, Clinton Street School Archives.
81 The slogan is attributed to the well-known ad man Jerry Goodis, who attended Clinton for one year before transferring to another school in the neighbourhood.
82 See Judith N. Shklar, *American Citizenship: The Search for Inclusion* (Cambridge, MA: Harvard University Press, 1991).

4. Clinton, 1950–1965

1 "Ceremony of Laying the Cornerstone for the New Clinton Street Public School (Junior)," 20 October 1965, Clinton Street Public School Archives, Folder J.
2 Alex Zeidman, *Good and Faithful Servant: The Biography of Morris Zeidman* (Burlington, ON: Crown Publications, 1990).
3 Scholars of immigration have noted that the distinction between first- and second-generation immigrants is sometimes rather artificial, as children who are born to immigrant families shortly after their arrival in the new country are counted as second generation, even though their experience of acculturation is quite different from that of the child who is born to parents who have been in the new country for many years. For this reason, scholars have developed the category of "one-and-a-half generation" – children who are born to immigrant parents within the first (usually) five years of their residence in the host country. A significant number of Clinton students would fit into this category.

4 Quoted in Triadafilos Triadafilopoulos, *Becoming Multicultural: Immigration and the Politics of Membership in Canada and Germany* (Vancouver: University of British Columbia Press, 2012), 58.

5 Cited in ibid., 64–5.

6 See ibid., 61.

7 Harold Troper, "Becoming an Immigrant City: A History of Immigration into Toronto since the Second World War," in Paul Anisef and Michael Lanphier, eds., *The World in a City* (Toronto: University of Toronto Press, 2003), 29.

8 Ibid., 38.

9 Franca Iacovetta, *Such Hardworking People: Italian Immigrants in Postwar Toronto* (Montreal: McGill-Queen's University Press, 1992), 24.

10 Triadafilopoulos, *Becoming Multicultural*, 62.

11 This was the formulation of Watson Kirkconnell. See Triadafilopoulos, *Becoming Multicultural*, 62, which draws from Richard J.F. Day, *Multiculturalism and the History of Canadian Diversity* (Toronto: University of Toronto Press, 2002), 162.

12 Triadafilopoulos, *Becoming Multicultural*, 62.

13 Iacovetta, *Such Hardworking People*, 28.

14 Ibid., 22.

15 Ibid., xxi–xxii.

16 "New Neighbours from Other Lands," Grade III, Social Studies, Cat. No. SS7, Stencil #101, Toronto District School Board Archives, Social Sciences, Curriculum, presumed date 18 October 1960.

17 Iacovetta, *Such Hardworking People*, xxi.

18 John E. Zucchi, *Italians in Toronto: Development of a National Identity, 1875–1935* (Montreal: McGill-Queen's University Press), 45.

19 See Zucchi, *Italians in Toronto*, chapter 2.

20 See Jordan Stanger-Ross, *Staying Italian: Urban Change and Ethnic Life in Postwar Toronto and Philadelphia* (Chicago: University of Chicago Press, 2010), chapter 2.

21 Ibid., 27.

22 Roberto Perin, *The Many Rooms of This House: Diversity in Toronto's Places of Worship since 1840* (Toronto: University of Toronto Press, forthcoming), chapter 4.

23 Ibid.

24 For most of the period covered by these chapters on European Clinton, the school's catchment area ran from Markham Street on the east to Grace Street on the west and from Bloor Street on the north to College Street on the south. This is almost a perfect match for two census sub-tracts (42 and 43 until 1961 and 57 and 58 thereafter) that are bounded by Bloor (north), College (south), Bathurst (east) and Grace (west).

25 Canada, Census, Population characteristics by census tracts, Toronto (1951) and General population characteristics by census tracts, Census Metropolitan Area of Toronto (1961).

26 R.D. Gidney, *From Hope to Harris: The Reshaping of Ontario's Schools* (Toronto: University of Toronto Press, 1999), 27.

27 See R.D. Gidney, *How Schools Worked: Public Education in English Canada, 1900–1940* (Montreal: McGill-Queen's University Press, 2012), Table 2.1, 13.

28 This is a central theme in Gidney, *From Hope to Harris*.

29 C.C. Goldring, "What Happens to Education?," 29 April 1958, TDSB Archives, Goldring Papers.

30 Gidney, *From Hope to Harris*, 28.

31 This is something of an educated guess. Montrose opened in September 1963. Between September 1962 (1,132) and September 1963 (901), Clinton suddenly lost 230 students. The most sensible interpretation seems to be that this drop in enrolment reflects new boundaries and a new school.

32 Kenneth Carson, "Clinton St. Opening, Recognition of Official Guests, Etc.," 21 November 1966, 2, Clinton Street Public School Archives, Folder J.

33 Jack Quarter, "Clinton School," 25 February 1980, Clinton Street School Archives, Folder J.

34 Carson, "Clinton St. Opening," 1.

35 See letter from M.K. MacDonald (Acting Superintendent of Public Schools) to the Management and Property Committee, Toronto Board of Education, 13 September 1964. Clinton Street Public School Archives, Folder J.

36 Carson, "Clinton St. Opening," 4. One of the reasons for the miscalculation seems to have been that the planners at the Toronto Board of Education believed that some significant number of school-aged children would attend a new Catholic school, St Lucy's, that was about to be built across the street from Clinton, thus reducing demand for spots in local public schools like Clinton. See MacDonald's letter (cited in the previous note).

37 The best historical account of Catholic education in Toronto is Robert T. Dixon, *We Remember, We Believe: A History of Toronto's Catholic Separate School Boards, 1841–1997* (Toronto: Toronto District Catholic School Board, 2007).

38 According to figures compiled by James Lemon, enrolment in public elementary schools in Toronto rose modestly from about 60,000 pupils in 1951 to 77,000 pupils in 1966, then declined steadily to 42,000 in 1983. Catholic school enrolment at the elementary level, on the other hand, grew rapidly from about 12,000 in 1947 to almost 83,000 in 1975, which levels remained steady through to the early 1980s. Because Lemon's enrolment snapshots are not taken from identical years, it is hard to compare precisely, but the basic trend – public enrolment down, Catholic enrolment

way up – is clear. See James Lemon, *Toronto since 1918: An Illustrated History* (Toronto: Lorimer, 1985), Table V, 195.

As to funding, Robert Stamp notes that, throughout the 1950s and 1960s, Catholic schools in Ontario worked "at a financial disadvantage. This was primarily due to low municipal assessments on the property of separate school supporters, plus the continued denial of a share of corporation taxes." See Robert M. Stamp, *The Schools of Ontario, 1876–1976* (Toronto: University of Toronto Press, 1982), 215–16.

39 In order to provide a large enough sample size to make meaningful comparisons, I used the period 1950–1990 to calculate and compare the "transfer in" and "transfer out" rate. The percentage of students who transferred between the public and Catholic systems was about the same; in all, about 15 per cent of all students who transferred schools moved between systems. But the absolute number of students transferring out (551) was much higher than the number transferring in (337), which is why this phenomenon relieved enrolment pressure on Clinton when enrolments were high (between the 1950s and mid-1960s), then helped to deepen the trend of enrolment decline thereafter.

40 Gidney, *From Hope to Harris*, 36.

41 C.C. Goldring, "Are We Hitting the Target in Our Educational Effort?," address given at the Ontario Urban and Rural School Trustees' Association, 21 June 1955, Toronto District School Board Archives, Goldring Papers, 1.

42 Goldring, "What Happens to Education?," 9.

43 Neil Sutherland, *Growing Up: Childhood in English Canada from the Great War to the Age of Television* (Toronto: University of Toronto Press, 1997), 192. A slightly different version of this argument appears in Neil Sutherland, "The Triumph of 'Formalism': Elementary Schooling in Vancouver from the 1920s to the 1960s," in Sara Z. Burke and Patrice Milewski, eds., *Schooling in Transition: Readings in Canadian History of Education* (Toronto: University of Toronto Press, 2012), 375–97.

44 R. McArthur, "Message from Our Principal," *Clinton Chronicle*, April 1961, 2. Clinton Street Public School Archives, Folder Q.

45 Ibid., 2.

46 Glenna Davis, "Voice of Clinton," *Clinton Home and School Association Bulletin*, April 1955, 2. Clinton Street Public School Archives, Folder R.

47 Ibid., 3.

48 Gidney, *From Hope to Harris*, 77.

49 Noel Pollard, "Message from the Principal," *Clinton Chronicle*, April 1960, 3. Clinton Street Public School Archives, Folder Q.

50 "Message from Miss Farley," *Clinton Chronicle*, May 1959, 4. Clinton Street Public School Archives, Folder R.

51 Franca Iacovetta, *Gatekeepers: Reshaping Immigrant Lives in Cold War Canada* (Toronto: Between the Lines, 2002), 13.

52 Ibid., 19.
53 Ontario, Report of the Royal Commission on Education (1950), 5.
54 See Gidney, *From Hope to Harris,* chapter 2.
55 C.C. Goldring, "Some Trends in Education." Radio broadcast 11 March 1950, 4. Goldring papers, Toronto District School Board Archives.
56 Loren Lind, *The Learning Machine* (Toronto: Anansi, 1974), 29.
57 Goldring, "Are We Hitting the Target in Our Educational Effort?," 11 (emphasis added).
58 Northrop Frye, ed., *Design for Learning* (Toronto: University of Toronto Press, 1962), 4.
59 Ibid., 3.
60 W.R. Douglas, "Non-English Speaking Pupils," *Clinton Home and School Association Bulletin,* June 1949. Clinton Street Public School Archives, Folder H.
61 Ibid.
62 Ibid.
63 J.E. Parsons, "New Canadians at Clinton," *Clinton Home and School Association Bulletin,* November 1952.
64 John Bishop, "Clinton School Paved Way for New Canadians," *Toronto Telegram,* 19 May 1961.
65 Ibid.
66 Goldring, "Are We Hitting the Target?," 11.
67 Pollard, "Message from the Principal" (emphasis added).
68 Lind, *Learning Machine,* 29.
69 Ibid., 27.
70 Jane Gaskell and Ben Levin, *Making a Difference in Urban Schools: Ideas, Politics, and Pedagogy* (Toronto: University of Toronto Press, 2012), 72.
71 C.C. Goldring, *Canadian Citizenship* (Toronto: J.M. Dent, 1948), 289.
72 Troper, "Becoming an Immigrant City," 34.
73 Ian Wallace and Angela Wood, *The Sandwich* (Toronto: Kids Can Press, 1975).
74 *The Sandwich* was inspired by an event that occurred in the life of one of the authors, Angela Wood, while working as a teacher's assistant in a school. The school in which the incident occurred was in Scarborough (one of Toronto's "near" suburbs), not Clinton. The authors and Kids Can Press chose Clinton as the site for the book because they understood, as co-author Ian Wallace explained to me, that Clinton was a very good example of "a 'multi-cultural' and 'inner city' school" that was "on the cutting edge of the 'multi-cultural' movement in Canada" at a time when most governments "weren't interested." So while the book was published in the 1970s, it was intended to reference the roots of multiculturalism, which is why it is appropriate to discuss it with respect to Clinton in the 1960s. Nominated for the City of Toronto Book Award, *The Sandwich*

ultimately sold about 30,000 copies. Ian Wallace, e-mail to author, 21 July and 11 August 2015.

75 On gender and education in English Canada during this era, see M.L. Adams, *The Trouble with Normal: Postwar Youth and the Making of Homosexuality* (Toronto: University of Toronto Press, 1997), especially chapter 2; on women teachers, see Kristina R. Llewellyn, *Democracy's Angels: The Work of Women Teachers* (Montreal: McGill-Queen's University Press, 2012). I heard from several interviewees how their mothers would use pieces of pasta to help their young children master elementary addition, subtraction, multiplication, and division.

76 Imogene Walker, interview by author, 4 February 2015.

77 Iacovetta, *Gatekeepers*.

78 Walker, interview by author.

79 Ibid.

80 The literary allusion is to Keats's poem *Ode to a Nightingale:* "Perhaps the selfsame song that found a path / Through the sad heart of Ruth, when, sick for home / She stood in tears amid the alien corn." The reference to Ruth seems particularly appropriate in this context since, like Ruth, the immigrant students Ms Walker was teaching may well have identified with the plight of someone who found herself "sick for home."

81 Walker, interview by author.

82 Robert D. Putnam, *Bowling Alone: The Collapse and Revival of American Community* (New York: Touchstone/Simon and Schuster, 2000).

83 *Clinton Home and School Association Bulletin*, various years, Clinton Street Public School Archives, Folder R.

84 "Home and School Minutes, 1957–1960," Clinton Street Public School Archives, Folder R.

85 Letter to Parents, Home and School Minutes, 1957–1960, Clinton Street Public School Archives, Folder R, n.d.

86 Ibid. The musical entertainment for the evening also crossed cultural boundaries: "To add to the evening's entertainment we have for your pleasure, Mr. Nathan Appleby, operatic tenor and well known singer of Italian songs. He will be accompanied at the piano by Mrs. Lilian Levy Sher."

87 Speaking Notes, Clinton Home and School General Meeting, 4 November 1957, Clinton Street Public School Archives, Folder R.

5. European Clinton, 1965–1975

1 Stratton Holland, "They Study for the Space Age – in an 1863 School," *Toronto Star*, 1 July 1967.

2 For a beautiful photographic history of the Good Friday procession, see Vincenzo Pietropaolo, *Ritual* (London: Black Dog Publishing, 2016).

3 See Jordan Stanger-Ross, *Staying Italian: Urban Change and Ethnic Life in Postwar Toronto and Philadelphia* (Chicago: University of Chicago Press, 2010), 31.

4 Ibid., 31.

5 Toronto Board of Education Research Department, "Immigrants and Their Education," May 1965, 12.

6 Carlos Teixeira and Victor M.P. Da Rosa, eds., *The Portuguese in Canada: Diasporic Challenges and Adjustment*, 2nd ed. (Toronto: University of Toronto Press, 2009), 6, Table 1.1. According to figures drawn from the 2006 census, just over 70 per cent of Canadians who self-identify as being of Portuguese ethnic origin live in Ontario, and just under 70 per cent of these live in the Greater Toronto area. To frame this demographic portrait slightly differently, in 1971 approximately 15 per cent of residents in west central Toronto (some 18,235) reported Portuguese ethnicity. A decade later, in 1981, 31 per cent (or 31, 645) so reported. See Carlos Teixeira and Robert A. Murdie, "On the Move: The Portuguese in Toronto," in Teixeira and Da Rosa, eds., *The Portuguese in Canada*, 191, 200.

7 For an evocative narrative portrait of what it was like growing up as a Portuguese-Canadian boy in downtown Toronto, see Anthony DeSa, *Kicking the Sky* (Toronto: Doubleday, 2013).

8 Teixeira and Murdie, "On the Move: The Portuguese in Toronto," 194.

9 Figures compiled from the annual lists of teaching staff, gathered and published by the TBE. Available in the Clinton Street School Archives.

10 Kenneth Carson, "Clinton St. Opening, Recognition of Special Guests, Etc.," 6, 21 November 1966, Clinton Street Public School Archives, Folder J.

11 Office of the Director of Education, Toronto Board of Education, untitled report on ESL in Toronto schools, 3 December 1965, 42. TDSB Archives. There were another eight teachers involved with ESL teaching at the Main Street School, which had been created as a school whose entire remit was to teach immigrant children.

12 See Loren Lind, *The Learning Machine* (Toronto: Anansi, 1974), 30–1.

13 Clinton provided 8.75 hours per week of dedicated, withdrawn ESL teaching. The system average was approximately 2 hours per week of withdrawn instruction. See TBE, report on ESL, 1965, Table 9, 41.

14 Toronto Board of Education, "Summer Session for New Canadians," TDSB Archives, File TBE – Curriculum – New Canadians – 1970. The growth in this sort of summer school was dramatic. In 1963 the program ran in three "centres." By 1968 there were 14, and by 1971 a total of 21 such summer programs.

15 Lind, *Learning Machine*, 41.

16 Cited in Donald J. Nethery, "A Survey of the Toronto Board of Education's Response to the Education of Immigrants from the 1840's to the 1930's,"

TDSB Archives, n.d., 1. Nethery was the chief archivist for the Toronto Board of Education for many years and occasionally produced such topical reports that drew on the archival collections he was responsible for maintaining.

17 See ibid., 1.
18 Toronto Board of Education, "English as a Second Language," 26 June 1970, 1. TDSB Archives, TBE-Depts-English as a Second Language.
19 Lind, *Learning Machine*, 27.
20 Ibid., 33.
21 Ibid., 29.
22 The TBE's research department actually produced two versions of the same report, a shorter, somewhat more philosophical version that was entitled "Immigrants and Their Education" and that was completed in May 1965. The longer, data-richer version of the report was produced in December 1965 and was untitled. For clarity, I will refer to the first version as "Immigrants and Their Education" and to the second as "ESL in Toronto Schools."
23 Research Department, TBE, "ESL in Toronto Schools," 61 (emphasis added). This is one of the earliest uses of the term "multi-culture" (in this case as a noun) that I found at the TBE.
24 TBE, "Immigrants and Their Education," 1.
25 Ibid., 12.
26 Ibid., 16.
27 Ibid., 12.
28 Ibid.
29 Ibid., 4 (emphasis added).
30 Ibid., 12.
31 David L. Sam and John W. Berry, eds., *The Cambridge Handbook of Acculturation Psychology* (Cambridge: Cambridge University Press, 2006).
32 TBE, "Immigrants and Their Education," 12. Subsequent quotations in this paragraph come from the same page of the same document.
33 See the discussion and references in Anna C. Korteweg and Triadafilos Triadafilopoulos, "Is Multiculturalism Dead? Groups, Governments and the 'Real Work of Integration,'" *Ethnic and Racial Studies* (2014): 1–21; and Matthew Wright and Irene Bloemraad, "Is There a Trade-off between Multiculturalism and Socio-Political Integration? Policy Regimes and Immigrant Incorporation in Comparative Perspective," *Perspectives on Politics* 10, 1 (March 2012): 77–95.
34 TBE, "Immigrants and Their Education," 3.
35 Ibid., 4. Subsequent references in this paragraph are drawn from the same page and source.

36 George Grant, *Lament for a Nation: The Defeat of Canadian Nationalism* (Toronto: McClelland and Stewart, 1965).

37 Royal Commission on Bilingualism and Biculturalism, *Book IV: The Cultural Contribution of Other Ethnic Groups* (Ottawa: Queen's Printer, 1969), xvii.

38 Christopher Armstrong, *Civic Symbol: Creating Toronto's New City Hall, 1952–1966* (Toronto: University of Toronto Press, 2015).

39 See C.P. Champion, *The Strange Demise of British Canada: The Liberals and Canadian Nationalism, 1964–1968* (Montreal: McGill-Queen's University Press, 2010), and William J. Smyth, *Toronto, The Belfast of Canada: The Orange Order and the Shaping of Municipal Culture* (Toronto: University of Toronto Press, 2015).

40 See Jane Gaskell and Ben Levin, *Making a Difference in Urban Schools: Ideas, Politics, and Pedagogy* (Toronto: University of Toronto Press, 2012), chapter 3.

41 The Royal Commission on Bilingualism and Biculturalism was created by Prime Minister Lester Pearson in 1963. It published a preliminary report in 1965, which became the subject of public hearings and led, ultimately, to a four-part final report. The first volume of the final report, entitled *Bilingualism in Canada: Its Foundation* (Ottawa: Queen's Printer, 1967) was published in the fall of 1967. The fourth, entitled *The Cultural Contribution of Other Ethnic Groups* (Ottawa: Queen's Printer, 1969), saw the light of day two years later. In effect, the final report provided intellectual scaffolding for the change from "biculturalism" to "multiculturalism," the policy embraced by the Trudeau government in 1971. On the commission's approach to questions of assimilation, integration, and acculturation, see the Introduction to Volume 4, 3–14. For a recent critical appraisal, see Eve Haque, *Multiculturalism within a Bilingual Framework: Language, Race, and Belonging in Canada* (Toronto: University of Toronto Press, 2012).

42 R.D. Gidney, "Instructive Parallels: Looking Back to Hall-Dennis," in Geoffrey Milburn, ed., *"Ring Some Alarm Bells in Ontario": Reactions to the Report of the Royal Commission on Learning* (London, ON: The Althouse Press, Faculty of Education, University of Western Ontario, 1996), 32.

43 Ontario, Department of Education, *Living and Learning: The Report of the Provincial Committee on Aims and Objectives of Education in the Schools of Ontario* (Toronto: Newton, 1968).

44 Gidney, "Instructive Parallels," 35. See also Robert Stamp, *The Schools of Ontario, 1876–1976* (Toronto: University of Toronto Press, 1982), 216–24.

45 Robert Vipond, "The Civil Rights Movement Comes to Winnipeg: American Influence on Canadian Rights Talk, 1968–1971," in Stephen Newman, ed., *Constitutional Politics in Canada and the United States* (Albany, NY: State University of New York Press, 2004), 89–107.

46 Ontario, Department of Education, *Living and Learning*, 49.

47 Ibid., 62.

48 Gidney, "Instructive Parallels," 38.

49 Ontario, Department of Education, *Living and Learning*, 10.

50 Ibid., 180.

51 Ibid., 179.

52 Gidney, "Instructive Parallels," 25.

53 Ontario, Department of Education, *Living and Learning*, 62.

54 Stamp, *Schools of Ontario*, 218.

55 Ontario, Department of Education, *Living and Learning*, chapter 5, "The Learning Experience." The quoted phrase is taken from "the one fundamental recommendation" of the committee, 179.

56 Ontario, Department of Education, *Living and Learning*, 23.

57 Ibid., 24.

58 Ibid., 25.

59 Ibid., 27.

60 Ibid., 108.

61 Ibid., 109.

62 Ibid.

63 Ibid., 27.

64 Ibid., 111.

65 Ibid., 30.

66 TBE, "Summer Session for New Canadians," chapter 2, n.p.

67 Ontario, Ministry of Education, *Multiculturalism in Action*, 1977, 2. This guide built on the curricular architecture developed by *The Formative Years* (1975), which in turn was, in part, a response to the Hall-Dennis report.

68 Harold Troper and Morton Weinfeld, "Diversity in Canada," in Harold Troper and Morton Weinfeld, eds., *Ethnicity, Politics, and Public Policy: Case Studies in Canadian Diversity* (Toronto: University of Toronto Press, 1999), 9.

69 Harold Troper, "Becoming an Immigrant City: A History of Immigration into Toronto since the Second World War," in Paul Anisef and Michael Lanphier, eds., *The World in a City* (Toronto: University of Toronto Press, 2003), 46.

70 Canadian Jewish Congress, *Religious Education in Ontario Schools*, Brief submitted to the Royal Commission on Education, 19 September 1945, 10.

71 Nathan Glazer, *We Are All Multiculturalists Now* (Cambridge, MA: Harvard University Press, 1998).

72 Bernard Yack, "Multiculturalism and the Political Theorists," *European Journal of Political Theory* 1, 1 (2003): 108.
73 *The Corporation of the Canadian Civil Liberties Association* v. *The Minister of Education and the Elgin County Board of Education* (1990) 71 O.R. (2d) 341.
74 *Multani* v. *Commission scolaire Marguerite Bourgeoys* (2006) 1 S.C.R. 256. The Canadian Supreme Court has not always been as accommodating, however. In a 2009 case, *Alberta* v. *Hutterian Brethren of Wilson Colony* (2009) 2 S.C.R. 567, the court was asked to rule on the validity of an Alberta law that requires all drivers to have their photographs appear on their licenses. The Hutterites maintained that the requirement violated their belief that photographs are graven images and so contrary to the Ten Commandments. In a 4–3 decision, the court sided with the Government of Alberta and refused any accommodation.
75 Yack, "Multiculturalism," 109.
76 Angela Febbraro, e-mail to author, 9 July 2012.
77 Ontario, Ministry of Education, *The Formative Years*, 4.
78 Ibid., 20.
79 Will Kymlicka, *Politics in the Vernacular: Nationalism, Multiculturalism, and Citizenship* (Oxford: Oxford University Press, 2001), 21.
80 Ibid., 22.
81 Ontario, *Multiculturalism in Action*, 2.
82 Mary Waters, *Ethnic Options: Choosing Identities in America* (Berkeley, CA: University of California Press, 1990), 147.
83 Ibid., 154.
84 Sergio Mateus, interview by author, 20 February 2015.

6. Global Clinton, 1975–1990

1 "Welcome to Clinton Street Public School," Clinton Street School Archives, 1986, 17.
2 I have used fathers only here, largely because, until about 1960, the student registration cards typically provided information only about fathers. In order to ensure comparability, therefore, I used fathers throughout. As a check, however, I also produced indices from 1960 to 1990 that included both fathers and mothers. I found no major differences in the pattern. Indeed, if anything, the trends were even more pronounced.
3 Kathleen Rex, "Empty Classrooms Used for Special Programs," *Globe and Mail*, 23 February 1978, T2.
4 Fernando Mata, "Latin American Immigration to Canada: Some Reflections on the Immigration Statistics," *Canadian Journal of Latin American and Caribbean Studies*, 10, 20 (1985): 27–42.

5 See Lucia Lo and Shuguang Wang, "Settlement Patterns of Toronto's Chinese Immigrants: Convergence or Divergence?" *Canadian Journal of Regional Science* 20 (1997): 49.

6 Enrolment data were compiled from annual audits produced by the Ontario Ministry of Education. See Ontario, Ministry of Education, Information Systems and Records Branch, *Public School Enrolment* (1966–88). For the earlier period, I used data compiled by the Toronto Board of Education. See *Public School Enrolment Books: Attendance Statistics* (1933–67), TDSB Archives, 2003–0377. There is a difference between enrolment (the number of children who have registered at a school) and attendance (the smaller number of students who are present on a given day). The TBE "books" (in fact, they are typewritten records on carbon paper, embalmed between pieces of cardboard and held together by loose-leaf rings) use both terms for the *same* statistics. The provincial publications, on the other hand, clearly state that they are tracking enrolment. It would appear that the TBE data refer to enrolment, not attendance, because on the few years for which I had both ministry- and TBE-generated figures, the Ontario and Toronto numbers correspond precisely.

7 The calculations in this paragraph are derived from census data from 1961, 1991, and various years in between. As noted in chapter 4, the boundaries of two census sub-tracts (42 and 43 in 1961, 57 and 58 thereafter) match the boundaries of the Clinton catchment area almost perfectly. See Canada, Census, Metropolitan Area of Toronto, various years (1961, 1971, 1976, 1981, 1986, and 1991). The breakdown of population (by age, for instance) appears in supplementary publications. The titles for these pamphlets vary slightly, but typically the title is something like "Selected Characteristics by Census Tracts."

8 Between 1975 and the late 1980s, Clinton's enrolment declined by 53 per cent. During the same period, the population at Montrose Public School fell by 70 per cent and at Grace Street Public School by 65 per cent. Ultimately, Grace School was closed.

9 Between 1975 and 1988, enrolment at St Francis and St Lucy's declined by about 47 per cent. In this case, the "old" St Francis School eventually closed so that K-8 students who wanted a Catholic education were streamed to St Lucy's (on Clinton Street). It remains there, though, confusingly, it is now called St Francis. Figures tabulated from Ontario, Ministry of Education, Information System and Records Branch.

10 See Irene Bloemraad, *Becoming a Citizen: Incorporating Immigrants and Refugees in the United States and Canada* (Berkeley: University of California Press, 2006).

11 Centro Organizzativo Italiano (hereafter COI), "Brief Re Centro-Clinton Day Care Centre," 4 March 1974, 1. Clinton Public School Archives.

12 George Ben, letter to John G. Anderson, 19 February 1974. Ben was the local alderman; Anderson was the commissioner of social services for Toronto.

13 COI, "Brief," 2.

14 COI, "Brief," 3.

15 Rex, "Empty Classrooms," T2.

16 COI, "Brief," 3.

17 Ibid.

18 Maria Azevedo, interview with author, 22 May 2015.

19 Andrew McIntosh and Ann Rauhala, "Doing It the Right Way: The Sunny Side of Child Care in Ontario," *Globe and Mail*, 6 February 1989, A11.

20 Jason Ellis and Paul Axelrod, "Continuity and Change in Special Education Policy Development in Toronto Public Schools, 1945 to the Present," *Teachers College Record,* 118 (February 2016): 5.

21 *Orde Street Junior Public School Centenary Yearbook, 1915–2015,* 21–2.

22 Ellis and Axelrod, "Continuity and Change," 20.

23 C.G. Stodgill, "Special Education Facilities in Public and Secondary Schools Operated by the Toronto Board of Education," 1 October 1956, cited in Ellis and Axelrod, "Continuity and Change," 8.

24 Ellis and Axelrod, "Continuity and Change," 5.

25 The Metropolitan School Board (MSB) was created by the Government of Ontario in 1954, which established a federation of eleven Toronto-area boards of education, including the Toronto Board of Education. One of the goals of the Metro board was to pool resources in areas such as special education to make it possible for smaller, suburban school boards to mount programs. The TBE preferred to run most of its own programs, but it did participate in some MSB initiatives. Ellis and Axelrod, "Continuity and Change," provide a good summary.

26 These snapshots are drawn from several sources: annual lists of teaching staff produced by the school board (on file at the Clinton Street Public School Archives); Clinton Street Public School, Annual Report, 1978 (Clinton Street Public School Archives); and "Welcome to Clinton Street Public School," 1986.

27 See Ellis and Axelrod, "Continuity and Change."

28 Add to this a "gifted" program that began as an enrichment program, one day per week, for some grade 6 students.

29 Marlene Danicki, interview with author, 6 March 2015.

30 "Welcome to Clinton," 18.

31 "Annual Report, 1978," 1.

32 Ibid., 2.

33 Jane Gaskell and Ben Levin, *Making a Difference in Urban Schools: Politics, Ideas, and Pedagogy* (Toronto: University of Toronto Press, 2012), 82.
34 "Welcome to Clinton," 4.
35 "Annual Report, 1978," 2.
36 "Annual Report, 1978."
37 Richard Reed Parry, e-mail to author, 1 May 2015. Mr. Parry is best known as a core member of the indie rock band Arcade Fire.
38 "Annual Report, 1978."

7. Global Clinton and Heritage Languages

1 Toronto Board of Education, "The Bias of Culture: An Issue Paper on Multiculturalism," 25 October 1974.
2 Toronto Board of Education, "Draft Report of the Work Group on Multicultural Programs," 20 May 1975 (hereafter MP); and Toronto Board of Education, "Final Report of the Work Group on Multicultural Programs," 12 February 1976.
3 Toronto Board of Education, "Draft Report of the Sub-Committee on Race Relations," 1978; and Toronto Board of Education, "Final Report of the Sub-Committee on Race Relations," 1979.
4 Toronto Board of Education, "Draft Report of the Work Group on Third Languages Instruction," 1981; and Toronto Board of Education, "Final Report of the Work Group on Third Language Instruction: Towards a Comprehensive Language Policy," March 1982.
5 TBE, "Draft Multicultural Programs," n.p. The quotation is from the statement by Prime Minister Pierre Trudeau before the House of Commons, 8 October 1971.
6 Jim Cummins and Marcel Danesi, *Heritage Languages: The Development and Denial of Canada's Linguistic Resources* (Toronto: Garamond, 1990), 36–7. See also Jack Berryman, "Implementation of Ontario's Heritage Languages Program: A Case Study of the Extended Day Model" (PhD diss., University of Toronto, 1986).
7 Toronto Board of Education (TBE), "Final Report ... on Third Language Instruction" (1982), 2.
8 Ibid., 2.
9 Ibid., 1, 3.
10 Toronto Board of Education (TBE), "Draft Report ... on Multicultural Programs" (1975), i.
11 Ibid., i.
12 Ibid., 5 (emphasis in original).
13 Ibid., 24 (emphasis in original).

14 Ibid., 57 (emphasis in original).

15 Ibid., 58–9.

16 Ibid., 2.

17 Jane Gaskell and Ben Levin, *Making a Difference in Urban Schools: Ideas, Politics, and Pedagogy* (Toronto: University of Toronto Press), 72.

18 TBE, "Final Report … on Third Language Instruction" (1982), 1.

19 TBE, "Draft Report … on Multicultural Programs" (1975), 55.

20 TBE, "Final Report … on Third Language Instruction" (1982), iii, iv.

21 Ibid., 1.

22 TBE, "Draft Report … on Multicultural Programs" (1975), 58.

23 TBE, "Final Report … on Multicultural Programs" (1976), 22.

24 TBE, "Draft Report … on Multicultural Programs" (1975), 1.

25 TBE, "Final Report … on Multicultural Programs" (1976), 21.

26 TBE. "Final Report … on Third Language Instruction" (1982), 2.

27 Ibid., 29. See also TBE. "Final Report … on Multicultural Programs" (1976), 26.

28 TBE. "Final Report … on Third Language Instruction" (1982), 2.

29 TBE. "Final Report … on Multicultural Programs" (1976), 4.

30 Ibid., 4–5.

31 Ibid., 6.

32 TBE, "Draft Report … on Multicultural Programs" (1975), 57–66.

33 TBE. "Final Report … on Third Language Instruction" (1982), 3.

34 TBE, "Draft Report … on Multicultural Programs" (1975), 79a.

35 Ibid., 79b–80.

36 Ibid., 83.

37 TBE, "Final Report … on Multicultural Programs" (1976), 26.

38 Clinton Street Public School, "Annual Report" (1978), 2.

39 Cummins and Danesi trace the twists and turns in these policies very well. See Cummins and Danesi, *Heritage Languages*.

40 Ibid., 39.

41 TBE, "Draft Report … on Multicultural Programs" (1975), 54c.

42 TBE, "Final Report …on Multicultural Programs" (1976), 23.

43 Ibid., 23–4.

44 Cummins and Danesi, *Heritage Languages*, 37.

45 "Man Charged with Assault," *Toronto Sunday Sun*, 25 March 1984. TDSB Archives, TBE – Curriculum – Heritage Language – 1980–1985.

46 TBE, "Final Report … on Multicultural Programs" (1976), 23.

47 TBE, "Draft Report … on Multicultural Programs" (1975), 54a.

48 Rosario Marchese, interview by Scott Kilian-Clark, 1 March 2013.

49 TBE, "Final Report … on Multicultural Programs" (1976), 21.

50 Ibid., 24.

51 Ibid., 25.
52 Cummins and Danesi, *Heritage Languages*, 15.
53 *Toronto Star*, "Don't Balkanize Schools," 2 June 1980. TDSB Archives, TBE – Curriculum – Heritage Language – 1980–1985.
54 See, for example, Randall Hansen, "Assimilation by Stealth: Why Canada's Multicultural Policy Is Really a Repackaged Integration Policy," in Jack Jedwab, ed., *The Multicultural Question: Debating Identity in the 21st Century* (Montreal and Kingston: McGill-Queen's University Press for Queen's School of Policy Studies, 2014), 73–88. Several other chapters in the same collection betray the same tendency. See, for instance, Richard J.F. Day, "(Never) Coming Out to Be Met? Liberal Multiculturalism and Its Radical Others," 127–48, and Yasmeen Abu-Laban, "Reform by Stealth: The Harper Conservatives and Canadian Multiculturalism," 149–72.
55 Clinton Street Public School, "Annual Report" (1978), 2.
56 Clinton Street Public School, "Study Group Report to the CECA Steering Committee," January 1984, 1–3. Clinton Street Public School Archives, File R CECA, Minutes 1980s.
57 Clinton Street Public School, "Study Group Report," 4.
58 Clinton Street Public School, Clinton Education Community Association (CECA), letter to Rosario Marchese, school trustee, 5 February 1985. Clinton Street Public School Archives, Folder R, CECA, Minutes 1980–1985.
59 At least this is how the Clinton parents interpreted Mr Marchese's reaction. CECA, letter to Marchese, 5 February 1985.
60 See Clinton Street Public School, CECA, "The Consultative Process: Integrated/Extended Day Heritage and Concurrent Program," n.d. Clinton Street Public School Archives, Folder R, CECA Minutes, 1980–1985.
61 I could find no written record of the actual vote results or of the turnout. Oddly enough, I found a report from one of the area superintendents in which he provided the winning percentage in a couple of other schools, but about Clinton there were no figures. When I asked former Clinton parents who had been involved in the issue, most thought that the final vote was something in the neighbourhood of 55–60 per cent opposed, 40–45 per cent in favour. Comfortable but not overwhelming seems to be a good way to describe it.
62 Jim Clarke, interview by author, 16 June 2015.
63 Sally-Beth MacLean, interview by Scott Kilian-Clark, 2 April 2013.
64 Clinton Street Public School, "Welcome to Clinton" (1986), 20. Clinton School Archives.
65 Ian Wallace, e-mail to author, 21 July and 11 August 2015.

66 Beatrice (Spiegel) Minden.

67 Clinton Street School, "Welcome to Clinton" (1986), 12.

68 Caroline Parry, *Let's Celebrate! Canada's Special Days* (Toronto: Kids Can Press, 1987).

69 Caroline Parry, e-mail to author, 29 April 2015.

70 MacLean, 2013.

71 MacLean, 2013.

72 On these distinctions, see Will Kymlicka, *Multicultural Odysseys: Navigating the New International Politics of Diversity* (Oxford: Oxford University Press, 2007), 83–5; and David Miller, *On Nationality* (Oxford: Clarendon Press, 1995), especially chapter 5: "Nationality and Cultural Pluralism."

73 Will Kymlicka, *Multicultural Odysseys*, 61.

74 Ibid., 64.

75 Ibid.

76 Michael Ignatieff, *Blood and Belonging: Journeys into the New Nationalism* (Toronto: Viking, 1993).

77 Kymlicka, *Multicultural Odysseys*, 65.

78 P.E. Trudeau, Statement to the House of Commons on Multiculturalism, 8 October 1971.

79 Government of Canada, *Shared Values: The Canadian Identity* (Ottawa: Ministry of Supply and Services, 1991), cited in Wayne Norman, "The Ideology of Shared Values," in Joseph Carens, ed., *Is Quebec Nationalism Just?* (Montreal and Kingston: McGill-Queen's University Press, 1995), 139.

80 TBE, "Draft Report ... on Multicultural Programs" (1975), i.

81 Bernard Yack, *Nationalism and the Moral Psychology of Community* (Chicago: University of Chicago Press, 2012), 30.

82 Benedict Anderson, *Imagined Communities: Reflections on the Origin and Spread of Nationalism* (London: Verso, 1991).

83 Yack, *Nationalism*, 69.

84 Ibid.

85 Ibid., 28.

86 Cited in ibid., 29.

87 TBE, "Bias of Culture," 1974.

88 Eric Hobsbawm and Terence Ranger, eds., *The Invention of Tradition* (New York: Cambridge University Press, 1983).

89 Hansen, "Assimilation by Stealth."

90 See Abu-Laban, "Reform by Stealth"; Day, "(Never) Coming Out to Be Met?"; and Eve Haque, "Multiculturalism, Language, and Immigrant Integration," all in Jedwab, ed., *The Multicultural Question*, 203–23.

8 Conclusion

1 See Gerald Tulchinsky, "Family Quarrel: Joe Salsberg, the 'Jewish Question,' and Canadian Communism," *Labour/Le Travail* 56 (Fall 2005): 149–73; and Ester Reiter, "Secular *Yiddishkait*: Left Politics, Culture, and Community," *Labour/Le Travail* 49 (2002): 121–46. The Labour League Mutual Benefits Association was the social welfare arm of the Labour League, which "fulfilled the needs for a progressive social community and schooling for children, providing its members with medical, unemployment and mortuary benefits, and a credit union, which was quite radical at the time." The Labour League was dedicated to preserving and fostering Yiddish culture through the creation of such things as the Toronto Jewish Folk Choir (whose conductor lived around the corner on Palmerston Boulevard) and Camp Naivelt (where the Travellers folk group was created). In 1944, the Labour League merged with another labour organization to form the United Jewish People's Organization (UJPO). The quotation is taken from the Winchevsky Centre website, www.winchevskycentre.org. Accessed 31 May 2016.

2 Toronto District School Board, Organizational Development/Research and Information Services, *Kindergarten–Grade 6 Parent Census: School Report – Clinton Street Junior Public School*, March 2013. Over the entire TDSB, 26 per cent reported family incomes of over $100,000. In the cluster of nearby schools, called Clinton's "family of schools," the percentage of high-income households was 33 per cent.

3 See figure 6.3 in chapter 6.

4 Where at Clinton 10 per cent of students are first generation, in Toronto as a whole the rate is 20 per cent, and in Clinton's family of schools 22 per cent.

5 The precise figures are 73 per cent (Clinton), as compared to 37 per cent (Toronto schools as a whole).

6 David Rayside, Jerald Sabin, and Paul Thomas, *Religion and Canadian Party Politics* (Vancouver: University of British Columbia Press, forthcoming 2017).

7 Peter Loewen and Daniel Rubenson, "Support for Conservatives' *Niqab* Ban Is Deep and Wide, even among Immigrants," *Ottawa Citizen*, 9 October 2015. Similar results were recorded by Vote Compass, a democratic engagement initiative. See Vox Pop Labs, Vote Compass, "Niqab," 19 September 2015. Nor are these views simply the product of election campaigning. According to a recent, non-election cycle poll commissioned by the *Toronto Star*, "67 per cent [of Canadians] believe immigrants should be screened for 'anti-Canadian values.'" See Bruce

Campion Smith, "Canadians Favour Screening Immigrants," *Toronto Star*, 10 September 2016, A1.

8 See Clifford Orwin, "Stephen Harper's Veiled Attack on Religious Freedom," *Globe and Mail*, 18 February 2015.

9 See, for instance, Wayne Sumner, *The Hateful and the Obscene: Studies in the Limits of Free Expression* (Toronto: University of Toronto Press, 2004). In this context, it is interesting that when a French administrative tribunal struck down the "burkini ban" in a French town in the summer of 2016, the court essentially applied a utilitarian risk analysis to conclude that burkinis neither posed a significant public risk nor inflicted any significant harm. See "France's Burkini Ban Overturned by Highest Court," cbc.ca/news/world/burkini-ban-france-overturned-1.3736823, 26 August 2016.

10 This phrase is taken from an e-mail sent by the Conservative party as part of its fundraising campaign before the 2015 general election. Cited in Steven Chase, "Niqabs 'Rooted in Culture That Is Anti-Women,' Harper Says," *Globe and Mail*, 10 March 2015.

11 Ibid.

12 Canada, House of Commons, Bill S-7, *An Act to Amend the Immigration and Refugee Protection Act, the Civil Marriage Act and the Criminal Code and to Make Consequential Amendments to Other Acts*.

13 Lucas Powers, "Conservatives Pledge Funds, Tip Line, to Combat 'Barbaric Cultural Practices,'" cbc.ca/news/politics/Canada-election-2015-barbaric-cultural-practice-law-1.3254118, 2 October 2015. The timing of this announcement – about two weeks before the general election – suggests strongly that the Conservatives believed these initiatives would pay electoral dividends by galvanizing fear and anti-Muslim sentiment.

14 Chris Alexander, Minister of Citizenship and Immigration, remarks in the House of Commons, 16 June 2015, accessed at https://openparliament.ca/bills/41-2/S-7.

15 Irene Bloemraad, *Becoming a Citizen: Incorporating Immigrants and Refugees in the United States and Canada* (Berkeley: University of California Press, 2006.)

16 See, for instance, Matthew Wright and Irene Bloemraad, "Is There a Trade-off between Multiculturalism and Socio-political Integration? Policy Regimes and Immigrant Incorporation in Comparative Perspective," *Perspectives on Politics* 10, 1 (March 2012): 77–95; and Will Kymlicka, "Testing the Multiculturalist Hypothesis: Normative Theories and Social Science Evidence," *Canadian Journal of Political Science* 43, 2 (June 2010): 257–71. One troubling trend in Toronto, however, is growing residential segregation. On this see David Hulchanski, *The Three Cities within Toronto:*

Income Polarization among Toronto's Neighbourhoods, 1970–2005 (Toronto: Cities Centre Press, University of Toronto, 2010).

17 Bernard Yack, "Multiculturalism and the Political Theorists," *European Journal of Political Theory* 1, 1 (2003): 109.

18 This is the formulation made famous by the German chancellor, Angela Merkel.

19 Margaret Wente, "What's the Matter with Belgium?" *Globe and Mail*, 27 November 2015.

20 For a particularly subtle version of this argument, see Janice Stein, "Searching for Equality," in Janice Stein, David Robertson Cameron, John Ibbitson, Will Kymlicka, John Meisel, Haroon Siddiqui, and Michael Valpy, *Uneasy Partners: Multiculturalism and Rights in Canada* (Waterloo: Wilfrid Laurier University Press, 2007), 1–22. Christopher Cochrane has noticed that, with respect to opinions about same-sex marriage, there is a significant divide within the Muslim community in Canada between those who are educated in Canada and those who are not. As he notes, "Canadian-born Muslims with a university degree are no more opposed than other university-educated Canadians to the legal recognition of same-sex relationships. It seems that the school is more important than the Mosque as a source of Muslim-Canadian opinions about same-sex relationships." Christopher Cochrane, "The Effects of Islam, Religiosity, and Socialization on Muslim-Canadian Opinions about Same-Sex Marriage," *Comparative Migration Studies* 1, 1 (2013): 174. See also Stephen White, Neil Nevitte, Andre Blais, Elisabeth Gidengil, and Patrick Fournier, "The Political Resocialization of Immigrants: Resistance or Lifelong Learning?" *Political Research Quarterly* 61, 2 (June 2008): 268–81.

21 Will Kymlicka, "Marketing Canadian Pluralism in the International Arena," in Linda White, Richard Simeon, Robert Vipond, and Jennifer Wallner, eds., *The Comparative Turn in Canadian Political Science* (Vancouver: University of British Columbia Press, 2008), 107.

22 Martel apparently made the comment in the course of accepting the Man Booker Prize in 2002. It was picked up by conservative commentators, among them Michael Bliss. See Michael Bliss, "The Multicultural North American Hotel," *National Post*, 15 January 2003, A14. The image, it turns out, is an old one. As Luigi Pennacchio notes, "an editorial in *The Globe* newspaper argued: foreigners could not be allowed to use the school system to propagate their own culture, since by doing so Canada would no longer be a nation, it would, instead, become a 'polyglot boarding-house.'" See Luigi Pennacchio, "The Defense of Identity: Ida Siegel and the Jews of Toronto versus the Assimilation Attempts of the Public School and Its Allies, 1900–1920," *Canadian Jewish Historical Society Journal* 9, 1

(Spring 1985): 56. The phrase "polyglot boarding-house" is taken from an editorial in *The Globe*, 7 January 1919, 6.

23 For interesting examples of how this process of cultural adaptation plays out in the context of national holidays, see Matthew Hayday and Raymond B. Blake, eds., *Celebrating Canada, Volume I: National Holidays, Annual Celebrations and the Evolving Contours of Canadian Identities* (Toronto: University of Toronto Press, 2016).

24 Ernest Renan, "What Is a Nation?" cited in Bernard Yack, *Nationalism and the Moral Psychology of Community* (Chicago: University of Chicago Press, 2012), 29.

Index

Page numbers in italics followed by an f refer to figures and tables. Page numbers for notes indicate the note number preceded by an n.